The C   a Walloon Vo.anteer: August 8, 1941 – May 5, 1945

© Gerry Villani – 2019

"Water shapes its course according to the nature of the ground over which it flows; the soldier works out his victory in relation to the foe whom he is facing."

— Sun Tzu, The Art of War

Acknowledgements

This project couldn't have been completed without the help of some very important people. Their help, moral support, providing of crucial documents and documentation, and giving me permission to use some of their personal materials was crucial in accomplishing this book. You can't build an empire on your own! I want to give very special thanks to:

The late Untersturmführer Raymond Lemaire for leaving his personal stories on audio files as a testimony to his time as a soldier of the Legion Wallonie. May he join the army of all warriors in the afterlife.

Oberscharführer Dries Coolens, Schwerer Granatwerfer Zug 4.Kp./I. Btl/67. Rgt/III. SS-Panzer-Korps, for his friendship and sharing of his wartime stories.

My brother Martin Ridgway for writing the wonderful foreword. A loyal friend and fellow historian!

My brother Chadwick Clark for being my editor. Thank you so much for taking the time to review my work and making it look so much better!

My brother Andrea Sysyphus for creating such a beautiful cover for this book!

Tomasz Borowski, my Polish brother and author of *"Last Blood on Pomerania: Léon Degrelle and the Walloon Waffen SS Volunteers, February-May 1945"* and *"The Collapse of Pomerania"* for his endless support.

My brother Gary Grindstaff, for always supporting me when I was working on this book.

My NY brother Michael Shatkin, for his endless support and keeping an eye on the Facebook page! A more loyal friend is hard to find!

Stefan Willms, my German brother, for his support and for keeping history alive by guiding numerous people through the Hürtgen Forest every year.

I would also like to thank the following people for their endless support and believing in me while working on this project: Philip O'Brien, Michael Flynn, Gary Hanley, Jarred Crump, Axel Van Looy, Lance O. Adams, Cynthia Mahon, Kraig Jewell, Al Cameron, John Poole, Andy Van Billemont, Joel Edwards, Michael Falsey, Kim "Auratum" Blok, Jens Box, Ralf Stinkens, Johnny Drummond, Dominique Berrardelli, Paul Timms, Henny Lettinck, Hidde Jan Nieboer, Simon Cani, Steven Dieter, Robert Taylor, Danny Van Honste, John Uys, Thomas Mason, Patrick Krennerich, Karl Redmann, Richie Love, Sensei Steve Vinden, David Walker, John Theisen, Jay Warden, Alan Crook, Gary Hanley, Michael Held, Grégory Bouysse, and Gooch.

There are many more people I'd like to thank, but then the list of names would be several pages long. My apologies if your name is not here in the list, but know that I'm grateful for your help and support.

Last but not least, a super thank you goes to my wife and kids for their support and patience while I was writing this book. They are the foundation of my existence!

In loving memory of Eddy Dheere, 1950-2018, family man, entrepreneur, bon vivant, but most important of all a true friend.

"Qu'il est magnifique d'être homme quand on est homme."

Contents

Foreword

It was a total surprise and a great honour when Gerry asked me to write the foreword to his latest book. I think my reply was "Me? Seriously?" He was indeed serious, and I remember saying I would get on with it immediately. Gerry laughed and said I had several months before it was required.

Therefore, may I welcome you to the latest offering from Gerry Villani. I have studied the Waffen SS for nearly 40 years and I am still learning, looking for new information, and reading the tales of those men who served in the Waffen SS. Even now nearly 80 years since the beginning of World War 2, new information comes to light and sometimes old information is discovered to be incorrect.

I came across Gerry and his work through a friend when he sent me a picture of Gerry's book "Voices of the Waffen SS", having never heard of the author before I was pointed to his page on Facebook and ordered a copy. I was impressed with what I found in his book; here was a young author with a passion, who obviously had researched his subject and written a great book. "Soldiers of Germania", then "Germania's Assault Generation" followed, again both superbly well written books. Gerry's writing style is free flowing and easy to read, he takes you to the side of the men he is writing about.

The Waffen SS: for most people those words evoke images of atrocities and slaughter. Through his books, Gerry looks beyond those old outdated stereotypes and brings us the stories of the ordinary men who found themselves in extraordinary situations. He gives unknown men a voice, the chance to tell their stories before they are lost forever, and for this we should be grateful. It is easy for an author to revisit the same personalities and re-tell the same stories. Gerry does not do that - he searches for the tales that have never been told and brings them into the public domain.

In this his latest work he brings us the story of a Walloon, a man of Belgium who took up arms for "Rex and Belgium". This man was not a Nazi, but he was a patriot. He fought not just for Wallonia but for all of Belgium to protect it from Bolshevism. Like the vast majority of European volunteers in the Waffen SS, he did not fight for Germany he fought to stop the spread of Communism. When the Second World War ended and Europe was divided, the world then endured the Cold War. This must have been a slap in the face for those who fought trying in their view to protect Western Europe.

Whenever Wallonia is mentioned with regard to the Second World War, one name immediately springs to mind: Léon Degrelle. However, there was more to Légion Wallonie than Léon Degrelle…what about the ordinary men? Men who served alongside Degrelle? Gerry once again has done some amazing research and gives us the story of just one such man.

A man who was one of the first to join Légion Wallonie with his father. A man who took part in actions on the Eastern Front that have been largely forgotten. As you will read, he was wounded several times and suffered personal loss as the war progressed before finally becoming an officer in the Waffen SS. Gerry tells us this man's story. He has spoken to his family and been given access to letters and records so that now we can hear this remarkable story too.

So please pour yourself a glass of Single Malt, sit down and travel with this man as his story unfolds before you.

I give you "The Crusade of a Walloon Volunteer."

Martin Ridgway - East Yorkshire 2018

A Word from the Author

The most important political and military phenomenon of World War II is known as the Waffen SS. The Waffen SS were the ideological and military shock troops of a planned New Order for Europe. After the Germans began their crusade against communism, from every country in Europe thousands of young men joined this new army, their minds resolved that the destiny of their native countries was now at stake. "Rome or Moscow?" that was the question!

These men volunteered their lives in the fight against the Soviets believing that, after first destroying the Bolshevik threat, they would work together with their German comrades-in-arms to create a united Europe. Volunteers swelled the ranks of the Waffen SS which grew to include almost 400,000 non-German Europeans fighting on the Eastern Front alone! New foreign divisions were created and added to the strength of the Waffen SS, and soon the Reich Germans would be outnumbered in this new army. Despite the past efforts of Napoleon Bonaparte, the almost one million-strong Waffen SS represented the first truly pan-European army to ever exist. All Waffen SS soldiers were comrades-in-arms, and suffered the same wounds. The Waffen SS displayed again and again standards of courage, discipline, and self-sacrifice which must command the respect of any soldier or historian. These units fought their way to a combat reputation and fighting power second to none. Their iron reliability led to their employment as a military fire brigade, rushed from sector to sector to shore up collapsing fronts, or to sacrifice themselves in desperate counter-attacks, heedless of appalling casualties. On the other hand, there were units that were less successful on the front line who were used to fight partisan groups and special operations. These units became infamous because of their brutality, bestiality, and merciless killings of soldiers and civilians. When Hitler struck against the Soviet Union, many other European nations offered to raise a volunteer battalion to ensure a place of honor in Hitler's new Europe. Wallonia, the Francophone part of Belgium, was one of these to raise a battalion of volunteers in 1941. However, of these first 900 Walloon volunteers who left for the Eastern Front, amazingly only three survived the war - one of them was Léon Degrelle. Some 2,500 of his fellow Walloons died wearing the uniform of the Waffen SS while fighting the Soviets during that period.

About the Waffen SS, Degrelle has said, "If the Waffen SS had not existed, Europe would have been overrun entirely by the Soviets by 1944. They would have reached Paris long before the Americans. Waffen SS heroism stopped the Soviet juggernaut at Moscow, Kharkov, Cherkassy, and Tarnopol. The Soviets lost more than 12 months. Without the Waffen SS resistance, the Soviets would have been in Normandy before Gen. Dwight D. Eisenhower. The people showed deep gratitude to the young men who sacrificed their lives. Not since the great religious orders of the Middle Ages had there been such selfless idealism and heroism. In this century of materialism, the Waffen SS stand out as a shining light of spirituality. I have no doubt whatever that the sacrifices and incredible feats of the Waffen SS will have their own epic poets like Schiller. Greatness in adversity is the distinction of the SS."

After four nearly continuous years in the inferno of battle, his Legion was one of the last to retreat from Russia. This titanic struggle against the combined forces of communism and the "Allied democracies" is described in his famous epic, "Campaign in Russia", which earned him the name in Europe as "the Homer of the 20th century." And when Degrelle returned to Brussels after fighting communism for four years on the Eastern Front, he was given the largest mass welcome in Belgian history. Tens of thousands of Belgians lined the streets of Brussels to cheer the returning troops only a few months before the Allies invaded their country. However, Degrelle knew that he, as one of the fiercest foes of communism who had survived the war, was targeted for imprisonment for life. However, he would not bow to the conquerors.

This book is written to present the reader with a piece of history about the Walloon Legion during WWII, and in particular to present the story of one man, an Untersturmführer who was a member of the 28. SS-Freiwilligen-Grenadier-Division "Wallonien". It's not a justification about the crimes that some of the units or brigades of the Waffen SS have committed, nor is it to support the ideologies of a regime responsible for the killings of millions of people. Its goal is the preservation of history; history from the unknown side of WWII. The story of one man, and at the same time, a warning to future generations: a reminder that never again must such nonsensical dying happen!

Gerry Villani - 2019

Notes on Text

Military terminology: As far as possible, the military terminology used is that of the time and the army involved. An attempt has occasionally been made to translate that terminology to aid understanding.

Foreign words: Where non-English words are used, they are written in italic unless in common usage, and the English translations are given immediately afterwards.

Place names: Particularly in regards to place names in the Soviet Union, I have stuck with one spelling which is in most cases German. Some of the place names cannot be found on current maps since their names were changed during the course of history.

Introduction

To understand the drive of certain Walloon volunteers, it is necessary to understand the political situation in Wallonia, the Francophone part of Belgium, during the pre-war years and during WWII. One of the most important, and maybe one of the most significant, right-wing parties in Wallonia was the Rexist Party. The Rexist Party (French: Parti Rexiste), or simply Rex, was a far-right Catholic, nationalist, authoritarian, and corporatist political party active in Belgium from 1935 until 1945. The party was founded by a journalist, Léon Degrelle, and unlike other fascist parties in Belgium at the time, advocated Belgian unitarism and royalism. The party initially ran in both Flanders and Wallonia, but never achieved much success outside Wallonia and Brussels. Its name was derived from the Roman Catholic journal and publishing company, "Christus Rex" (Latin: Christ the King).

The Rex high point was the overwhelming victory - with 21 of 202 deputies (with 11.4% of the vote) and twelve senators - in the 1936 election. Never a mass movement, it was on the decline by 1938. During the German occupation of Belgium in World War II, Rex was the largest collaborationist group in French-speaking Belgium, paralleled by the "Vlaams Nationaal Verbond" (VNV) in Flanders, founded by Staf De Clercq in 1933. By the end of the war, Rex was widely discredited, and was banned following the liberation of the country.

Modelled initially on Italian Fascism[1] and Spanish Falangism[2], it later aligned more closely with German Nazism. The Party espoused a "right-wing revolution," and the dominance of the Catholic Church in Belgium, but its ideology came to be vigorously opposed by the leader of the Belgian Church, Cardinal van Roey, who called Rexism a "danger to the church and to the country."

---

[1] Italian Fascism (Italian: *fascismo*) was the authoritarian political movement which ruled Italy from 1922 to 1943 under the leadership of Benito Mussolini. German Nazism, under Adolf Hitler, was inspired by Italian Fascism, but only came to power ten years later in 1933. Similar movements appeared throughout the world including Europe, Japan, and Latin America between World War I and World War II.

[2] Falangism took formal shape in 1933–1934 after the founding of a new political movement called Falange Espanola (Spanish Phalanx). Falangism is the Spanish variant of the fascist doctrines that gained vogue in Europe during the 1930s.

Ideology

The Rex ideology, which was loosely based on the writings of Jean Denis[3], called for the "moral renewal" of Belgian society through dominance of the Catholic Church, by forming a corporatist society, and abolishing liberal democracy. Denis became an enthusiastic member of Rex and later wrote for the party newspaper, Le Pays Réel. The original program of Rexism borrowed strongly from Charles Maurras' integralism. It rejected liberalism which it deemed decadent, and was strongly opposed to both Marxism and capitalism, instead striving for a corporatist economic model, idealizing rural life and traditional family values.

In its early period - until around 1937 - Rexism cannot accurately be categorized as a fascist movement. Rather it was a populist, authoritarian, and conservative Catholic nationalist movement that initially tried to win power by democratic means, and did not want to totally abolish democratic institutions. The party increasingly made use of fascist-style rhetoric, but it was only after Degrelle's own defeat in a by-election in April 1937 that it openly embraced anti-Semitism and anti-parliamentarism, following the model of German Nazism. Historian and fascism expert Roger Griffin only considers the Rexist Party during the German occupation of Belgium as "fully fascist"; until then he considers it "proto-fascist."

The Rexist movement attracted support almost exclusively from Wallonia. On October 6, 1936, Degrelle made a secret agreement with Rex's Flemish counterpart, the Vlaams Nationaal Verbond (VNV; Flemish National Union). Both movements strove for a corporatist system, but unlike the Rexists, the VNV sought to separate Flanders from Belgium and to unite it with the Netherlands. The Flemish side cancelled the agreement after just one year. It also faced competition from the ideologically similar (but explicitly anti-German) Légion Nationale (National Legion) of Paul Hoornaert.[4]

Pre-war politics

---

[3] Member of the far right Catholic movement in Belgium that would become the Rexist political party in 1935. He published "Principes Rexistes" and "Bases Doctrinales de Rex" the following year, arguing for a new hierarchical structure for Belgium as a means to a greater Belgium. He collaborated with the German occupation administration during the war.

[4] A Belgian far right political activist. Although a pioneer of fascism in the country, he was an opponent of German Nazism, and after joining the Belgian Resistance during the German occupation, died in Nazi custody.

The Rexist Party was founded in 1935 after its leader Léon Degrelle had left the mainstream Catholic Party which he deemed too moderate. It targeted disappointed constituencies such as traditionalist Catholics, veterans, small traders, and the unemployed. In the Depression era, it initially won considerable popularity - mostly due to its leader's charismatic appearance. Its greatest success was when it won 11.5% of the vote in the 1936 election. Therefore, the Rexist Party could take 21 of the 202 seats in the Chamber of Deputies, and 8 out of 101 in the Senate, making it the fourth-strongest force in Parliament, behind the major established parties (Labor, Catholic, Liberal). However, the support for the party was extremely localized: Rexists succeeded in garnering over 30% of the vote in the French-speaking province of Luxembourg, compared to just 9% in equally French-speaking Hainaut. Degrelle admired Adolf Hitler's rise to power, and progressively imitated the tone and style of fascist campaigning, while the movement's ties to the Roman Catholic Church were increasingly repudiated by the Belgian clergy. Rexism received subsidies from both Hitler and Mussolini.

Degrelle ran in the April 1937 Brussels by-election against Prime Minister Paul van Zeeland of the Catholic Party, who was - to avoid victory of the Rexists - supported by all other parties, including even the Communists. Jozef-Ernest Cardinal van Roey, the Archbishop of Mechelen and primate of the Catholic Church of Belgium, intervened, rebuking Rexist voters and calling Rexism "a danger to the country and to the Church." Degrelle was decisively defeated: he lost by 20 to 80 percent.

Afterwards, Rexism allied itself with the interests of Nazi Germany even more strongly, and incorporated Nazi-style anti-Semitism into its platform. At the same time, its popularity declined sharply.

In the 1939 election, Rex's share of votes fell to 4.4%, and the party lost 17 of its 21 seats, largely to the mainstream Catholic and Liberal parties.

Second World War

With the German invasion of Belgium in 1940, Rexism welcomed German occupation, even though it had initially supported the pre-war Belgian policy of neutrality. While some former Rexists went into the underground resistance, or (like José Streel[5]) withdrew from politics after they had come to see the Nazis' anticlerical and extreme anti-Semitic policies enforced in occupied Belgium, most Rexists, however, proudly supported the occupiers and assisted German forces with the repression of the territory wherever they could. Nevertheless, the popularity of Rex continued to decline. In 1941, at a reunion in Liège, Degrelle was booed by about a hundred demonstrators.

In August 1944, Rexist militia were responsible for the Courcelles Massacre.[6]

Collaboration

Closely affiliated with Rex was the Légion Wallonie, a paramilitary organization which later became the "Wallonien" Division of the Waffen SS. After the start of Operation Barbarossa, the Légion Wallonie and its Flemish counterpart, the Legion Flandern, sent thousands of volunteers to fight against the Soviet Union. Degrelle took command of the Wallonien division, where he fought on the Eastern Front. Whilst Degrelle was absent, nominal leadership of the party passed to Victor Matthys.

End of Rexism

From the liberation of Belgium in September 1944, the party had been banned. With the fall of Nazi Germany in 1945, many former Rexists were imprisoned or executed for their role during collaboration. Victor Matthys and José Streel were both executed by firing squad, Jean Denis (who

---

[5] An early member of the Rexist movement. In 1936, he was made the editor-in-chief of all Rexist publications. During the occupation, he collaborated with the Germans despite having earlier reservations with Nazism. In Jan 1943, he resigned from the Rexist Party after clashing with Rexist leader Degrelle.

[6] In the morning of August 18, 1944 twenty Belgian civilians were killed at the town of Courcelles by members of the Rexist Movement. After the Normandy landings in June 1944, tensions between German authorities, collaboration movements and the resistance grew more intense, in particular in the Walloon province Hainaut. Among the culprits of the massacre were the main national leaders of Rex, in particular Victor Matthys, Louis Collard and Joseph Pévenasse. Of the 150 participants of the massacre, 97 were identified, 80 were arrested and tried by the Belgian justice. On November 10, 1947 27 of them were executed.

had played only a minor role during the war) was imprisoned. Degrelle took refuge in Franco's Spain. He was convicted of treason in absentia in Belgium and sentenced to death, but repeated requests to extradite him were turned down by the Spanish government.

Collaboration in the Reich: German-occupied Europe

Collaboration in German-Occupied Europe has long excited the interest of historians and others. This has been especially so in France where the works of Ory, Dioudonnat, Brunet, and many others have contributed to a fuller understanding of the various pro-German groupings. In addition, the works of a number of historians have been devoted but not limited to Quisling's activities in Norway, Mussert's Nationaal-Socialistische Beweging (National-Socialist Movement) in the Netherlands, Nationalist movements in Flanders (e.g. VNV, DINASO), and the Czech and Slovak collaborationist groupings. But significant gaps in our knowledge of collaboration remain and this thesis is intended to make a small contribution towards resolving this problem by analyzing a movement which, though small in size, was of considerable importance because of its wartime activities and the curious amalgam of Catholic authoritarianism and Germanic National-Socialism which motivated its supporters.

It would seem impossible to exaggerate the importance of WWII. For many, its events remain all too clear a memory and throughout Europe it is still - almost 80 years later - the central historical event which overshadows the occasionally rather drab post-war history of the Continent. Its power to fascinate even those too young to have experienced it at first hand is amply demonstrated by the huge volume of literature, films, and television programs devoted to aspects of the war, while the political divisions which it created within European countries show few signs of disappearing. WWII is thus, in a very real sense, part of the present rather than of the past; no element of its legacy remains more powerful than collaboration. The image of those men and women who turned their backs on their countries in order to assist the German armies has entered popular memory as a key element of the war, helped by the photographs and newsreels of the retribution meted out to the collaborators after the liberation. Thus, collaboration in its various political, intellectual, and economic forms has come to stand - along with the genocide of the Holocaust - as representative of the evil revealed during those years and with which present European generations still seek to come to terms. But collaboration was of course far from entirely novel. The wars of the Ancient World and those of medieval and early-modern Europe

17

abounded with examples of traitors who, for reasons of personal greed or revenge, chose to assist an enemy. But the collaboration of WWII was in important respects different from these historical precedents. The ascendancy of nationalist loyalties which occurred throughout Europe during the 19th century created a very different moral climate in which to betray one's nation was regarded as a uniquely serious crime. Secondly, many collaborators were not merely isolated opportunists, but the advocates of a political cause. Collaboration was thus collective in these cases, and could not merely be explained by the individual motives of those involved. Hence, collaboration, unlike treason, is emphatically modern. There were isolated examples during WWI - notably in Flanders [7] and Poland [8] - of groups who assisted the Germans or the Western powers in order to further their own nationalist goals, but ideological collaboration was essentially a creation of WWII. From Quisling in the north to the Greek fascist groups in the south, and from Vichy and Paris in the west to the Ukrainian nationalists and General Vlasov's pro-German Russian army (*Russkaya Osvoboditel'naya Armiya*, abbreviated as POA - *ROA* - Russian Liberation Army) in the east, groups of collaborators emerged throughout Europe. Only Poland of the Occupied European countries did not produce a pro-German movement of some importance.

The Rexist movement operated in German-occupied Belgium (Wallonia) from 1940 to 1944. Led by Degrelle, this largely francophone political grouping emerged soon after the defeat of 1940 as an enthusiastic advocate of an agreement with the German conquerors. By January 1941 it had voiced its categorical support for the Nazi cause. At first shunned by the German authorities who distrusted both its Catholic inspiration and its young inexperienced leaders, Rex subsequently succeeded in winning the confidence of the Nazi leaders, and by the time of the German retreat from Belgium had established itself as one of the principal pro-German groupings within Nazi-occupied Europe. Rex was not a creation of WWII but a movement whose

---

[7] In the period of 1914-1918, Belgium had its own specificity, the most evident and well-documented form of ideological-political collaboration: *Flamenpolitik*. The Germans promoted the Flemish language and culture, and encouraged the Flemish movement to envisage separation. The German administration eventually split Belgium into Flemish and Walloon sections in March 1917, but only a minority of Flemish separatists (about 15,000) and even fewer Walloons were involved in this "*activism*", which was opposed by most Belgians.

[8] There were a few small revolutionary groups who sought to use the crisis of 1914 to recreate Poland. Some of them had been operating for decades, mostly in Russian-occupied Poland. Pro-German groups were eager to fight against Russia - until Germany overran all of Russian Poland in early 1915.

origins lay in the political life of inter-war Belgium. Like most European countries, Belgium experienced in these years the emergence of a number of movements opposed to the democratic political structures which had been gradually established after the state's foundation in 1830. Some of these - such as the Communist party - were on the left of the political spectrum, but throughout the inter-war period, the principal threat to the status quo was to come from the right. In the immediate post-war years, a number of small authoritarian nationalist leagues, such as the Jeunesses Rationales and the Legion Rationale had already been established, but at the end of the 1920s a more substantial challenge began to emerge.[9] This had its origins in the disenchantment of many young Catholic students and intellectuals with the system of parliamentary democracy. They were especially critical of the Catholic party which with almost 40% of the vote, was an unavoidable element of almost every government, and which saw its role as the protector of the institutions of the Catholic world.[10]

Belgium, though the vast proportion of its population was nominally Catholic, was a largely secular society in which substantial sections of the population - notably the working class of the industrial regions - had lost all contact with the Church. Instead of refighting the stale clerical-anticlerical battles of the 19th century, these young militants believed that the Church and the Catholic party should seek to reconquer the modern world for the Catholic faith.[11] Many of these young critics were active in the Association Catholique de la Jeunesse Belge (ACJB - Association of Belgian Young Catholics) which had been set up by the Church after 1918 as an organization for young Catholics. Composed largely of the offspring of the middle classes, this vast movement was dominated by an intense, rather narrow spirituality which, at the instigation of the Catholic hierarchy, established a clear distinction between the spiritual and temporal worlds. Yet, although excluded from political action, the emphasis which the ACJB placed upon the cultivation of personal faith encouraged many of its adherents to look on the

---

[9] L. Schepens "Fascists and Nationalists in Belgium 1919-40" in S.V. Larsen, B. Hagtvet, and J.P. Myklebust "Who were the Fascists?" (Bergen, 1980), pp 501-516; F. Balace "Fascisme et catholicisme politique dans la Belgique francophone de l'entre-deux-guerres", Handelingen van het XXXII Vlaams filologencongres (Leuven, 1979), 146-164.

[10] E. Witte and J. Craeybeckx - La Belgique politique de 1830 a nos jours (Brussels, 1987) p 157.

[11] M. Claeys-Van Haegendoren "L'eglise et l'etat au XXe siècle, *Courrier hebdomadaire du CRISPS*, 542-543 (1971); E. Defoort "Le courant reactionnaire dans le catholicisme francophone Belge 1918-1926", *Revue Belge d'histoire contemporaine VIII* (1977), 81-149.

outside world as corrupt, and to heighten their dissatisfaction with the worldly maneuverings of the Catholic party.[12]

At the end of the 1920s and in the early-1930s, a number of small movements were launched by former members of the ACJB anxious to bring about a re-spiritualization of society. With titles such as L'Esprit Nouveau, La Cité Crétienne, and Pour l'Autorité, they all shared the same concern to build a truly Catholic Belgium. Many were strongly influenced by the ideas of Charles Maurras, but his influence was declining by this time and many of these militants found their inspiration in the writings of Charles Péguy, Paul Claudel, and even of Henri Bergson. The spirit of these groups was both reactionary and revolutionary. They protested that their aim was to work within the modern world, and they often admired the social achievements of Mussolini. But in many cases, their vision of an ideal society still retained a nostalgic, almost ancient regime character. At heart, they were often unwilling to accept the complexities and pluralism of an industrial, urban society, and instead they took refuge in St. Augustine's vision of a harmonious Catholic city.[13]

Rex was, in origin, one of these movements for Catholic renewal. Its leader, Léon Degrelle, was the son of a prosperous brewer from the small town of Bouillon in the Belgian Ardennes where his father played a leading role in the local Catholic party.[14] Like many sons of the Catholic bourgeoisie, Léon attended the University of Louvain where he became a prominent figure in student politics and journalism. His energy and enthusiasm soon attracted the attention of the Catholic hierarchy, and in 1930 the head of the ACJB, Mgr. Picard, invited him to take over the direction of a small Catholic publishing house.[15] Reflecting the popularity in student circles of the cult of Christ the King, this enterprise was called Christus Rex, and from the outset Degrelle used it to build a popular Catholic press which reached out to a wider audience than the existing rather pious middle-class titles. During the subsequent years, he published with some success a number of popular periodicals as well as sensationalist pamphlets and cheap editions of novels.[16]

---

[12] E, Gerard "La responsabilite du monde catholique dans la naissance de l'essor du rexisme", *La Revue Nouvelle* (Jan, 1987), 67-77; G. Hoyois *Aux origines de l'Action Catholique; Monseigneur Picard* (Brussels, 1960).

[13] G. Carpinelli 'Belgium' in S.J, Woolf (Ed,) *Fascism in Europe* (London and New York, 1981) pp, 283-306; R, De Becker - *Le livre des vivants et des morts* (Brussels, 1942); C. Soetens and P. Sauvage - *Les annees trente aux Facultes Saint Louis* (Brussels, 1985).

[14] J-M. Etienne "Les origines du rexisme", *Res Publica* IX (1967), 87-110.

[15] P. Vandromme - *Le loup au cou de chien* (Brussels, 1978), pp 13-53; G. Hoyois "Mgr. Picard et Léon Degrelle", *Revue generale belge* XCV (Nov. 1959), 83-94.

[16] G. Hoyois - *Aux origines de l'action Catholique*, pp 146-18; G. Newes "The Belgian Rexist Movement before the Second World War."

At the offices of Christus Rex in Louvain, Degrelle surrounded himself with young men who like him had been active in Catholic student life, and who shared his desire to construct a more heroic and engaged Catholic faith in Belgium. These Rexists (as they soon came to be known) used the publications of Christus Rex to preach their ideas of spiritual renewal. By 1933, Degrelle had assumed sole control of the publishing house, and it was at this stage that his ambitions began to expand. He started to hold public meetings, and the Rexist periodicals took on a more political character. Concerned by these developments, the Catholic Church withdrew from all official sponsorship of Rex, though it continued to look with sympathy on the activities of these young enthusiasts. Nevertheless, Degrelle became more outspoken in his criticisms of the Catholic Party, and in 1935 he decided to challenge its leaders directly. In November, Degrelle accompanied by a group of enthusiastic young supporters, burst in to a meeting in Courtrai (Kortrijk) of the leaders of the Catholic party, and harangued them on their complacency and corruption.[17] This coup de Courtrai, as it became known, brought Degrelle wide publicity, but he had not yet decided to break with the Catholic party. Rex remained no more than a dissident group within the Catholic world, and its support was drawn almost exclusively from young Catholics who shared his belief that the leadership of the party needed renewal. The decisive break with the Catholic hierarchy only took place during the subsequent winter. Pierlot, the head of the Catholic party, refused to enter into negotiations with the young rebels, and although at a local level there were many examples of Rexists continuing to receive encouragement from priests and Catholic politicians alike, no national compromise between Rex and the party proved possible.

---

[17] J-M Etienne - *Le mouvement Rexiste jusqu'au 1940* (Paris, 1968), pp 14-29.

Degrelle at a party speech - date and location unknown

With a general election imminent in May 1936, Degrelle belatedly decided to contest these elections as an independent political force.[18] This decision brought about a substantial transformation in Rex. Though its leaders and many of the militants who ran the local Rexist sections which sprang up during the winter of 1935-36 were still young Catholics, the movement also experienced an influx of more seasoned right-wing politicians who had lost patience with the ability of the Catholic party or the small patriotic leagues to articulate their demands. In addition, the Rexists acquired the support of a number of lower middle-class pressure groups, composed mostly of tradesmen and independent professionals who had felt the full weight of the depression and who were anxious to obtain redress for their essentially economic grievances.[19] The ideology espoused by this rapidly expanding movement was, not surprisingly, an amalgamation of diverse and even contradictory ideas. In essence, the Rexists stood for a vaguely defined political and moral transformation of Belgium. The secret of Degrelle's success at this time lay in his skillful exploitation of a series of financial

---

[18] E. Gerard "La responsabilite du monde Catholique", *La Revue Nouvelle* (Jan, 1987), 70-71.
[19] J-M. Etienne - *Le mouvement Rexiste*, pp, 64-66; "Echec aux politiciens" - Interview between Carl Peeters and Jose Gotovitch, March 24, 1972, C2GM.

scandals which had shaken public confidence in the probity of politicians and which Degrelle used to launch a wide-ranging critique of the Belgian political system. He insisted parties were corrupt cliques which served their own interests rather than those of "le pays réel" and he called for a flexible and "depoliticized" system of government which would be more responsive to the wishes of the people. Thus, far from advocating a statist authoritarian regime, the Rexists wished to establish a network of devolved corporations through which the people would be able to exert effective control over their lives. Central power would be exercised by the King who would act as the symbol of authority and as the guardian of the national interest.[20] These political demands were complemented by a number of social and economic policies. Reflecting their intellectual origins in the social Catholic movements of the late 19th century, the Rexists were intensely conscious of the injustices in modern industrial society and advocated social reforms which, while retaining intact private property, would, they hoped, resolve the deep sense of alienation felt by the Belgian working class. Hyper capitalism, as represented by the financial trusts and economic conglomerates, was another "bête noire" or black sheep of Rex. They were held responsible both for much of the corruption in public life as well as for the sufferings of small businessmen, and the Rexists advocated economic reforms which would guarantee the rights of small traders against the rapacious practices of the economic elite.[21] But beyond these specific policies, the Rexists still saw their final goal as the moral and spiritual transformation of Belgium. Thus they called for a *"revolution des ames"* (revolution of the souls) which would create a new era of justice and social reconciliation. Selfish individualism and class war would be abolished and the spiritual influence of the Church liberated from its partisan ghetto in order to become the guiding spirit for the entire population. Whether this Utopian and insubstantial ideology qualified Rex as a fascist movement remains open to question.

Definitions of fascism, like the proverbial crock of gold at the end of the rainbow, always seem to evade the grasp of historians anxious to give clear form to what is perhaps the most overused term of the 20th century political vocabulary. In fact, no single satisfactory definition will ever prove possible as, far from being a monolithic political movement, fascism was a

---

[20] e.g., *Annales parlementaires de Belgique* – Senat - July 2 and 9, 1936, Speeches of X. De Grunne.
[21] *Ibid*, Chambre de Deputes, June 25 and October 29, 1936, Speeches of C. Leruitte; J-M. Etienne *Le mouvement Rexiste*, pp, 92-95.

complex and highly diverse amalgamation of divergent social and intellectual trends. There was no clear division between fascism and traditional conservatism or, for that matter, between certain elements of fascist ideology and mainstream socialism. No convenient litmus test can thus be devised which would enable a movement to be categorized as fascist or democratic, and fascism is perhaps best regarded as an all-pervading spirit which influenced to varying degrees wide areas of the inter-war political and intellectual life of Europe.

Perhaps not surprisingly, the supporters of Rex generally denied that it was a fascist movement. But the Rexists certainly were much influenced by various foreign political and intellectual trends. Though the reputation of Mussolini in Catholic circles had declined somewhat by the 1930s, his social and corporatist ideas were much admired by the Rexists, and both Fascist Italy and Franco's Spain were the object of much uncritical praise in the Rexist press. In addition, representatives of Rex - including Degrelle - visited both Spain and Italy, and in 1936 Rex received considerable financial assistance from the Italian government.[22] Links also existed between Rex and the Nazi leaders, and in the summer of 1936 Degrelle was able to visit Germany where he was received by Hitler. Little of substance resulted from their meeting, though Degrelle remained in intermittent contact with the German leaders and received a small amount of financial support from them. None of this contact did, however, have much impact on Rexist attitudes towards Nazism. It remained in the mid-1930s an alien Germanic creed of which they knew little and which they looked on as the product of a culture entirely different from their own.[23] Instead, like all francophone Belgians of the era, the Rexists turned instinctively towards Paris. The ideas of Maurras as well as of other French Catholic and nationalist writers had an enormous impact on Rex. The language of Rex was saturated with concepts borrowed from French political thought, and these ideas clearly did much to define the movement's early character.[24]

---

[22] J-M Etienne - *Le mouvement Rexiste*, pp 113-114 ; J. Gerard-Libois and Jose Gotovitch - *L 'an 40* (Brussels, 1971), p 34; Interview between Jean Vermeire and J. Gotovitch March 25, 1971; pp 22-23, C2GM ; *Le P.R.* - September 21 1940, p, 1; "M. Serrano Suner..." January 1 and 20, 1943, p, 3, "Rex ou Moscou.".

[23] E. Krier "Le rexisme et l'Allemagne 1933-1940", *Cahiers V*, 173-220 ; R, De Becker "La collaboration en Belgique", *Courrier hebdomadaire du CRISPS*. 497-498 (1970), 9-10.

[24] P.M. Dioudonnat "*Je suis partout: les Maurrassiens devant la tentation fasciste*" (Paris, 1973), pp. 139-154; R. De Becker *Op. cit.* 11 and 21.

The Rexists themselves were, however, always at pains to stress their specifically Belgian character. The greatest influence on Rex was ultimately the intellectual life of inter-war Belgian Catholicism and in particular, the consensus amongst the young that parliamentary democracy was an outmoded, ineffectual system. When they looked to the international scene, the Rexists regarded themselves not as the agents of fascism, but as a movement of Catholic renewal which had many affinities with other groups elsewhere in Catholic Europe, notably in Austria, Slovakia, Spain, and Portugal. It is impossible to characterize the Rexist movement of 1936 as simply fascist. Certainly, many of the ideas now associated with fascism were to be found in Rex, but like many other inter-war political movements, it fell into a "no man's land" between fascism and democracy. Indeed Rexists such as Jose Streel insisted that they were the advocates of a third way between fascism and democracy, and it is perhaps such a definition which best does justice to the volatile fusion of simple populism, authoritarian nationalism, and Catholic idealism which characterized the Rexist movement of this period.

Rex meeting notification

Légion Wallonie recruitment poster
"The Legion is the army of the people"

History of the Walloon Legion

The Walloon Legion (French: Légion Wallonie) was a collaborationist volunteer unit recruited from Belgium's French-speaking population in Wallonia and Brussels during the German occupation of World War II. The Walloon Legion served in the Wehrmacht, and later in the Waffen SS, on the Eastern Front in both front line and reserve duties.

Concept and formation

Before the outbreak of World War II, fascism was quite popular in Belgium, particularly in the French speaking region of Wallonia. Léon Degrelle, owner of a newspaper and ardent Catholic, had founded the Rexist party in 1930. The Rexists watched the rise of Adolf Hitler's NSDAP in Germany through the 1930's, and campaigned strongly for similar changes in their own country, some even fighting for the establishment of an independent Walloon nation. When the Germans launched Fall Gelb in May 1940, the Belgian authorities placed Degrelle in custody to prevent him assisting the advancing enemy by raising dissent. Soon after Belgium's capitulation, Degrelle was released and he immediately set about the work of furthering the Rexist party's aims of an independent Walloon state. Despite his efforts, Degrelle's Rexists were largely ignored by the Germans, who were focusing their efforts on rousing the Flemings to their cause. Degrelle, seeing that Germany was not interested in his Rexists, began using his excellent oratory powers to gather a fighting force together for the expected crusade against Bolshevism.

The unit had its origins in Corps Franc Wallonie (Walloon Free Corps), consisting of men from the Formations de Combat (the paramilitary arm of the Rexist Party). The German occupation authorities ordered the formation of the Wallonische Legion for service in the east. Command of the Legion, which had absorbed the Corps Franc Wallonie, went to Captain-Commandant Georges Jacobs, a retired Belgian colonial officer.

Léon Degrelle, the leader of the Rexist Party, who later became known for his service with the Legion, requested to be commissioned as an officer; he was denied for lack of military training, forcing him to sign up as a private. On August 8, 1941, the Legion, now 860 strong, was sent to Meseritz in East Prussia for basic training. In early October, the Legion was incorporated into the German Army (Heer) as the Wallonische-Infantry Battalion 373. On October 15 it was ordered to the front to operate as a part of Army Group South currently advancing through Ukraine.

Part of the Heer

Upon its arrival at the front, the Battalion was assigned to the rear area to participate anti-partisan duties. At this stage, the German commanders saw the little Battalion as a political statement, rather than a combat worthy formation, and so were hesitant to commit it to a major action.

Degrelle inspecting new volunteers of the Sturmbrigade Wallonien, Namur 1943

After a brief stint serving under Panzergruppe 1, the Battalion was attached to the 17.Armee (17th Army). During this period, the Walloons were the subject of ridicule by their German counterparts, and several complaints were filed with the OKW (Wehrmacht High Command). The Battalion suffered casualties during the winter of 1941-42, and the combination of this and the German ridicule of the Walloons meant that the Battalion's morale plummeted. To make matters worse, on 10 December all the Battalion's heavy weapons were confiscated and distributed to combat units. With the Walloons close to outright mutiny, the Germans appointed a new commander, Belgian staff-officer Hauptmann Pierre Pauly and attached a German liaison officer.

Before the effects of this change could take effect, the Battalion was thrown into the line to halt a Soviet breakthrough near Dnepropetrovsk on the Donets River. Fighting alongside the SS-Division Das Reich's Germania Regiment, the Walloons defended the village of Gromovayabalka[25] from attacks by large enemy forces. After a second attack on 28 February, 1942 took most of the village, Pauly rallied his men and in fierce house to house fighting recaptured the position. The Battalion was relieved on March 2. During this action, the Walloons had lost over a third of their strength, but gained the respect of their Heer counterparts. Among those who received decorations was Léon Degrelle, who was also promoted to Feldwebel for his bravery in the action.

The action at Gromovayabalka had restored the battalion's morale, and soon after Pauly was replaced by Hauptmann Georges Tchekhoff, a former Imperial Russian naval officer who had immigrated to Belgium after the October Revolution. More recruits from the Rexists arrived to restore the strength of the Battalion, and in May 1942 it was attached to the 97th Jäger Division. Hauptmann Lucien Lippert replaced Tchekhoff as the formation's commander, and he proved popular with the men. During the Battalion's formation, Degrelle was finally commissioned as a Leutnant.

During the Fall Blau[26] offensive into the Caucasus, the Walloons were positioned to guard the assault's supply lines, seeing little action. In early August, the Walloons were called upon to clear a small village. During this battle, Degrelle was awarded the Iron Cross second class. In late August, the Battalion was pulled out of action and posted to flank security. During this time, it came into contact with Felix Steiner's SS-Division Wiking.

---

[25] Hromova Balka, Gromovaya Balka, or Gromovayabalka in the Oleksandrivs'kyi district, Donetsk Oblast, Ukraine. The town is located near Holubivka, Zoloty Prudy, and Ocheretyne.

[26] The Wehrmacht's name for its 1942 strategic summer offensive in southern Russia between June 28 and November 24, 1942 - the continuation of Barbarossa. Championed by Hitler, Operation Blue involved a two-pronged attack against the rich oilfields of Baku in today's Azerbaijan, as well as an advance in the direction of Stalingrad, an industrial city and transportation nexus along the Volga River, to cover the flanks of the advance towards Baku. The Germans and their allies had 1.3 million men, 1,900 tanks, and 1,610 aircraft. Facing the Axis armies were 1.7 million Soviets, with another one million in reserve, 3,720 tanks, and roughly 1,670 aircraft.

Degrelle and Steiner got along well, and Degrelle was impressed by the ethos of the Waffen SS. In December, Degrelle was ordered to Berlin to coordinate the formation of a second Walloon Battalion, but Degrelle had already decided to take his Walloons to the Waffen SS.

From the Heer to the Waffen SS

On June 1, 1943 the Legion Wallonie was transferred to the Waffen SS from the German Army (Heer) and given the title of SS-Freiwilligen Sturmbrigade Wallonien. The formation of the brigade had started at the Pieske training center near Meseritz. The Legion Wallonie had originally been recruited by the Waffen SS in 1941 only to be turned over to the Wehrmacht later in the fall of 1941 when the SS High Command decided that the Walloons were not sufficiently "Germanic" to qualify for the Waffen SS. By 1943 all of this had changed mainly to two things:

1) The incredible performance of the battalion-sized Legion on the southern sector of the Eastern Front in 1942.
2) Degrelle, who had risen through the ranks in the Legion from private to lieutenant and his brilliant performance on the front lines wasn't lost on either Himmler or Hitler.

As a result, Degrelle was able to convince both Himmler and Hitler to have the Legion Wallonie incorporated into the Waffen SS. The Legion's first commander in the Waffen SS was Oberst and former Belgian Army Staff Officer, now Sturmbannführer, Lucien Lippert with Hauptsturmführer Degrelle as second-in-command. In October, the Wallonien was re-designated 5.SS-Freiwilligen-Sturmbrigade Wallonien, and was to be equipped as a fully motorized brigade with a complement of 250 vehicles. By November 1943, the Wallonien was deemed fit for combat, and was sent to the Ukraine to fight alongside the Wiking, which was now designated the 5.SS-Panzer Division Wiking.

Lucien Lippert and Degrelle in 1943 just before their transfer to the Waffen SS

Dnjepr battles

On December 24, 1943 the Soviets launched "Operations for Ukraine, Right Bank", an operation aimed at clearing the area west of the Dnjepr of German forces.[27] Involving four Ukrainian Fronts and one Byelorussian Front, these operations would last until April 24, 1944. The Wallonien and the Wiking, along with eleven other German divisions of 1.Panzer Army and 8.Army were positioned in a salient based on the western bank of the river, and so were naturally the first target for the Soviet operations.

---

[27]On December 24, 1943 the troops of General of the Army N. F. Vatutin's 1st Ukrainian Front initiated the Zhitomir-Berdichev Operation. With powerful strikes, they routed the opposing forces of the 1st and 4th panzer armies and liberated Rado-myshl', Novograd-Volynskii, Zhitomir, Berdichev, and Belaia Tserkov'. By January 14 they had advanced 80-120 km west and southwest and enveloped the enemy's Korsun'-Shevchenkovskii grouping from the northwest. The Czechoslovak 1st Brigade under L. Svoboda fought alongside the Soviet troops at Belaia Tserkov'. To close up the breaches in the defense, the German command had to bring up 12 divisions to the area of operations from the reserves and from other sectors of the Soviet-German front.

Soviet forces occupied the strategically important forest near Teklino, and threatened to sever communication lines between Smila and Cherkasy. After three failed assaults by the Wiking, its commander ordered the Wallonien into action. The day before the assault, skeptical Wiking veterans posted signs around the assembly area: "The Wallonia Circus - Free Shows tomorrow from 0600h to 0800h."

In temperatures below freezing, with two feet of snow on the ground, Wallonien attacked across an open field towards the forest, clearing the tree line and advancing into the forest, being halted just short of their objective. Realizing that enemy reinforcements were reacting quickly to any attack and stalling the Wallonien's attacks, Lippert ordered a dozen three-man machine gun teams to infiltrate the enemy lines and take up positions covering the route the Soviets used to bring up reinforcements. He then ordered the Wallonien to attack again. Over 700 Soviet log-pits and bunkers were destroyed during the attack. Despite this victory, the Soviets soon encircled the forces of XLII and XI Army Corps near Korsun.

Korsun-Cherkasy Pocket and Narva

While Wallonien and Wiking were engaged defending the brunt of the Soviet attack, several Soviet Tank formations had advanced along the side of the salient and succeeded in encircling the German forces.

During the battle of the Korsun-Cherkasy Pocket, the Wallonien was tasked with defending against Soviet attacks on the eastern side of the pocket. After the 105.Regiment of the 72.Infanterie Division became exhausted defending Novo-Buda from Soviet attacks, the Wallonien was sent to relieve them. While General der Artillerie Wilhelm Stemmermann, the overall commander for the trapped forces, moved his forces to the west of the pocket in readiness for a breakout attempt, Wallonien and Wiking were ordered to act as a rearguard. During the desperate fighting, Lippert was killed. Degrelle quickly took command of the brigade, and after repulsing all Soviet attempts to break through near the town of Novaya-Buda, the Wallonien began withdrawing one platoon at a time under cover of darkness. Advancing through Hell's Gate, the brigade came under heavy enemy fire with little or no cover. Of the brigade's 2,000 men, only 632 survived the carnage of the Korsun-Cherkasy Pocket. For his actions in the battle, Degrelle was awarded the Knight's Cross and promoted to Sturmbannführer. Degrelle, who had become one of Hitler's favorites, was

Walloon volunteers in the Cherkasy pocket, December 1943

confirmed as commander of the brigade with ex-Belgian army Colonel, Sturmbannführer Franz Hellebaut in tactical command. A propaganda campaign was launched which successfully portrayed Degrelle as a hero to pro-German Europeans. The gravity of the Korsun disaster was downplayed, and Degrelle took an active role in promoting the Wallonien, addressing 10,000 people at the Brussels Sports Stadium. When he was awarded the Knight's Cross in Berlin, Hitler said to him of the Korsun affair "You had me worried." The veterans of the 6.SS Freiwilligen Sturmbrigade Langemarck, the other Belgian SS formation, caustically remarked that they too had suffered at Korsun, but they had no Degrelle to make a fuss about it.

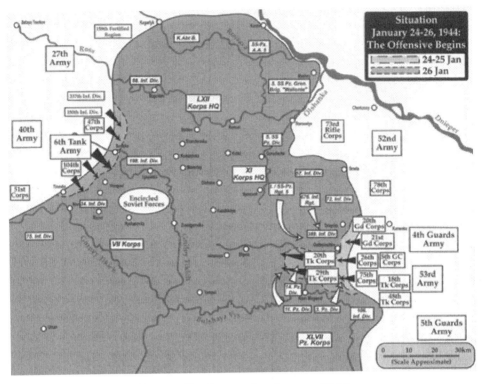

Korsun-Cherkasy pocket, January 1944

The ragged remains of the Wallonien was sent back to SS-Übungsplatz at Wildflecken to be reformed. Large numbers of new recruits were arriving thanks to the propaganda campaign, which had been augmented by a widely attended march of the Wallonien survivors through Brussels. In June 1944, the Battles around Narva (Known as the Battle of the European SS) were beginning to go badly for the German Army Group Nord. A 440-man battalion of the Wallonien was sent to Estonia to assist in the defense of the Tannenberg Line. Operating under SS-Obergruppenführer Felix Steiner's III (Germanic) SS Panzer Corps, the battalion was thrown into the line near Dorpat, attempting to halt a Soviet breakthrough at Pskov. On August 10, the battalion joined Kampfgruppe Wagner, and for three weeks fought against Soviet tank, infantry, artillery, and air attacks. By the end of the month, only 200 men remained. After Operation Bagration, Army Group Nord began to fall back into what would be known as the Kurland Pocket. During the retreat, the battalion escaped entrapment by leaving through the port of Reval on the Baltic. During this period, the leader of the Panzerjäger platoon, Untersturmführer Léon Gillis, received the Knight's Cross for his actions in single-handedly destroying several T34s. In early August, Degrelle was flown out of the Kurland Pocket to receive the oak leaves to his Knight's Cross for his actions during the Battle of Narva. The shattered remnants of the Battalion were sent back to join the rest of the brigade, now located at Breslau.

Final battles

As was the case with the Langemarck, the allied invasion of Belgium in 1944 had resulted in an influx of new volunteers. Together with the Langemarck, the Wallonien Sturmbrigade was upgraded to become the 28.SS-Freiwilligen-Grenadier-Division Wallonien in October 1944. Despite this upgrade in Status, the actual strength of the Wallonien remained that of a reinforced brigade; around 8,000 men. The division was first sent to Southern Hannover then to Braunschweig to continue training. The new Walloon recruits were joined by Frenchmen from the LVF and Spaniards of the Blue Division. Most of the new recruits lacked any military training, so only about 4,000 men were ready for action. These men were formed into a Kampfgruppe and sent to the region near Stargard and Stettin in Pomerania, joining the XXIX Panzer Corps, a part of Felix Steiner's XI SS Panzer Army.

The Wallonien was scheduled to take part in Operation Sonnenwende, the major offensive to relieve German troops encircled at Arnswalde. Wallonien was to operate in the area between Miedwie Lake and the Plönesee (Jezioro Płoń), covering the flank of the main attack. The offensive was launched on February 15, 1945 and met with initial success. However, after the III SS Panzer Corps reached Arnswalde, the situation changed and the Soviet defense began to solidify. Despite the XI Panzer Army causing heavy casualties, the offensive stalled. In savage fighting, the Wallonien sustained heavy loses as well as inflicted heavy losses, and eventually began a fighting withdrawal.

Pomerania February-March, 1945. From left to right: Ustuf Georges Suain, Ustuf Léon Gillis, Ustuf Desire Lecocq, Oscha Van Isschott, and Sturmmann Collard

The Soviet counter-offensive, launched on March 1, pushed back the Wallonien before it, and over the next few weeks was in almost constant combat until it reached the Oder near Stettin. The Wallonien, fighting alongside the Langemarck, managed to hold a thin strip of land on the eastern bank of the Oder until it was forced back across the river in early April. At this point, the Walloons held a council of war and released those volunteers who no longer wished to continue the hopeless fight. Twenty-three officers and 625 men chose to remain, and they assembled in one last battalion, plentifully equipped with machine guns, Panzerfausts, mortars, and automatic rifles. At the end of March, a second battalion was formed from men of the artillery and engineer units who had come forward from their technical schools, but this formation appears to have never been committed to battle. The Langemarck, who had also consolidated their remaining troops into two heavily armed battalions and an artillery section, was merged with the Wallonien under command of its tactical leader, SS-Sturmbannführer Franz Hellebaut. Joining the Belgians was one German battalion and a section of tank destroyers. Langemarck's SS-Standartenführer Schellong commanded the artillery and one of the Flemish battalions.

After the final Soviet offensive of April 20, 1945, the Belgians held as best they could, but were soon swept aside by the advancing Soviets. After several unsuccessful counter-attacks, the Belgian units realized all was lost and Degrelle ordered his troops to make for Lübeck, where they eventually surrendered to British troops. He then drove with his bodyguard into Norway. After that he flew to Spain where he spent the rest of his life in exile. Degrelle died in 1994.

The Crusade Begins

The history of the Legion Wallonie has already been written by many historians. The work has been done, so I'm not going to do that again. My name is Raymond Lemaire and I was a member of the Legion Wallonie from August 8, 1941 to May 5, 1945. The following is simply a recital of my personal story of what I experienced during that period of almost 4 years. These are personal memories which I had written several years after the war when the details about the conflict were still fresh in my memory. Since then about 400 pages of written memoires are "sleeping" in my drawer at home, and I thought maybe this document could interest someone sooner or later. Maybe some parts could be a little lengthy or less interesting, however I wouldn't change anything in my story because it is about a period of my life where I was between 18 and 23 years of age. And these years of my life are somewhat a bit too precious to me to leave certain details out. Every book has its preface and there's one to make me remember everything:

> *"Celui qui n'est pas révolutionnaire à 20 ans montre qu'il n'a pas de coeur; celui qui est encore révolutionnaire à 30 ans montre qu'il n'a pas de tête!" (The one who is not revolutionary at the age of 20 shows that he has no heart; the one who is still revolutionary at the age of 30 shows that he has no brain!) - signed Maurice Barrès.*[28]

It certainly is some sort of fate that the famous writer wrote down such a brutal judgment, but it is quite obvious that this quote's stiffness prevents it to be definite. The aggression of this picture, rather quite simplistic, only has the goal of influencing the mind and to impose a reality which is much subtler, much more balanced. It is undeniable, apart from a few exceptions, that it seems that age nourishes the character of a man and encourages him to remain calm and to reflect on things. So it is totally normal, or it looks like it, that after a certain time it builds an indispensable spontaneity in the pursuit of an ideal. I said that it looks like it because in reality time is not the immediate cause of this evolution, however changes and improvements of the situation and the conditioning of each, are. Time is the only factor that allows these two causes to develop. In fact, the evolution wouldn't continue after the age of 20 with men where the condition of time remained the same and who provide the exceptions that I just had mentioned

---

[28] French writer and politician, influential through his individualism and fervent nationalism.

earlier. It shows that time is there for nothing, and these exceptions are scarce.

The previous observation is not the only way to bring us to this theory. It is also known that life is the only possession of an idealist of 20 years of age, and that it is easier to risk one's life instead of endangering the few advantages obtained through one's existence. All of this says that Mr. Barrès is right, to a certain extent, and it is human and natural that it is actually so. Mind you that a lot of people have interpreted too liberally this principle, and they imagined that if one wasn't a revolutionary at the age of 30 it's because they were wrong 10 years earlier. This reasoning, if we can actually call it like that, is completely wrong. Did we make a mistake or did we do something stupid when we were idealist at the age of 20? Did we have to be ashamed, regret what we did, or blame ourselves? Absolutely not! Because the idealism at this age is but a virtue; it is courageous, it is sincere, and it is clean. And those who sell themselves by claiming and affirming that at the age of 20 they already had the brains but simply lacked the heart and often courage are in complete denial. The men that are pictured here are the ones that would repeat what they had done many decades ago and that would simply be inadmissible under the penalty of condemning themselves of having acted in a certain way.

We can regret the fact that we made a mistake or committed a crime. We can attempt to regret an experience which required a certain sacrifice. It is absolutely unthinkable that a man of whatever age could deny the fact that he stood up for something for which he risked many years of his life just like thousands of Walloon Legionnaires have done on the Eastern Front from August 1941 to May 1945, and from which 2,500 are resting somewhere between the Caucasus and the Baltic Sea. Denying all of this would not only endanger one's own honesty and courage, but mainly disgrace the memory of the ones that paid the ultimate price on the battlefield. The ones that lost that 20-year-old heart to allow those 30-year old to have some brains. It would be a sacrilege!

Les Bourguignons - August 1941

On Friday August 8, 1941, a parade of 1,000 men marched in Brussels, most of them in black uniform, which were combat units of Léon Degrelle, with music of the Wehrmacht Heer in the front followed by a couple hundred Rexists, Germanophiles, and other sympathizers. Amongst the crowd on the parade route were about 100 visibly disapproving citizens of Brussel as well. These were 1,000 volunteers who had enlisted to go and fight communism on the Eastern Front which had opened one month earlier on June 22 with an attack initiated by the troops of the Third Reich against Soviet Russia. It was the Belgian Legion Wallonie, it was the "Bourguignons." This name was adopted by us to point out a Walloon Legionnaire. Many times, we were at meetings with Léon Degrelle where he talked about the history of Belgium. A particular part of this history was about the Dukes of Bourgogne (Burgundy), Philip the Good, and Charles the Bold, who in the 15th century ruled over our provinces.

On June 22, 1941 an opportunity arose for Belgium to claim its place in a new Europe. Degrelle reminded us that one day we would be masters of our own country again just like in the glorious days when our provinces were under the rule of the Dukes of Bourgogne. The emblem of the Walloon Legion was the "Croix de Bourgogne" in red on a black background fringed with gold. The flags of the companies had a red "Croix de Bourgogne" on a white background with an armored arm holding a sword. For outsiders this was the symbol of the Walloon Legion, but in our circles we called ourselves "Bourguignons." Bourguignons was a cry of courage, a war cry, but also a reminder of the greatness and wealth which our provinces haven't known for the last five centuries. Our education system tried to hide this history in every Belgian school. For Léon Degrelle, being a Belgian was to be and to see big. For him Belgium was richness, the greatness of the Dukes of Bourgogne, but also their authority and discipline.

A Democracy Called Belgium

The greatness, the authority, discipline…lots of principles which make it almost impossible to have them penetrate in the spirit of the masses, the masses who gargle in the universal suffering of the so called "Belgian sauce." Universal suffering: it is this bone that you throw to the dog to prevent it from growling. The price of tranquility is who will permit certain politicians, somewhere, to wallow in the dirt of a regime in which they cheerfully violate a constitution which is willing enough under the watching eye of a king who doesn't even have the power to have this constitution respected. This is what they call democracy in Belgium! This blessed regime in which sinister politicians continuously make the people believe that they are indispensable and that their disappearance would be catastrophic for the country which at that point would be abandoned to the dictatorship of the fascists. For these politicians it's not about being a Belgian and to get out of this political mess. No, they will always, with the least cleanliness and order, try to form a group which is supposed to be in service of the people and form a clique of vigilantes to riot. There you have the decrees and classes; you are the fascist, the dogs that want to hurt us. Again, a nice "party" justice, isn't it, Mr. De La Fontaine?[29]

And the Belgian sheep herder was satisfied, and he still didn't understand that it was he who invited the wolf inside the barn when every four years he went to "blacken the box" (in Belgium they had to vote with ballots by blackening a box with a pen or pencil behind the name of the party/person they wanted to vote for), proud of his rights to vote, overwhelmed, deceived but happy. My father and I were both members of the Legion Wallonie. What were we going to do in this prison called Belgium? Who were we to take action? My father was a WWI volunteer and a hardened patriot. He was a small Christian employee, a simple man, very honest and disgusted by the current political situation, and he was tempted to

---

[29] A professor of international law, a senator in the Belgian legislature for thirty-six years, a renowned bibliographer, a man of wide-ranging cultural achievements, he was noted, most of all, for his fervent and total internationalism. His interest in reform eventually led him into politics. A socialist, La Fontaine wrote for the movement, spoke at meetings, joined in founding *La Justice*, a socialist paper. Elected to the Belgian Senate as a socialist, he represented Hainaut from 1895 to 1898, Liège from 1900 to 1932, and Brabant from 1935 to 1936. He was secretary of the Senate for thirteen years (1907-1919) and a vice-president for fourteen years: third vice-president (1919-1921), second vice-president (1921-1922), and first vice-president (1923-1932).

give them a big whack with a broom. Rexist that he was, he followed Léon Degrelle since 1936. I was 18 years old and I wasn't really interested in politics, however raised in the mindset of my father, as a witness of his sincerity, I have to recognize that I was enthused by a couple of meetings held by Léon Degrelle at the Palais des Sports where my father had attended. During these occasions I was strongly impressed by the hate of thousands of reds who were waiting outside the building where the meeting took place to spit their insults and stupidity on the people that wanted to go home peacefully.

These two parties that clashed so violently before the war were losing steam at the beginning of 1940. The Rexists, due to the abandonment of its voters in 1936, were maneuvered by the clever propaganda of the politicians. Now desperately seeking a solution to pull the country out of the mud in which they had thrown it, they didn't hesitate to search for infamous tactics like Léon Degrelle in the eyes of their voters. Their means were strong and they knew how to use them, and I can only say that they practically reached their goal. The communists had already received some blows during the last little while. During the last couple of years, some stories were told about little father Stalin. Since 1936, and the next three following years, similar propaganda had been orchestrated around the Spanish civil war which had pitted Franco against the reds. This anti-communist propaganda was ultimately confirmed by the victory of the Generalissimo. Closer to us during the war, France tried to pull itself out of the bad experience it had had with the regime of the Front Populaire (the Popular Front was an alliance of left-wing movements, including the French Communist Party, the French Section of the Workers' International, and the Radical and Socialist Party, during the interwar period) who had left the nation in a vegetative state. And then, the icing on the cake, was the German-Russian pact of 1939 (Molotov-Ribbentrop) which had created a certain level of consternation among the allied parties.

On May 10, 1940 the German invasion of Belgium had reunited all the Belgians in shock just like thousands in France. On May 28 the capitulation of King Leopold III marked the beginning of the Belgian disunity, a disunity that still continues to exist today. It still connects the optimism to split Belgium which can't change the mind of these bigheaded people of the regime who think they prepare for the better, but who actually are the evidence that they are responsible for the mess that we call democracy and the anarchy that we call freedom. This is what reigns our country today. The capitulation of France marked the last victory of the Blitzkrieg of the German Army which confirmed that Germany was the strongest nation in Europe, and that the future could be led under its directions. Now with some exceptions to the case, mostly for sentimental reasons that aren't really important, who wanted to oppose to such force? Pro or con? Rejoiced or terrified? Based only on these facts, who would dare to question the final victory of Germany in June 1940? However certain things changed this conviction influenced by propaganda, by certain events that had occurred, the failure of the Battle of Britain, etc. Certain feelings were awakened and the majority of the anti-Germans, by tradition and also democratized by the universal suffering, regained hope and were convinced that Hitler would be beaten in the end. What was finally seen was, but with the final result of not going to those that hoped for it, the impression of a great strategist who had seen it right. He had seen nothing at all and they who believed in him were only guided by their personal feelings. The minority in Europe, about twenty percent, was convinced or deemed it quite possible that the German victory of June 21, 1941 wasn't only a victory by the Nazis or other idiots. The writings and speeches by historians or politicians who experienced the events are quite numerous to give evidence of these facts.

Those of August 8, 1941

My father and I were against the political regime in Belgium. Even today I'm still against the current regime. However, nor my father or myself were Nazis. We only believed in a German victory. At that time our behavior was completely normal as it was the correlation of our beliefs. These are all the reasons in a nutshell, all the events and circumstances which made my father and I join the ranks of this Walloon Legion which on August 8, 1941 embarked for a painful but wonderful adventure. Approximately thousands of volunteers had responded to the call to arms since August 8. Those of August 8 weren't exactly that high in numbers. They came from all places, from the cities, and from the countryside. They had left everything behind and no distinction was made about age or physical appearance. All of them ran and crawled through the woods and plains as they simulated real combat. They were all for one and one for all! This is how those of August 8 became soldiers. They entered this new world by crossing this bridge over the shadows; they launched themselves into combat in the Ukraine. Nature wanted to kill them with a harsh winter, however they were there to fight! They crossed the icy rivers and when they left all these obstacles behind, they resumed their war towards the "Valley of Thunder", also known as Gromovayabalka. Like legendary heroes they marched through this living hell, and after this long and torturous road, this was the place of their sacrifice. It was an infernal stay composed of cold, death, and fear. Every painful day was succeeded by a night of horror. And in the morning the battle would start all over again. Death was orchestrating the carnage, and through shrapnel it was showing its real face. On the front line they were about 2,000 strong but after a teeth clenching battle, only 500 survived. These men knew what real hell was as they would perish through the fire of the bombs and bullets or were going to kill. They had to win or lose, fighting one against four with death joining their ranks while covered in dust and blood. However, the enemy was strong. Already defeated during the first two assaults, two battles where they fought man to man, the Walloons prepared, after a day of heavy fighting, for a third assault under heavy fire and machine gun fire. They were near giving up the last obstacle, succumbing to the overpowering forces of the enemy, when a miracle came down from the skies which instantly made death switch camps. The black birds of death dove down while making a screaming noise and the Bourguignons regained their courage and continued their assault. While feeling the heavy resistance, the enemy fled without glory. When the night finally covered the plains, the Walloons were holding victory. The next day a man count was held, and like in Gromovayabalka, only 301 of those from August 8 survived the ordeal.

Of course, they knew other adventures on the front. During the spring, settled in their positions, reviving like nature, they were already thinking about action. And when combat was the order of the day, again they rushed into Gemblenskaya and they occupied the entire sector. In pursuit of the retreating reds through the dusty roads they arrived at a river with slow moving water. It was the Donets River at Barashovka that reinforcements arrived. It were members of "La Jeunesse" (the youth), pure of heart and with a distant gaze, radiant of glory and pride who came to shake their hands. They arrived dashing, full of pride, ready for action and for victory without imagining for a moment that they came to steal the glory which was guarded until then under jealous care by those of August 8.

Soon they were thrown into a new glory and the war took them on a new adventure making them forget the wounds of the past. The veterans were mixed with the newbies, black with sweat and dust, and all marched through the plains and the higher elevations, crossing rivers and creeks until they reached the mountains. There, all united, were only but the Bourguignons. Months of combat action surely gained respect between the veterans and the newcomers. Now there were, united by the events at the front, only soldiers who were all proud to be called Bourguignons. However, we had to honor those who lived their moment there on the battlefield without hope of coming out alive of this white hell on earth. Never had soldiers suffered so much as those who threw themselves into combat during the harsh winters - fighting madness every day. And those of August 8 were there, those who ran after the war, those of the Valley of Thunder, those of Gromovayabalka. One day in November, during a small break between battles, somewhere in the woods they were all given a medal. From that day until the last, one was always able to distinguish those legionnaires of August 8. During the next four years they went through fire and machine gun fire, their numbers diminishing after each of 15 to 20 battles. Everywhere they were radiating glory and sacrifice, they rest now in a sleep without end which will give them peace after all. Forsaken by the gods jealous of our immense victory and only having their eyes to cry. Defeat has claimed victory marked by a blind destiny, and still they were able to keep their head held high while looking the beast in the eyes. Beaten, humiliated, tortured…but never have they submitted. Their contempt and their dignity have defeated all their enemies. Today after several decades and having only the memories of those who've experienced the suffering, one by one they're disappearing, rejoining the ranks of our great army without forgetting their motto "Meine Ehre Heißt Treue" (my honor is loyalty), and to never have betrayed their comrades. Today only a few of August 8, 1941 remain alive.

I would live this adventure until the end, until May 5, 1945, the day that the last group of Walloon volunteers surrendered at the western front to the Americans just a few minutes before their final encounter with the Russians. But why? From a speech of Léon Degrelle: "Belgian Nationalists, stay idle and sterile when millions of Europe's sons are running into combat. Here we are, the hands reaching to the weapons which will make us comrades of blood and greatness, of those who will liberate Europe and the world! We are leaving because for us Europe is sacred, it's the flower of civilization, the country of leaders of peoples. We are leaving because our country is involved like all the other countries in Europe! He who dares to refuse to fight for his people is a traitor and a deserter! Finally we are leaving and our hearts are filling with happiness, with thoughts that our Fatherland would manifest its presence again!"

For the majority, to most of our compatriots we were traitors who had no other goal but to deliver our country to Nazi Germany. But why would we wait one year? Why did we attend an event which we were able to give another meaning besides the war Germany was fighting? Simply, why would we go to risk our lives thousands of kilometers away from home when it would've been easier and less dangerous for each and every one of us to exercise the role of valet and traitor in our own country? This way it would've been the blood of our compatriots that would've flown, not ours! It is easy to maintain the spirit of the old ones and to create, in the spirit of the youth, the idea that the legionnaires weren't fighting in Russia as a valet of Germany with the evil intention to betray Belgium. We didn't join the German Army to help the Nazis conquer Europe and to impose their indoctrination. This wouldn't be serious at all! Germany has lost the war with us, however she could also have been able to win the war without us. Similarly, the Allies could've been able to win the conflict without the help of the Brigade Piron (the 1st Belgian Infantry Brigade, named after its commander Jean-Baptiste Piron, was a Belgian and Luxembourgish military unit in the Free Belgian forces during World War II) or Division Leclerc (the French 2nd Armored Division, commanded by General Philippe Leclerc, which fought during the final phases of World War II in the Western Front). Both formations, just like ours, had the same intention: to help one power to reach its objective. In both cases the same methods were used to reach an identical objective which only differed in the initial point of view. Unfortunately, the animals suffered of the plague…

Initiation

So here I was at the Legion Wallonie. After one year since my return from the middle of France on August 3, 1940, in the streets of Brussels I observed the German military of all components and all ranks. Only their insignia were different. What I noticed was that not a single one of them was smoking cigarettes and their uniforms were impeccable. The way they saluted and how they presented themselves in public showed me that they were of a rigorous discipline! And this was only the discipline of soldiers that were just walking around off duty! Some of the well-informed people said that the military training would be one of a kind. We would experience that sooner than later! At the Palais des Beaux Arts a small ceremony was held to welcome us into the German Army. One thing that astonished us was the fact that it seemed to us that the officer who presented us to the German General was only a low-ranking officer. In fact, he was the commander of a military band and he was just introducing us to the General. Our train left at the Gare du Nord (North Station in Brussels) in the early evening only to stop ten minutes later at the station of Schaarbeek where we received bowls of soup and books for the road by female supply service auxiliaries. The soup was more like a puree, it was so thick and its taste was even worse than the cheapest soup from a can which were sold at any grocery store. The books, the bread, the cheese, the sausages and meat, the canned sardines, etc. lasted us for another two weeks after our arrival at the Meseritz (aka Regenwurmlager - located in Poland, 80 km east of Frankfurt an der Oder) military training camp. All of incomparable quality! The trip took two days until Sunday afternoon. At every stop, day or night, in an important station we would get more "puree" soup. The impression was of that of the best but we always said that such treatment had to be compensated by a service even more sensational, and that we didn't lose anything while waiting.

Welcomed by an officer and a couple of NCOs, we walked the 2 km that separated the train station and the camp, Regenwurmlager[30]. I always asked myself why they named the camp earth worm. Maybe there was a correlation with the countless hours we spent on our bellies moving around in the camp. The first couple of days were reserved to get installed and to be permanently assigned to your infantry unit. Then we received our first theoretical lessons and we had our first contact with our instructors. The ranks, the salute, the presentation, the internal regulations, etc. - things we all had to learn. Furthermore, we were equipped and armed. People always told me that in certain armies clothing was distributed despite the use of common sense and without worrying about the size of the soldier and the uniform he would receive. However, in the German Army the army tailors distributed the effects like tailors of a high-end clothing store. They examined every person with an expert eye then they disappeared into the shop and returned with a uniform that corresponded exactly with the measurements of the soldier. It was out of the question that this uniform would have a wrinkle in it, and I've seen cases where they retouched tunics immediately. I knew one unique case where they had to make a helmet for a soldier of the 1st Company who had the biggest head of the entire German Army. His size did not exist! So, the first three weeks this man had to participate in all exercises with a garrison cap. Then the helmet finally arrived. It was carefully packed. It was a real cooking pot in which we could've made soup for the entire platoon! But the circumference of his heads was not his only unique quality as a soldier. He was also an elite shooter, a sniper.

Everyone at the Legion Wallonie received the rank that he previously had in the Belgian Army. My father was an NCO and since I had no previous military experience, I was just a regular soldier. Same for Léon Degrelle, he had no previous military experience, however it was obvious that because he was a political leader they offered him a rank and function outside our troop. But he refused! [31] The only distinction he accepted was the one of being

---

[30] The East Wall or Ostwall/Regenwurmlager is an extensive underground fortification bunker system constructed by Germany between 1930 and 1943, about 120 km east of Berlin. Although at that time very much part of Germany, the location has, since the end of the WWII been part of Poland. The Ostwall was a system of underground bunkers interconnected by tunnels and corridors with a total length over 100 km, which included almost fifty above-ground firing points. Some of the tunnels are more than 70m deep. Long lines of anti-tank "dragon's teeth" were built, and the tunnel system had its own power plant, hospital, armaments factory, barracks, and underground electric railway. In the 1930s an associated military training camp (Truppenübungsplatz) was established for the training of troops.

[31] Joining as a Private he earned his stripes from Soldier 1st Class to General for exceptional bravery.

promoted to Soldier 1st Class which changed absolutely nothing to his status as a recruit. He was the first machine gunner of the 1st Group, 1st Platoon of the 1.Kp. That was all. With this rank he went through training like all the other recruits. He did the same exercises and same chores like all of his comrades and until the end of the first campaign, which ended with the battle of Gromovayabalka, he lived the life of a simple soldier enduring the same hardships, the same tiredness, and the same sufferings which were the evidence of his exemplary courage and morale.

I was also a machine gunner of the 1st Platoon. At least ten times I shared the same loaf of bread with him, the same straw bale, the same lice. He was afterwards promoted to the rank of warrant officer (adjudant in French), and soon he was made an officer with the title of company commander. Finally, he was made commander of the Legion Wallonie after the death of Commander Lipper at Tsherkassy. But even then, he never shied away from the action, from a battle, or any form of danger in which the Legion Wallonie participated. Later when the Legion became a brigade and when it finally got divisional status, the Legion was split into different components. However Degrelle was always with that component that went into action. In June 1944 when he was in Paris, he learned that a Kampfgruppe of the Legion, without his knowledge, was about to engage in Estonia. Hitler ordered him not to expose himself again in battle. He became outraged and refused to obey Hitler's order. He received this order after Tsherkassy from the Führer himself when he was awarded the Ritterkreuz (Knight's Cross). Degrelle immediately left Paris behind the wheel of his car and joined his legionnaires in Tartu (Estonia). When he returned, Hitler would add the Eichenlaub (Oak leaves) to his Ritterkreuz and not because his name was Léon Degrelle but because he deserved it! When he fled to Spain in the first days of May 1945 not even one Walloon volunteer was found on the front lines. With them Degrelle had participated in the last fights at the Oder front.

Was Degrelle a traitor and a war criminal? Among all political leaders of that era, regardless of their nationality, who had a certificate of good citizenship and were first class patriots, I'd challenge you to give me the name of a single person who behaved the same and who risked his life so

He engaged in 75 man-to-man combat actions, and was wounded on numerous occasions. He was without a doubt one of the most famous Waffen SS volunteers.

many times like Léon Degrelle, knowing that he was not obligated to do so. On the contrary, for a moment it was forbidden for him to engage in the military, however he never paid any attention to this prohibition. That he was morally obligated to adopt a certain behavior, we have to admit, that it is questionable. Ever assuming that he fulfilled a moral obligation, the question remains: who made him, who did it at the price this would cost? Perhaps his ambition pushed him to take these risks to become someone important after the war if he would survive? Come now! In 1945 at the Oder Front, any Belgian or other foreign volunteer knew, even Léon Degrelle, that no award and no honor would wait for them. The only thing to save at that time was your own life. So why did we stay? To betray Belgium? One has to be stupid, thick headed, or incurable to believe such enormities. It is dumb, it is ridiculous! What value would such conduct have for us when thousands of men would go into battle to risk their lives for years for the fun of betraying their country? A traitor risks nothing, anyways not his own life! We have never betrayed anything. If we were capable of betraying our country, we would've betrayed our new master as well when we realized that victory was changing camps. Because only rats will abandon a sinking ship and we were no rats and Germany wasn't our ship! Some evidence to the contrary: in the occupied countries the increase of members of the resistance was proportional to the Allied successes. Allow me to quote something; this quote is no form of critique, but only confirms what I was talking about. It is an extract of the editorial of "Pourquoi Pas" ("Why Not") number 24/96 of the September 29, 1966 edition dedicated to King Leopold III:

"The truth, something we could've said and should've said sooner to the entire country however could it be supported in 1945 in the euphoria of victory of which all were very proud of but who had risked nothing to get to this victory. In 1945 all the Beulemans and "Chanchai" [32] declared that they have been resistance fighters since May 28, 1940. By saying so and repeating it different times they honestly believed what they were saying. And this is how the perspectives we were talking about were forged."

No comments necessary! Isn't it surprising to observe that against all apparent logic the number of the Legion Wallonie increased in time when Germany's star started to fade? This observation about the resistance puts

---

[32] Beulemans is a common name in Belgium; "Chanchai" is unknown to the author and couldn't be retrieved in the archives of the Belgian resistance - most likely here it means socialists.

the unusual character of their progression into the spotlight. That the progression of the numbers of the Legion Wallonie proportionally inversed based on the successes of the German Army on all fronts was not of the nature to let one reflect with an objective mind. Isn't it some sort of proof that the legionnaires who were engaged at the front had a clear conscience in relation to their patriotic duty? They would have done it even if the future of Belgium wasn't at stake because they rightly thought that under these circumstances the fact to consider was not to help Nazi Germany but merely a contribution that was going to save Europe of a great misfortune that could happen to her at any time.

All these legionnaires were soldiers, and Léon Degrelle behaved like a soldier, from the first day to the last one. A soldier! Even if he had nothing military in him because, according to the troops' jargon, he was perfectly incapable of leading two men through a farm's courtyard. The Prussian discipline gave him diarrhea, and foremost he did not bear the Germans in his heart. There was no doubt about the fact that he felt like a brother-in-arms of the Germans. He admired certain German soldiers and certain German politicians, but it stopped right there. Léon Degrelle had nothing, but absolutely nothing, that made him a Germanophile. It wasn't because he yelled "Heil Hitler!" In January 1941 in Liege (Belgium) that he was Hitlerian[33] . The "Heil Hitler" of Léon Degrelle was a show off of his fist and I know that Marshal Petain never had been, not even in 1940, a Germanophile and even less of a Hitlerian. And if there are still some idiots that are lost in the fog of their nonsense and that are still convinced of their beliefs it would be about time to revise their judgments! And that once and for all they know that our feet were meant to march and not to think! If on one hand, like it's generally pretended, Léon Degrelle would've been the heir apparent of Hitler in Belgium since 1936, and on the other hand if he would've been just a Gauleiter when Germany occupied Belgium, he would have been that since his return to Belgium from a French prison in August 1940 [34]. We didn't have to wait for Germany's final victory!

This was not what Léon Degrelle wanted. That he wanted to become "the chief" wasn't a secret at all. The chief between parentheses and not just

---

[33] Relating to or characteristic of Hitler or the policies of the Nazi party.
[34] Degrelle was placed under arrest by the government out of fear that he would collaborate with the Germans. German troops discovered him in a French prison - the concentration camp of Vernet in the French Pyrenees - and he was immediately released.

as a title. And even when they had nothing else to offer him, and even if they had, it wouldn't have worked with him. He would've waited for the moment or opportunity where he could have the chance to conquer the right to discuss as equal to equal with the chief of the German state, as this one would be called, if he would win the war and was called up to organize Europe. This opportunity was given to him during the German-Russian war which he felt coming because one day we would have to get there anyways. He took advantage, not only by seeing the other go, but by going to war himself. This war against Bolshevik Russia wasn't the best opportunity which had never presented itself as a right to conquer, a right which no one ever had the intention to recognize before. But for us it fulfilled all the conditions. Most likely there would have been a better explanation by logic and by opportunity to justify this war against Russia. Logic: we were anti-communist. Opportunity: it was the way to conquer the necessary authority to claim something which would be morally impossible for us to refuse. Germany contracted a debt towards us to recognize that which she had promised before. And cheerfully we would use this way with a clear conscience. Another proof that we didn't just engage like the valet of the enemy to help him in his war was that we could have done it one year earlier without any other given reason. Not even one legionnaire who fought during the 15-day campaign in 1940 or during the conflict of 14-18 would have joined the German Army to fight France or England. For us it was clearly a way which was amply justified by the simple fact that we represented Belgium. There was no other reason to look for at any moment under any circumstances. So here you have the reason why thousands of legionnaires went to fight in Russia. Here you have the reason why they died; 2,500 of them!

The soldier Léon Degrelle, not even militaristic in the slightest bit, received a lot of merits during the months of his military training. The strict rules of the German discipline were obligatory for all ranks under any circumstances and we, not morally nor physically, would have suspected way before that this German Infantry School would have been just like that. The reason why is very simple: people have seriously exaggerated about the tenure of the German officers and NCOs. If we didn't have a difficult time during our military training it wasn't because we were volunteers nor because Léon Degrelle was with us. No, it was because our company was comprised of men of all ages and of any physical condition. All fit for duty of course, and all had passed the medical tests which were held in Brussels. There were, mixed in every unit, youngsters of 18 years of age - like myself - and veterans from the First World War, aged 35 plus years just like my father. And even if it was easy to get myself prepared morally and physically it wouldn't have been the same for the veterans of the other war who beside their age were wearing a dozen of Belgian medals on their German tunics. This didn't go unnoticed with the German instructors. And since it was impossible to establish a system that would favor both age groups, we youngsters were going to enjoy a regime favorable for those who were older and that didn't have the same moral and physical flexibility in their bodies.

It must be said that the spirit of the instructors, without exception during our training, was exemplary until the end and surely contributed to the fact that we were all successful in our training. I attended two training schools: one was the SS school for assault engineers in Dresden,[35] and the other one was the school for SS officers in Prague[36]. In this last one all the youngsters were submitted to suffer the Prussian discipline which was applied in every method of instruction by middle aged officers and NCOs. How many times didn't I wish, just like all the rest of the recruits, to be in any situation at the front instead of being at the SS-Junkerschule! The food at the Regenwurmlager was plenty and in general of good quality. After hours we were able to obtain beer and alcohol in the canteen. And chocolate at will! The first month we were not allowed to leave the training camp and the following month, one by one, we obtained one afternoon of leave.

Now the closest village, Meseritz, was located 8 km from the camp. It was one of those typical German villages in which it would be catastrophical to "release" fifty Bourguignons at once! There was another camp in close proximity to the village, a camp which we would occupy upon our return from the Caucasus, and some barracks at the edge of the village. I was able to go on leave with my father under the false pretense that he couldn't speak a word of German and that he had to go buy a couple of things in town. After a few hours of leave in this foreign village, to which we were not accustomed

---

[35] Kaserne für den SS-Pionier-Sturmbann und die SS-Pionierschule, Dresden-Trachenberge.
[36] SS-Pz-Gren.Schule/Junkerschule Beneschau/Neweklau/Prag. The SS-Panzergrenadier Schule was at the Czech village of Prosetzchnitz which in early 1944 was renamed Kienschlag. Kienschlag and the school formed part of the larger Böhmen/Beneschau Troop Training Grounds complex. Men who were being considered for officer training were sent to Kienschlag to attend pre-training courses (actual officer training courses were also held there for foreign officer candidates, especially French-language courses for Walloons, Frenchmen, and Romanians).

with the local habits and people's minds, one had to adapt quickly. This was an easy task for the Bourguignons! But under these circumstances, on top of that, we were accompanied by a fatherly figure who wasn't there to have fun. In this case I recommended the formula to have one representative for him in the store to help him out. Most likely a positive outcome was assured. And if after his shopping he would have left me to return to the camp on his own, he would have doubtlessly gotten lost in town. So every time he would distance himself from me, I had to pretend not to notice him so he could keep his dignity. Then one night I suggested that my NCO father to return to the camp, and he was delighted to hear my suggestion. This was October 1941 and I wouldn't see an eastern village like this in the next ten months.

For two months the military training went at an accelerated tempo without any major incidents. Every now and then during a weapons inspection, one of us would be send to a "session" of sleeping in the upward position (standing) which was ordered by an NCO instructor who always had a severe and strict attitude. Even those that underwent this punishment carried big smiles on their faces, for the more one smiled during such punishment the less long it would last. It was something they taught us from the beginning. Under no circumstances did I portray a bad mood. Everything was done with a big smile and everything I had to undergo was with a light heart. To learn to endure and to suffer a lot was to learn the limits of the moral strength which commanded the physical force. We surely would need this soon!

In an infantry battalion like ours, the company commanders were always on a horse. They were always riding a horse in front of the company. Our commander, Captain Van Damme[37], veteran of 1914-18, was asthmatic, but he continuously smoked cigarettes, leaving him out of breath all the time. On the morning of our first march, 35 km in total, my father - whose discretion wasn't his main quality, rejoiced himself at the front to the group with some of his comrades which would comment about the bad behavior of "the old one" during this exercise. The old one was in proximity of the group and he overheard the uncharitable remarks made to his address. He pretended to have not heard a thing. The next morning at 0700h during the departure of the battalion, all the commanders mounted their horses. But our

---

[37] Commanding frontline officer 1st Company: Capt-Cdt Albert Van Damme (August '41 - January '42).

commander walked into the camp, feet on the ground and confident to march the entire 35 km. Every now and then he even permitted himself to march to the front of the company and join my father in the 3rd Platoon while viciously calling him out: "So Lemaire, everything OK?!" Then he would join the front of the group and continue this way until the end of the march. He would mount his horse again in the late afternoon to cross the camp's gate. This was for him a huge personal success, and the story went around in the entire battalion. From that day on his exhausting cigarettes appeared to have less of an odor. We performed battalion-sized exercises which showed that our unity was certainly developed, which constituted a homogeneous whole capable to finish its mission. Every one of us was capable to assemble and disassemble every infantry weapon with his eyes closed! We had acquired individually, and in group the precise movements which made our troop look like a well-oiled machine. We were ready! And we asked to let us prove that we were ready. Impatiently we were counting the days to leave the Regenwurmlager. I was able to celebrate my 19th birthday on October 13 at the camp just before we left Meseritz on the 17th.

850 men and 14 officers which formed the Wallonische-Infanterie Batallion 373[38] disembarked on November 3, 1941 at Dnjepopetrowsk after a 17-day long trip with relative comfort. 40 men and 8 horses in one train car. Then the march to the east had started.

---

[38] The Wallonische-Infanterie Bataillon 373 was formed on August 8, 1941 from Belgian Walloon volunteers. Unlike some other volunteer formations, the volunteers kept their ranks from the Belgian Army when joining the Wehrmacht. It was upgraded and transferred into the Waffen SS in June 1943 as SS-Sturmbrigade Wallonien.

Lemaire (middle) on a train - location unknown

The Winter of 1941-1942

We walked our way into the war. Dnjepopetrowsk was the end of the train line in the east, and the River Dnjepr constituted a border between two worlds. On the right bank civilization ceased to exist. On this foggy morning of November 6, 1941, the Walloon Legion assembled at the 1,800 m long bridge which spanned across the river. In a short speech Léon Degrelle quickly told us about what we were about to accomplish when we would cross this bridge into the unknown and being thrown into an unforgettable adventure. We started marching and company after company we crossed the river in silence with an unexplainable feeling. The words of Léon Degrelle had touched us in the right place and we felt really good. But we were about to be detached from something that had always given us a sense of security, something that connected us to many things, something we would never think about until now. In the next few minutes every man felt abandoned, every man found himself alone in between a handful of comrades, alone in between thousands and thousands of soldiers who fought for many different reasons but with the same goal for the same cause which inspired our ideal. Completely alone in the moment when meeting death, something each and every one of us was walking in to, abandoned by the majority of their compatriots in the general misunderstanding that one's sacrifice would be like treason. Alone, thinking what would happen in the future knowing that one day we would become the victims of hate, hate coming from the ones that one day we would give our lives for. How many among us, and in what circumstances, were going to cross this river again in this conquest that would cost so many lives and was adding an extra obstacle between Europe and the Bolshevik realm? But what if time itself would drag itself through the sand which has the same color as our thoughts? It is during that moment that it will liberate us and bring us back to present realities.

Rapidly Russian nature, which didn't work in favor of the aggressor against Russia, brought us back to order. At a high tempo the streets in the town made way for the roads in the steppes. These roads became very muddy because of the continuous rain. We had to travel 30 km which under normal circumstances is not a very long trip. Since then, I walked more than 2000 km in Russia at all times during all seasons! Never have I travelled under normal circumstances. This simply doesn't exist in Russia. Our first experience was going to be very hard since those 3 weeks that we spent on the train seriously impacted our physical condition and our training. Also, the rain changed all the roads into an indescribable mess in which moving your feet up would become more and more difficult as the mud was sucking your boots down. If only that would've been the problem. Every carriage, pulled by Brabander horses (Belgian heavy horse), was mounted on pneumatic tires which had done the work on the roads of Belgium, France, and even on the dry and dusty roads the months before. But now they were not keen to move through this mud. After a couple of kilometers, the horses were completely exhausted and were incapable to get out of the mud pools on their own. The vehicles were all stuck now. Ten to twelve men had to constantly place themselves behind a carriage and push it forwards, just to see it immobilized again 100 m down the road.

The night also surprised us when we were just a couple of kilometers distant from our destination. It increased the confusion in the already dislocated columns. This was the image of the advance of a victorious army. How would it be during retreat under the same conditions? But at that time no such thoughts were allowed at all! But the horizon of the soldier was limited to the neck of the soldier marching in front of him. Sometimes this neck would disappear. The next thing you knew, you were helping your comrade out of a big puddle of black water in which he was laying; black water to which shit and brothels looked like respectable places. It wasn't over yet! When it was your turn you would disappear in a big black hole and at that moment you had to count on your neighbor to help you out. The ones in the worst situation were the NCOs or messengers who from the beginning of the campaign seemed more privileged because they were issued bikes. This morning they still had an attitude of being important when they passed the column sitting straight on their saddle. They were quickly disillusioned when riding their bikes became impossible. For hours they were carrying their bikes on their shoulders. Have you ever tried to push a bike through the mud for 15 km? That mud, if you could actually call it mud, was the Russian gook once the rain would hit it. After the last 5 km, with mud up to your helmet and extremely exhausted feeling every muscle ache, we arrived in front of a big building which was, within the past couple of weeks, transformed into some sort of hotel for us. The place was offering us just more than mediocre sleeping quarters. We were in the suburbs of Novomoskovs'k (Ukraine), an industrial city where we would spend the next three days. These days gave us the chance to dry and sort things out and to regain a human shape again. And of course, joining the community to which we belonged since this morning…the German army during its campaign.

The region was weakly occupied by our troops, and partisans already had made their presence visible all over the place, especially behind our lines. During the dark and gloomy night, a very hard and deafening sound of an explosion was heard, followed by an intermittent red glow. An abandoned vehicle, broken down or stuck in the mud, was sabotaged by a shadow. These shadows were always very busy during the Russian nights - very active! During the night one had to be very careful in the rear lines. We insured ourselves with sentinels who patrolled the area. The rest of the time we remained very close to the bathrooms where we could clean ourselves, our uniforms, and our weapons. The third day my company, the 1st Company, was transferred to occupy a town at the edge of a forest called Karabinovka. The weather hadn't changed at all, and these 25 km were the same agony as our first trip. We again arrived at night in the same condition as days ago. There was nothing reserved for us to sleep, so for the first time we had to sleep in the local houses which were still occupied by their habitants. These houses were, and let's not have the fear to use certain word, constructed of dried cow shit and dried mud which was built around a frame of twigs and sunflower stems. The entire house was covered with this type of "masonry". Small squares were incorporated into the walls which were used as windows but which were impossible to open. Styling the whole house was a roof resting on multiple crooked beams. Sometimes between the ceiling and the roof there would be an attic which was accessible with a ladder. Here the provisions for the winter, like sunflower seeds and winter squash, would be stocked. The Russians never seemed to cease to eat these seeds during the day. With an incredible precision, they threw a dozen sunflower seeds into their mouth, cracking them one by one with their teeth and spitting out the empty shells which most of the time would stick around their mouth. I've never seen a Russian spit out one seed. Neither would you say a parrot, however he could only take one seed at the time in his beak. These sunflower seeds are excellent since they were lightly grilled; they had a large quantity of fat from which they would make oil, a bit peculiar in taste, but very much appreciated. The houses were very easy to maintain or to repair, and they had a simple layout. The main entrance would give access to the stables, and only one wall would separate it from the living room. Inside, a door would give access to both compartments. Sometimes when an architect would have keen imagination, he would place a window in between the two compartments. The furniture was old and simple. Everything was made out of wood: there would be a big closet, a table, chairs, and sometimes a bed…which were the remains of the luxury of a certain era gone a long time ago. What served us as our bedroom, we called it the dovecote. In between the stables and the living room there was a large wall and an alcove where the entire family would sleep on old blankets. Everything was infested with bugs and after spending a couple of hours in such a house, each and every one of us was covered in lice. One would only get rid of them in a hospital or a delousing center before returning back to Germany.

We were assigned a couple of houses and we made our way in. Can you imagine ten pair of hobnail boots making their way in, destroying the floor inside? This was just the beginning for these poor people, and many times we would hear them say "Ne voyna khorosho!" meaning war is not good. But good or bad, war is war! We would spend three weeks in this village which was already occupied by an Italian company. The neighboring forest was occupied by partisans, and our task was to patrol day and night. During the day I ran through every bit of that forest but I never did see one partisan. One night one of our patrols exchanged fire somewhere between the town and the forest. General alert! Everybody rushed into action, but the shadows had already evaporated. Around November 15 it stopped raining. The sky opened up, the air became much cooler, and the soil hardened up. Here we had the first signs of frost. During this time in Novomoskovs'k, where the rest of the battalion was located, the security posts of the 3rd Company of Lt Buyts was attacked by partisans. Result: four wounded - one mortally wounded. In the forest northeast of Novomoskovs'k, the 4th Company of Captain Dupré was able to destroy an enemy camp. This enemy was of course behind our lines. The mud of the fall stopped the eastward moving German troops, and where they stopped is where they had to remain. There were huge problems in providing rations and ammunition, and the more troops present the bigger the problems. Compounding the difficult campaign during these first five months, the victorious armies had sustained heavy losses in manpower and equipment. The units that had been fighting since June 22 were completely exhausted and had to be reorganized. We had to close the gaps and relieve the troops. With the approaching winter we would additionally have less manpower. Thus we were unable to form a permanent front which would normally require three times the available manpower.

The front consisted of isolated points[39] from the Donets in the area of Slovyansk, in the east in Artemivs'k and Horlivka, and also on the River Mius and Taganrog on the Sea of Azov. All these points were connected by patrols, but between two patrols sometimes 10 km would separate them from each other. Later some Cossack horsemen, more than one hundred men strong, would operate in our sector and would engage in attacks to which the toll would be heavily paid by the soldiers of the Italian company. On the 26th the rest of the battalion joined the rest of the company, and on the 27th the Walloon Legion was on the road again for a series of trips of 25-30 km long. The first stage brought us to Pavlohrad where we were greeted with music by the Italian troops under Colonel Luigi. After that we moved to Mezevaya, Petropavlovsk, and finally Slavyanka.

December 1 the snow fell for the entire night. None of the common places, none of the over-used clichés used to describe nature in our western countries, was comparable to winter in the Russian steppe. We had the impression that we were moving in cotton balls and that we had cotton in our ears. No sounds would resonate anymore as every noise was suffocated and absorbed. It was another universe where one would feel imprisoned as much as one was free, free to go where one would never be able to get out of. A prison of infinity! The perspective to travel a distance of 40 km in this new unknown environment wasn't made to stimulate a good mood. And soon this would become evident. After a couple of hundred meters, the most passionate predictions were beyond reality in every sense of the word. We ploughed through the snow waste deep and we advanced by stepping on the frozen mud. The steppes were flat which made it more difficult to recognize the roads. After a couple of passes, a frozen ball of snow would stick to the soles of your boots. Every now and then these snow balls had to be removed using a bayonet. Just like in the mud, our carriages had great difficulties advancing through the snow. Multiple horses fell down and broke a leg. Obviously, we had to shoot them at once. Men and animals made considerable effort though. Part of the carriages were abandoned on the road

---

[39] Tony Van Dijck, former Waffen SS soldier (Standarte Nordwest) and member of the Vlaamse SS talked about these "Stützpunkte" on the Eastern Front which were identical to these isolated points described by Lemaire. It was Himmler's idea to create these points, like fortresses, manned by members of the Waffen SS and Heer.

and the remaining horses were placed in front of other carriages. With two horses pulling, it made things a lot easier. But we had to come back sooner or later to recover the abandoned carriages.

Night was falling, and the 1st and 2nd Companies settled in a small village. The men were exhausted and empty and incapable of advancing any further. Since morning we had to chew on a piece of frozen bread which we had taken with us at our departure. The mobile field kitchens that accompanied every company were unusable due to the extreme weather conditions. These conditions would last for the remainder of our adventure. It was only at night, if the field kitchen made it, that we were able to eat and drink something warm. The field kitchen of the 1st Company might have arrived at its destination, but we were not there. So we had to be happy with the bread that we had. We had to defrost it and roast it over the fire. Sometimes we would find a couple of potatoes, hidden in one of the local houses. We would make mashed potatoes with water, no salt or butter - not because there wasn't anything better - but because it was warm and filling. We were going to cover about 100 km in harsh conditions in multiple stages in order to finally arrive at Cherbinovka, a small town in the basin of the River Donets on December 10. Here we would establish out winter headquarters (HQ), and we were staying in wooden barracks which were left behind in poor condition: the windows were all broken and the floor boards were disjoined. The whole building was a wind tunnel! And what a wind tunnel it was! Outside the snowstorms succeeded each other, and the wind howled over the steppe. For the past couple of days, the thermometer began to plunge at staggering speed, and it wouldn't stop until the beginning of January 1942 when it hit -48°C! Day and night a fire had to be kept burning in a small bin which was installed in the middle of the room, but which unfortunately only dispersed its heat in a 1 m radius. The worse was the fumes and smoke of the coals we were burning. We were exactly on top of a coal mine and there were several tunnel entrances in the vicinity to access the mine. But the Russians made sure before they left to destroy everything on the inside and leave slaughtered horses just at the entrance. When the wind would finally calm down, the smell that came from the rotting corpses in the tunnels was horrible and the air almost became unbreathable. I was about to experience a less painful period than my comrades. A scratch on my leg from a little while ago got infected and became an ulcer of about 4 cm in diameter, leaking all the time. It didn't bother me at all, but it was not something nice to look at. Since the care for such an injury couldn't be provided at the battalion infirmary, I was evacuated to the military hospital of Konstantinovska, a large city several kilometers away from the Legion's location. At the beginning of December Captain Dupré, commander of the 4th Company (4.Kp), arrived in the same hospital. During one of those terrible marches, he rode his horse into a field full of land mines and anti-tank mines. His horse stepped on a mine and was blown up in a thousand pieces; Captain Dupré had both his legs blown off. He died a couple of hours later, without complaining, but before he died he smoked one cigarette after the other to ease his pain. At the same time, another legionnaire was evacuated from the battalion for an unknown reason and I forgot his name as well. After a nice bath and an intense delousing process, we were well taken care of and installed side by side in a room occupied by half a dozen German soldiers, all sick or wounded. One of them had a part of his arm blown off due to the shrapnel from an exploded bomb.

One night I woke up and I heard something dripping in a corner. Drop by drop some liquid was dripping on the floor. My first idea was that one of my companions wet himself during his sleep. I got up and directed myself to the suspicious location where the liquid was dripping. My cry for a Sani (Sanitäter = medic) woke up the entire room and probably half of the hospital. When the light went on I noticed under one soldier's bed a large puddle of blood. The poor guy opened one of his wounds during his sleep and would've died that night if I hadn't woken up or if I had thought that one was just peeing in his bed and I wouldn't had deemed it necessary to get out of my bed for that. He was evacuated immediately and the next morning he was rolled back into the room, looking a little pale, but the transfusion saved his life. A couple of nice steaks and a couple of bottles of regional wine brought him back to normal in just a couple of days. The ordinary food was excellent, the care was perfect, and the doctors and nurses were good for the care of the two "Wallonen" (Walloons). Everything there was good and favorable for a good recovery. Admitted to the hospital around December 15, it was after Christmas that I was able to return to my battalion. I was unable to celebrate this event with my father and other comrades as I had hoped for. Also, my companion at the hospital wasn't ready to be released yet. On December 24 after dinner, our section doctor came into the room and distributed cigars, cigarettes, chocolate, and other goodies. Normally there was one bottle of French wine for two and to comfort the "Wallonen", but they had a bottle of Hennessey 3 star cognac which perfectly executed its mission. It was necessary, since I was 19 years old and it was my first Christmas far away from my loved ones. I couldn't even kiss my father who was only 10 km away. And on top of that the war was raging out there and I'm sure my companions at the hospital also wished they were somewhere else. We tried to make things better but despite the good will of every person and good humor there were, sometimes, moments of intense silence. But the wine and cognac chased away all our dark thoughts and then ruined everything again. It changed nothing at all. It's the harder experiences that benefit the best and it's the suffering of all sorts that forms one's character. Nobody had pushed me to go there! If I was there it was because I wanted to be there! So why ruin everything? Instead, let us drink! A few days later, fully healed, I left the hospital, but before I did a doctor lectured me about the Walloon Legion. He told me that if I wanted to do things right I had to go back to Belgium for a while to have my blood purified. The Walloon Legion wouldn't be in Russia that much longer and it was going to be repatriated soon. I had no news from the battalion, and I didn't know from where the Oberarzt received his information. I guessed he had invented it. I didn't understand a thing what he was saying and I didn't want to believe him.

We were all volunteers to fight against the Bolshevists. I would find it very unlikely that one or some of us would change his mind because up until now we've only beaten down the kilometers instead of the enemy! It wasn't our fault if we weren't at the locations where all the action happened. Then thinking about it, who would be able to fight in -40°C? When I arrived at Cherbinovka by taxi - I hired a driver by paying him with cigarettes and chocolate - it seemed that nothing had changed. The most important news announcement was that my father was in the infirmary because of a rash; not that severe but very annoying. After the formalities upon my return to the unit, I went to the infirmary which was located not that far from the Palace of Culture. An incident a few days later would make this location unforgettable for those who had known it. My father was doing well and he would be dismissed in no time. His question was if I had seen the commander. "No, I haven't seen him," I replied. "Why?" - "Well, he's gone!" Was is true what the Oberarzt told me at the hospital? I explained to my father the story I hadn't shared yet from the battalion Oberarzt about the repatriation of the Walloon Legion. Was it true or not? Well it better be!

My father explained in a couple of words what the next step was in the existence of the Walloon Legion. The highest ranking Belgian officer of the Legion from August 8, 1941 was Major Jacobs. A nice father figure whose greatest ambition was to smoke a big pipe which was balancing on his belt buckle. To cut a long story short, he was not the material to lead an infantry battalion into war.

I have to be honest that the difficulties experienced with the snow were terrible. The abandoned chariots would only rejoin us just before Christmas, and since Dnjepopetrowsk numerous sick soldiers had been evacuated, reducing the manpower to 650. We went through a harsh winter with the bare minimum of special equipment. Physically we were almost morally exhausted! Under those circumstances, and to keep the spirit and dynamics high, we needed a leader who was motivated and strong. These were not the qualities of our current commander. It was true, and most likely that the liaison officer of the general staff, Leutnant Leppin, was acquired and he had the right to make reports about us. We also have to add that he didn't really appreciate our company for some time. On the other hand, some officers, like my commander Van Damme, had had enough of this situation which didn't make things better. But it was the situation that there was nobody to trust with the command of the Walloon Legion. My Oberarzt was well informed, however he lacked the last bit of information. From Brussels came General Staff of the Infantry Captain Pierre Pauly, a Liegeois. He truly came down on us, and this is only but a weak expression, on December 30, 1941. I decided to open the envelope I had received from the Oberarzt at the hospital, and I took notice of a long medical record about all the care I had received and what caused the ulcer. The result was, what the Oberarzt actually told me, that I had to return to Belgium to receive proper alimentation which would regenerate my blood. He had recommended this explicitly to the Oberarzt of the Walloon Legion. My knowledge of the German language in those days wasn't bad at all, and I missed nothing on my record besides a word or two written in Latin. All forms of paperwork were very rare in Russia, especially for a soldier to carry them during a campaign. It is unnecessary to say how these could be used, envelope included! I was a volunteer for the second time, and I still resisted telling my story to my parents. Together with Captain Pauly, ten more volunteers arrived who celebrated the New Year with us without causing any problems. Some of the wounded like myself rejoined the battalion as well. On January 2, after six officers and fifty legionnaires left because of illness or unable to fight for other reasons, approximately 700 men were left over. Leutnant Leppin, the liaison officer, was replaced by Hauptmann Von Lehe. Everything fell back into place after that. The situation in general was as follows: 600,000 men held the Eastern Front over a front of 1600 km (radial distance!) from Leningrad to Taganrog at the Sea of Azov. Cherbinovka, occupied by the Walloon Legion constituted an anchor and point of retreat on the front line. The liaison was established 8 km northeast by a German unit and at 15 km south by an Italian Corps. Like college students, soldiers had their particular sense of humor. We had baptized Major Jacobs "PPM" or Pauvre Petit Major (sad little Major). The period that Captain Pauly was in charge was baptized as the era of Pierre Pauly, which effectively had started on January 2. Things that are taken back in hand under normal circumstances are certainly not that likeable. In our situation it was almost inhuman, but it was necessary. From now on Captain Pauly was addressed with "Sir" or "Monsieur le Commandeur."

The discipline, normally not that high of a standard during a campaign, and which was not strictly followed at the Walloon Legion, thoroughly revived like the discipline during military training. A military training that would be energetically resumed at the front. During three weeks at -40°C, every morning, there was a salute to the flag with a strict discipline and only with permission, when standing at attention, to look at your neighbor to remove an ice peg from his nose or any other part that was exposed. We had military exercises and defensive work until noon, and in the afternoon we had class. There was also cleaning duty and inspection of weapons and bedrooms just like in recruit class. Undeniably this regimen which seemed very harsh soon showed us its real benefits. Our rooms that we were so disgusted about in the beginning now looked very nice and welcoming after we came back from an exercise or from a guard post outside in the ice. The critique on and spirit of revenge about the new management slowly faded away and our hungry stomachs now appreciated more the field kitchens even if the food wasn't sometimes cooked properly. Community life came back to its senses and a new solidarity was born, bringing back the camaraderie which seemed to be lost a couple of weeks ago. It is undeniable that by the end of December the Walloon Legion was doomed. Everything was going sideways. It is with great certainty that our commander Pierre Pauly saved the Walloon Legion.

Without a doubt some thought that it was preferable that everything would've ended this was. I didn't think so. The end of this adventure under these circumstances would've been favorable for certain people. For these people every occasion was perfect to spit more venom and they hoped that none of us would make it back. Later these people would take our glory into question and would find every motive to despise us or who would be more than happy to ridicule us. To ridicule us was maybe something worse than the death penalty in 1945, instead of being treated as an imbecile in 1942. But life turned back to normal and organized at Cherbinovka for the better of all of us, morally and physically. My father was dismissed from the infirmary, all healed up and still very strong for an old WWI veteran. On a regular basis a small contingent left by sleds to go get rations for the battalion at 15 km in a town named New York. Why New York? It's a mystery! In this town Russian sleds and sled drivers were commandeered. One day during a ration run one of our soldiers, estimated that the sled wasn't going too fast, noticed a man close to the road who was yelling something. Assuming that the man didn't know any French, he was completely blown away when the sled came to a full stop as the man yelled at the legionnaires, and without a Ukrainian accent, his face all lit up: "Stupid little Walloons!" Our soldier was speechless. The Ukrainian man said this in a Walloon dialect. To the soldiers' surprise the man was an old miner who 25 years ago worked with Walloons in the Donets Basin. From his Walloon companions he still remembered some swearwords and phrases. Nothing more, but this event was funny enough that it went around in the entire battalion.

Like I said before, we had to remove rocks and dig in our positions as per orders of our new commander. One night when we were enjoying a well-deserved rest, a rumor brought us the terrible news that the Palace of Culture in town was on fire. I wouldn't doubt that each and every one of us was thinking what an unrepairable loss of architectural beauty it would be for Cherbinovka with the destruction of this building. Besides the building stood the community house of Horta which was already reduced to rubble. We were aware of this and it must be said that during our salute to the flag at 0700h in the morning, the distractions were quite uncommon when it had to be decided if the Bourguignons were going to face this Siberian cold of if they would go assist with the show in town. Immediately we discovered the disaster in all its horror when we arrived in town. From two windows on the second floor from which the blinds had been missing for a couple of years, thick and heavy smoke escaped. We were wondering what to do when the local fire brigade arrived at the scene. A dozen men arrived running and pushing a pump engine which was a cistern mounted on a chassis with four wheels like the ones that were in service in 1885. Four men, two on each side of the pump, ensured that the hose was full of water and ready to go. Or at least it should have. The frozen water in the cistern stopped the pump from working, and in the meantime the smoke coming from the two windows became thicker and thicker. So, were we going to assist in the destruction of cultural heritage of the town? Absolutely not! Because it is persistency that affirms the will of the men in action. The water was frozen so we were going to defrost it! And so, it was done! We took some doors from the building which were chopped into pieces by the axes of the fire fighters. We placed the doors under the cistern and lit them up, however we had to keep the keep the fire small. It was a genius plan and rapidly executed! But the elements were against the courage of our men. To defrost the water we required a couple of hours and doors were scarce. The cistern, on the contrary, started to become dangerous as well as it was made of wood and started smoldering so we had to abandon the idea. Soon the helpers and spectators were going to assist and witness an enormous catastrophe. But what happened next? A miracle! From the windows of the second floor some Bourguignons threw most of the old paintings, which had caught fire, out of the building. How they did it we will never know, but they threw them out of the windows and as soon as they hit the snow in front of the building they stopped burning. Thank God that all of us made it back safely to our unit where the memorable actions of our men and the local fire fighters of Cherbinovka were remembered.

Unfortunately, such incidents broke the monotony of our stay, just like another tragic event that brought us back to reality. We were soldiers and we made war. An Italian Corps occupied another post south of our positions. We knew the Italians since October 1941 from previous encounters. We Latins (same language group) were immediately sympathetic to each other because on the German side they didn't understand that we were made for other things than strictly Prussian discipline, when besides war there's the Chianti wine and love. Of course all of this existed, but not during war. And here in the Donets region in January 1942 we were at war. And you too, you charming Italians, were going to pay a high toll soon since you neglected this terrible reality. One night when their sentinels in one of their occupied towns were partying with Bacchus and Eros at the local hotel, a Cossack troop raided the unguarded town and captured all the Italians without problem. If my memory is correct, there was one man in town that witnessed this event. In all cruelty, in -40° C, they were stripped naked and they had to walk to the town center where they were doused with ice cold water. All of them died that night, almost instantly, victims of their Mediterranean temperament, more gifted for their love games than for the game of warfare. Victims of - and it has to be said - a guilty negligence with catastrophic results which had no measures with the insignificance of the course which had provoked all of this. This drama was discovered the next day by a patrol of one of the other connection points.

For the Walloons luck ran out as well because German warrant officers were now assigned to our units. For a couple of weeks we were aware of the danger of the Cossack, whose actions became more and more frequent, and which had had raised our alertness and audacity. What motivated these terrible horsemen, these terrible horsemen which had an admirable courage which we would see in the near future? During this harsh winter the Russians launched a major offensive and were able to breach the German defense lines in the Donets region, in Artemivs'k, and were threatening Konstantinovska where I had spent last Christmas in the hospital. The second offensive followed rapidly after the first offensive, but this time it happened at the Mius front. These operations had the objective of encircling the armies in the Donets region. But a counter-offensive was launched to prevent this Soviet attack with the direct and immediate result that the Walloon Legion had to gear up and get ready for battle. On the morning of January 27, the Walloon Legion left Cherbinovka during a violent snow storm which had been raging all night. Twenty kilometers were travelled with a lot of difficulties, but in the same relative order. The chariots that were previously causing the delays were now distributed to the platoons. Now every group had its own chariot to tow. Even if our commander Pierre Pauly sometimes would come up with the silliest ideas which he wanted executed in the smallest detail, we had to admit that these ideas in general facilitated our travels in a positive way and permitted us to obtain results we never had obtained before. Without a doubt he was the man in charge of the situation. The complete battalion arrived at Alexandrowka, and we were on high alert because of this famous Cossack cavalry, especially after what happened to the Italians. It is here in Alexandrowka that I would have contact with an officer who was unknown to me at that time, but whom we would speak a lot in the Walloon Legion and whom I, like many others, would admire and highly respect.

Just before midnight I was patrolling my designated sector. The orders were clear and strict, naturally, since the disastrous experience had proven a while ago that the lives of an entire company could depend on just one sentinel. I was in the proximity of an isba[40] close to the general staff when I observed a silhouette coming in my direction. Immediately with the rifle at the ready I called out and I engaged in the following dialogue: "Who's there?" "Leutnant Lippert" was the silhouette's answer while it was still moving towards me. "Leutnant please stand still and provide me with the password!" "Leutnant Lippert is not enough for you?" For me it was more than enough but it was not the password. "Come into this house of the general staff and it will be given it to you." Did he really forget the password? Well he certainly knew which part of our unit was housed there. Obviously he could've ignored me since he was the senior warrant officer of the battalion and Adjutant of the commander. He then entered the isba and came out seconds later. I hadn't moved at all and at a couple of passes from me he stopped right in front of me and gave me the first part of the password which was usually comprised of three passwords in the style of "Paris-Lyon-Mediterranean." Each person had to say a part and now, since the formality had been accomplished Lt Lippert asked me for my name. From that point onwards he would never forget my name!

In the morning of January 23, we left for a march of 28 km. The distance we had to travel was average compared to all of the other marches, but by the time we arrived at our destination it would've been the longest as we would need 3 days in total to get there. Just before noon when everything seemed to be going relatively well, a snowstorm came up with a magnitude I had never seen before! The storm lasted for 60 seemingly endless hours! Because of its violence, in just a couple of minutes everything had disappeared under a couple centimeters of snow. After one hour there was no way to tell where we were. The roads were completely gone now. A man who distanced himself 20 m from the column went missing, and to make it possible to find him back he had to fire his rifle in the air. We were marching

---

[40] A traditional log house of rural Russia, with an unheated entrance room and a single living and sleeping room heated by a clay or brick stove.

now without knowing where we were going, detaching us from the other. At night we arrived in a Kolkhoz where we spent the night. The storm was still raging, and there was nothing we could do but wait. We had to wait until the next morning to get back en route, and with a bit of luck we would find the road again. During 60 hours non-stop an incredible amount of snow had come down. In certain areas the wind had accumulated snow drifts of several meters high. Some of the houses were literally covered up to the roof with snow. You really had to know the exact location of a village to actually be able to find it first. En route we encountered other groups of our soldiers and the company was able to get back together. Suddenly on the horizon we noticed a compact group of silhouettes. We were just able to see that they were not hostile and when we came closer we noticed that it was our commander Pierre Pauly who was more than happy that he had found his 1st Company and Léon Degrelle. Part of the group that we saw were 200 Russians who were commandeered to work for us. Several minutes later the 1st Company entered a village while walking in between two walls of snow more than 2 m high and tens of meters long. It was January 25. We left on January 22 and since then we had covered 28 km. We arrived last, but we still received a warm welcome with at the same time a big breath of relief. Everyone else thought that the 1st Company had been captured by the Cossacks and that it underwent the same fate as the Italians. It became a bit of an obsessive fear, but it was justified because these horsemen were spotted all over the place and their numbers increased significantly to approximately 600! The size of a battalion! The state of alert was still in effect and a safety perimeter was placed around the camp. Besides that, we enjoyed a bit of well-deserved rest. The little Russian sappers were continuously guarding the white steppe except for when they were having a meal break. All dug in and behind their MGs, they would shoot at anything that would move in the steppe, forming small holes in the snow and creating dust clouds all over the place.

An immobilized airplane targeted by a MG does not cause such a big threat, but one just needs to know that and how to react effectively. On the contrary, only one volley of a plane's board cannon could engulf 5 or 6 houses without any hope for survivors. Besides the snow and wind, the long marches didn't cause any problems anymore like in the beginning of our campaign. It was just a matter of organizing now. We left on January 27 at 0700h and we marched 20 km, arriving around 1400h at Grivinobyl[41] where the air raid alarm was still in effect and on high alert. Now it was serious business! From the previous aerial attack, we could learn that these were not simple fighter planes but heavy bombers. They had destroyed many important parts of the town like depots and service buildings, typical for an aerial attack in a combat zone. The downside of the defense system was that if we were going to set ourselves on the defense for the air raids, our resupply zones would become, in just a couple of hours, a complete war zone and our role was to prevent such things from happening. Except for the 2nd Company, who was enroute with all the chariots, the entire battalion was now going to travel by train! At 2000h everybody was set and ready to embark, and the convoy started rolling until 1100h the next morning. I have never understood certain incidents and I still continue to challenge people that try to explain and justify these things. The distance we had to travel was 20 km but it seemed that our train was the only one travelling in the area for the last couple of days. But why didn't the train leave at 2115h to arrive at its destination one hour later? Why? Maybe I'm not very receptive to military scheduling, but I couldn't understand this at all, not even today. Evidently the train cars were not equipped for such a long trip, and even if the temperature mounted a little bit outside, it was still -30° C. Just try to sit or lay on a wooden floor in a train car which was meant for the transportation of goods and not for people without blankets or other winter equipment. What could we do? First, we were very happy to travel 20 km not on foot but now we were forced, during the entire duration of the trip, to run around in our train cars running distances of 50 km! This was the longest march of the entire winter campaign! And those that didn't run inside the train car and remained scated in a corner had to be evacuated after arrival because they were showing signs of frostbite to their hands and feet. Why did it take so long for such a short distance by rail? The explanation is simple because everything is simple in the army! When we were running our distance inside the train car, a new snow storm was raging outside covering the tracks with snow, approximately 1 m high. A snow plow in front of the locomotive made sure to clear the tracks for all the train cars that were following and to keep things safe, it had to be done at a slow speed. Why couldn't it be like

---

[41] This location is spelled phonetically, however the author was unable to find it on the map of the Ukraine. Some of the towns or villages from the period 1940-1945 have disappeared and cannot be found anymore on present day maps. It is assumed that this town was in the Donets area where the Walloon Legion was located in the winter of 1941-1942.

that every time we had to march? We could've get used to this! With the wind gusting and heavy snow coming down we arrived in a big Kolkhoz which was baptized Rosa Luxemburg[42], named after this Jewish-communist politician from Berlin. There the battalion was installed and one had to keep his eyes open in every direction since the tactical situation was more confusing. Despite the bad climate conditions, guard and patrol were provided on a regular basis. And to justify our vigilance one of our patrol units had to open fire on a Cossack unit which was distancing itself without resistance. The bad weather prevented all enemy aerial activities and we spent 10 days without having to worry about that. What was the situation at the Donets front at the beginning of February 1942? The second enemy offensive at the Mius was held back, but in the north the majority of the Russian forces occupied Barvenkovo and Konstantinovska. Supported by partisans and the air force, the light infantry and tanks were able to push deeply into the German defenses towards Pavlohrad and Grischino. These attacks were answered by targeted counter-attacks, and the serious threat towards the armies in the Donets was temporarily stopped.

The Walloon Legion together with the Croatian Legion under Colonel Markov formed a column of all types of light weapons and was in charge of the "cleaning duty" of the Samara River region. It was in company of these fearless and courageous soldiers that we would accomplish our last marches in this horrible winter during which the enemy fighter planes wouldn't leave us any opportunity to rest. The light bombers of English manufacture, recognizable by their semi-retractable landing gear, could've caused heavy losses to our column if they were operated by seasoned pilots. It was during one of their attacks that Léon Degrelle, while seeking cover, had his foot crushed by a chariot from which the horses were spooked by one of the planes. He had only a broken foot which was not too bad. What was worse was that another chariot filled with ammunition boxes and explosives had taken fire. It had been hit by an incendiary projectile and everything could blow up in seconds.

---

[42] Born March 5, 1871, Zamość, Poland, Russian Empire (now in Poland)-died January 15, 1919, Berlin, Germany. Polish-born German revolutionary and agitator who played a key role in the founding of the Polish Social Democratic Party and the Spartacus League, which grew into the Communist Party of Germany. As a political theoretician, Luxemburg developed a humanitarian theory of Marxism, stressing democracy and revolutionary mass action to achieve international socialism.

We all realized the danger, as did the Croatian Adjutant, a colossal man who commanded the PAK 37s. He took the burning ammunition box in his arms and went to put it down in the snow 50 m farther. The few seconds that this operation took seemed to last for ages. Ages which were nothing compared to this man's actions which put him with one leg already into eternity. The ammunition box exploded right after he rejoined us. He was short of breath because he had to run for his life. Three or four days later on February 16 we crossed the Samsara River. This river which could've been 50 m wide was completely frozen and permitted our lights trucks to cross on the condition that they left enough room in between them. When we were crossing the river, about 50 of us were putting pieces of blankets and pieces of coats on our horse's feet to make sure they wouldn't slip on the ice. Then an enemy bomber loomed up, taking the river as its target. The bomber carried one enormous bomb which was visible on the belly of the fuselage. This bomb could break all the ice and could throw all of us into the ice cold water. There was no way to escape and we would have drowned if this would be dropped on us. Our hobnail boots were not equipped with ice skates and didn't permit us to run to safety. It was out of the question that this plane wouldn't be able to hit us. He dropped his bomb with such precision right in the middle of our scattered group, and it had to make at least one victim. It was one of ours, comrade Pirret, a brave man from the region of Namur. The bomb swiped right next to him knocking him down. Gott mit uns! It was a miracle. Dropped at a low altitude the bomb wasn't able to turn its nose down to penetrate the ice. At 300 km/h it started sliding over the ice like a crazy out of control rocket and stopped at a few hundred meters from us. Shaken from what happened, our friend Pirret stood up and looked at our assistant platoon commander Jules Mathieu and said: "She came pretty close, eh Adjutant?!"

In the Ukrainian plains I twice noticed that after the spike of winter at the end of January beginning of February, there was an immediate defrosting of snow and ice. The temperatures climbed back up to 4 or 5°C. Since the soil was covered with a layer of ice and 1 m of snow, I will leave the rest to your own imagination. Within a couple of days, the bottom layer of ice was covered with several centimeters of water. Then suddenly a new cold snap would hit and freeze everything again overnight, vehicles included as they were all sunken into the water. During the defrosting period, the town of Blagodatsh was the theatre of heavy combat. An SS battalion of the

Germania Regiment, supported by tanks, initiated an attack on the village which was defended by a couple cannons. Several times the courageous men of the Cossack cavalry charged the Germans to protect their artillery positions. Hundreds of them were at the edge of the village but couldn't resist the brutal force of the SS troops. A piece of artillery was blown up by a direct hit from a tank. The operators of that piece of artillery were literally ripped to pieces. One of these men had his face "scalped" from his skull and the flesh was sticking to the cannon. It was missing all expressions... Another man was laying down on his belly while his face was looking at the sky. The frost overnight had kept them frozen in the positions that they fell. All the shredded meat laying around gave the impression that the location was a butcher shop. It was February 16, a day that the bombs were not exploding. In the meantime important enemy forces were concentrating south of Barvenkovo. We reckoned they would continue their offensive on the 28th. An advanced defense position was posted just north of the Samara River to prevent the enemy from crossing it. Kampfgruppe Tröger, which came as a reinforcement of the 100.Leichte Infanterie-Division of General Werner Sanne from which the command post was located in Stepanovka and the HQ in Bilopillia, also took position at the Samara River.

Baptism of Fire - Gromovayabalka!

On February 17 the Legion Wallonie was in position at Gromovayabalka northeast of Stepanovka. The point of support was in the kolkhoz, and the village nearby stretching approximately 2 km. It was the end of the suffering but the beginning of a martyrdom! This was it, the Walloon Legion entered the arena to perform this time. It was in the air for quite a while. For a couple of weeks, the Russians took advantage of their winter to fiercely attack the German positions, not thinking they were capable of doing so after they had received some terrible blows by the German Army. Nature wanted to slaughter them, and they were nearly defeated by winter: our victorious armies who in October and November 1941 were literally sucked into the Russian mud. Their trucks, their chariots, their cannons, and their field kitchens all sunk away in the muck from which only a foot soldier could be able to liberate himself. These German Armies saw by the end of November all their materials and equipment petrified as if it were the work of a magic wand because at night, without the smallest transition, it started freezing to -10° C after which the snow started to come down. During the days and weeks, the snow was levelling the steppe by covering and isolating all beings. There was nothing around you, nothing into infinity! Nothing but war which we were pursuing for months by foot for hundreds of kilometers. For months they lived at a distance from it in the isbas, but finally they would catch up with the war. It was the Valley of Thunder; it was Gromovayabalka!

We finally had arrived in this town on February 17, a small Ukrainian village which would terribly justify its name of "Valley of Thunder" or Gromovayabalka. A rain of artillery fire fell on us while we were flanked by a battery of Croatian volunteers operating their PAK 37s. They were going to live this living hell. Like legendary heroes they marched to the torture. After a long and terrible ordeal, it was the place of sacrifice. I followed the movement a bit like a sleepwalker. I had no fear, at least not yet because I hadn't fully realized what had happened to me. It was a little later when the situation calmed down that it started to sink in. Amidst the explosions, encouraged by our yelling NCOs, our faces were sprayed by the clouds of snow dust coming from the enemy shell impacts. The battalion commander was with us and everybody advanced towards the highest point of the village.

That was our objective. We had to advance only when the whistling of the enemy shells would disappear because of the constant explosions following each other almost every second. Around us we could see grey craters in the snow, hardened by the frost. The exploding shells flew into pieces and made different types of noises: the little ones made a whistling sound, and the bigger ones made a buzzing sound like big insects. I was stopped, kneeling with my back arched and head down. A Croatian Soldier squatted down with his head against my thigh. The Croatian soldier was already dead, his temple was crushed and his blood was already freezing on my uniform. Blood! Something I've seen flowing from tens of comrades, from my father, and from myself. It was an infernal stay made of cold, death, and fear. And after every horrifying day, a night of horror would follow.

We installed ourselves in some of the isbas which were going to become the graves for tens of our men. For ten days and ten nights there were aerial attacks, shelling, grenades, and tank projectiles fired at us. We had no rest, and it was freezing: -30°C! Our poor uniforms only provided temporary protection against the icy winds which penetrated our uniforms and bodies during hours of guard duty or patrols. Everybody was sick: dysentery, nervous breakdowns, fever, and lack of sleep. And the few moments of rest that we had during this war of hate we spent chasing hundreds of lice which were busy devouring our most intimate parts. We were sleeping in an area of a couple square meters with temperatures of -30° to -40°C. This time was spent constantly thinking that at any time a projectile would penetrate through the roof, shredding tens of bodies to pieces like it did in the neighboring isbas the night before with the 2nd Company, and like this morning with the 4th Company. Outside the closed door was the sinister steppe with a grey whiteness of corpses. The wind was howling death, the bullets were howling death, and the projectiles were howling death. Our positions were built out of blocks of ice which offered only minimal temporary protection against the wind, and that upon the condition of remaining immobilized, which meant having frozen feet within minutes. So one had to stay in position, had to stay covered, and keep the eyes open at all times. Sometimes in the snow storm silhouettes would appear at just a couple of meters away from us. If it's the enemy it would be too late if they were to engage in a confrontation, but if they were to shoot too fast, they risked killing a friend. A huge dilemma!

Many times situations were confusing with Croatian patrols coming from neighboring positions. Their uniforms were khaki just like the Russian uniforms. And when they combined it with white camouflage we wouldn't know the difference at all. Just the language was different than Russian. However, there were never any incidents. But there was no panic in between the Walloons. For most of them it was their first combat experience, like myself. One couldn't state that the conditions were favorable for a progressive initiation, no, everything was so sudden and every situation was so unexpected. Nothing was classic during this war. I had already been in this campaign for four months, but none of the situations so far resembled any of the infantry exercises during basic training.

It was not only the young ones that were disoriented. My father had served during 1914-1918, so he faced the danger in a more reasonable and phlegmatic way, but he was disoriented just like I was on how the events took form. My comparison with the fact that he already had fought for four years was totally wrong. For him and for the other "old dogs" as we used to call them, the suffering and death didn't have such an impact. They supported these facts with more moral force, and they approached it more calmly than we younger ones. So tired of fatigue, dusty, and full of vermin, we were acting like robots, only physically reacting to impulses from the outside. I was part of the 1st Platoon of the 1st Company (1.Kp).

Léon Degrelle was, just like me, a simple MG gunner in the same company. A couple of days before, as we already know, he fractured his foot during an aerial attack. Nobody was able to convince him that his place was at the hospital, and he stayed with us while having a big cast on his foot. Not for anything in the world would he have abandoned his position. For months now, he had never accepted any favors which could've spared him from this ordeal we had to go through. He went through the same army training at the same rank as mine without any considerations of the NCOs and instructors who, with him being just a simple soldier, wanted nothing to do with him. He was not gifted for the job as a soldier, and even less for the rigid Prussian discipline. Just like us he marched all the way carrying his MG. We marched for hundreds of kilometers in only a couple of months and which lead us to this famous Valley of Thunder. Here we were now, side by side on the beaten earth inside an isba. It was him with his broken foot who could lift our spirits all the time. There were Rexists, like my father, who had followed him for years. Then there were others who were never engaged in politics and who didn't know him until a couple of months ago. Personally I was too young to get engaged in politics, but I had accompanied my father to some very intense rallies. Since my 18th birthday in October 1940, I was part of the battle formations who were also some sort of militia whose duty was the security detail for Léon Degrelle at the party's rallies, and also as protection service in the Jeunesse Rexiste camps. On many occasions I was in his presence, and what struck me the most about him was that his person had a certain audacity and lots of nonchalance. Things that weren't precisely the best qualities of a combatant. Sometimes I thought to myself, and without a single doubt many others did the same, what would happen if things went wrong, which actually could happen one day? I have to admit in all sincerity that I was even more worried about my own behavior, and I owe it to the calmness of some of my companions that I was able to hold up during this first engagement. With Léon Degrelle, his audacity and nonchalance had transformed into lots of courage and a certain calmness which surely impressed all of us. It was then that I truly started to admire this man which later I would highly respect for his selfless actions for our Legion. That Léon Degrelle is considered to be a war criminal in Belgium leaves me indifferent. First of all because it still needs to be proven, and because I have the utmost respect for a man who risked his life hundreds of times with the only goal to lead by example. He was in a position that would've permitted him to observe everything from a distance and leave all the hard work to other in his advantage. But this was not the case at all! Some consider Léon Degrelle responsible for the loss of 2,000 lives on the Eastern Front. He never forced one single person to go there - he only accepted volunteers - and in 1945 he was responsible for handing out foreign worker passes to his troops, to find civilian for them, and to immobilize them so that they could disappear in nature. This way they would avoid being captured and could return home to Belgium or stay on a local farm. This is the truth and I know it for the simple reason that when I left the military academy in April 1945 for 15 days, I was a platoon leader for these poor guys. He witnessed all those that lost their lives because it was only in a very rare occasion that he wouldn't be at the front when his legionnaires were dying. He survived the war because of his own luck. Some say it was because of him being wounded six times - six insignificant wounds - while others, some of our own men, blamed him for abandoning the Legion and for saving his own life in Spain in 1945, and that he didn't undergo the same fate as his fellow legionnaires. But it was in his best interest not to undergo the same fate as his legionnaires because he wouldn't have survived for 12 hours. And his assassination wouldn't have saved a single one of his legionnaires. If we would've won the war and we would return to Belgium, I don't think I would've been a Rexist. Personally, I believe that one political party is one too many. I don't know if Léon Degrelle would've been a better politician than all the others. What is sure is that I continue to respect Léon Degrelle like all my other brothers-in-arms, and the ones that don't understand this have never seen men dying around them while fighting for the same cause.

Ten days had passed since our arrival in the village, ten days in which we lost track of time. Ten times 24 hours in which periods of clearness alternated constantly with periods of obscurity. There was no difference between day and night. Many times, the alarm had thrown us on the icy surface. But it was only reinforced patrols who wandered between our positions to taunt our defense lines which consisted of the pivotal point commanding the Samara River crossing and which could open the way to Dnepropetrovsk. However, we would be alerted of the decisive attack. Elements of the SS Germania were on high alert in the village of Ocheretyne 2 km northeast of Gromovayabalka. These men had taken Gromovayabalka, and we had hastily followed them. Since then, at Ocheretyne, they underwent daily attacks by the Russian infantry which the men of SS Germania were able to repel every time with an extreme courage almost too difficult to explain with words! One of our platoons assured the liaison between the two villages. Our men had seen them not that long ago. These men jumped to their weapons at the very last second, and they would only come out to fight man to man, pushing the Russians back, only to come back a little later to continue their game of cards or to continue reading their books. On the morning of the 28th there were only two handfuls of men left when it was decided that the German troops had to stop the Russian winter offensive on this day. On the night of the 27th all civilians were evacuated. The enemy learned that we were getting ready for them! Most of the civilians mainly women, children, and elderly people, were placed into the cowsheds upon our arrival at Gromovayabalka, since 40 soldiers would occupy most of the isbas. Just like us they had to undergo a rain of projectiles for a week, and they had nothing else to eat but sunflower seeds. All the other provisions were taken away from them by the retreating Russian Army. That night we gave them 30 minutes to reassemble at the rear of the village and to start walking to the closest village during the night in -30°C weather. The only thing that was left for them in the world were these four walls and a roof, but we had to force them out without any good explanation. For these villagers who only knew the Feldgrau uniforms for the past 10 days, it was the first act of barbarism. The only explanation we could have given them was the good one, and even then we would not have told them the truth. Would they have believed us if we told them the truth? We were not going to tell them that all hell was going to break lose in a little while and that nothing would be spared. That is, except for a couple walls, and that several tanks would be taking part in this ordeal. They knew this for sure! Since our arrival about 10 men were killed and about 50 were wounded. Because of this and because of sickness, our effective manpower dropped to 500. Medics, doctors, priests, soldiers...all were included. Together with us there was a German artillery group comprised of two 105 mm Infanteriegeschütze (infantry support guns, in this case most likely the *leichte Feldhaubitze* "light field howitzer"), two 75 mm Infanteriegeschütze, and one section of Croatian volunteers with two PAK 37s which were only able to scratch the mid-size tank of the Russians, the T34. We were part of the combat group under the command of Lieutenant-Colonel Tröger which was comprised of the following: the Legion Wallonie, one Croatian battalion, one SS Germania battalion, one Aufklärung Kompanie (Reconnaissance Company) on sleds, one group of German artillery (Infanteriegeschütze), heavy tanks, and a squadron of Stukas. We were all incorporated together in the 100.Leichte Infanterie Division under General Sanne.

One morning the battle finally started, and death was orchestrating the carnage and showed its real face through the blast of the machine guns. Our mission at Gromovayabalka was to hold for 20 minutes. Remember this well: 20 minutes that had to allow for the intervention of tanks and Stukas. On February 28 at -30°C we found ourselves crunched in our positions. But we wouldn't be able to hold our positions for much longer. The few leftovers of the SS Germania which hadn't yet been massacred hadn't had the time to put on their hats! They had no ammunition left, and they wished us lots of luck while informing us that we wouldn't have a chance to defend ourselves against the storm that was coming towards us.

When the charge started, there were two Russian Infantry Regiments, about 2,000 men, supported by 14 T34 tanks. We were only 500 strong, all traitors, wearing on our sleeve the Belgian tricolor shield which had the Burgundy cross drawn over it. These traitors were singing "Vers l'Avenir!" (Towards the future) and also the Brabançonne during battle! Traitors that were going to die while crying "Long Live Belgium!" In front of us there were 2,000 men against less than 500! On our positions a rain of fire and iron came down while we were trying to hold the lines. The Soviet artillery was firing at will now. Our PAK 37, useless against the Russian tanks, was blowing holes in the Russian infantry lines, but they quickly filled up again with new men. We MG gunners and rifle men had received orders to open fire only at the last moment. One T34 was already firing at our grenade launchers. One of them in position just a couple of meters away from my MG position, received a direct hit. The crew members were blown away, and the crew leader was found meters away, dead, half naked. The first cries of the wounded were heard, and they had to be transported immediately to the rear so that they could be evacuated to the battalion's infirmary. From there, rolled in blankets, they would be transported by sleds to the nearest hospital which was 10-15 km from the front lines. This was done by night obviously! During the day they would be the target of the little Russian fighter planes who would shoot at anything that moved on the steppe. And this was only the beginning! The Reds were now 50 m away from our positions, and this was the moment that our MGs and rifles opened fire. It was a real massacre. The first lines went down but soon they were replaced by the following lines. Soon we'd have to retreat! The Reds were shooting at us with explosive ammunition, and the only advantage was that it couldn't penetrate a block of ice or a reinforced wall. They were going to learn what hell is and they were going to perish in the fire! But they would also get killed by iron so we had to win or die. We were fighting with grenades and bayonets, and with the MG at the ready. Every isba was like a little fortress which we would defend dearly. The tanks that breached the positions of the 2nd Company and were occupying the north of the village were following the progression of the Red infantry in our sector, a sector which they wouldn't dare penetrate. The reason why was that the center of the village, after a couple of times of continuous cycles of frost - defrost - frost, was transformed into a really impenetrable barricade. We had turned our isba into a little fortress when at 50 m on our left one or two tanks opened fire at us. They blew our roof off, and most of the walls were damaged. We were able to save ourselves by crawling from under the debris covered in dirt, plaster, and blood. The Red soldiers were unable to capture or remove us from there!

The wounded which we had to leave behind, since we weren't able to evacuate them, were shot by the Russians with one bullet to the head! One of my high school friends, a Liegeois who operated the MG with me received a bullet in his stomach. We had to put him down in a corner inside an isba covered by several blankets and we had to leave without him. Two hours later we would find him again during the counter-attack. We were re-taking all the isbas one by one. Half the houses were severely damaged and most of them were missing their roof. During those two hours, the Reds had occupied all the, but none of them had searched that particular corner and had lifted the pile of blankets. Our wounded comrade had no complaints when we found him again, but he was suffering. He was a tough one but he would succumb to his injuries in the infirmary a few hours later.

They were fighting one against four. Death cleaned out their ranks, but they continued fighting, covered in black dust and red of blood. During this time in the sector of the 2nd Company, the tanks which had run low on ammunition were following our soldiers, crushing them under their tracks. In between two man-to-man battles, we observed the manhunt led by these 28t mastodons. The show was terrifying! Imaging how the effects were for these "actors", the ones chased by these tanks. Ironically this inhumane game would permit us to reconquer our sector.

A young German artillery lieutenant who had half of his left arm ripped off by an explosive bullet was able to recover one of the 105 mm cannons, and with the help of a few other men they engaged several enemy tanks who were massacring the 2nd Company. Multiple shots hit their targets! The Russian tankers were terribly shaken but the rounds were not made to penetrate such armor. But the tanks were afraid to show themselves now and they remained hidden behind the houses. Not for long though! The lieutenant who lost half of his left arm had lost most of his blood and died at his cannon. One hundred meters away from us we observed multiple Russian sleds approaching the tanks with new ammunition. Together with Sergeant Daras[43], the old Gardener of Léon Degrelle, we installed an MG inside what

---

[43] Francois Daras, born February 25, 1919 in Rostov o/t Don (Russia), joined the Legion Wallonie as a Sergeant or Unteroffizier. Later he was promoted to Untersturmführer. KIA at Koarovka on February

was left of a house. Some riflemen took position beside us just like in basic training. First, we shot the horses to immobilize the convoy of sleds, and then we shot the Red soldiers who were hastily trying to remove the carcasses so they could push the sleds 10 m farther to position them behind cover. It is crazy what an MG and a couple of old rifles could do! After a couple of minutes all of them realized that the ammunition would never make it to the tanks. The tanks went looking for the sleds and hooked them up so they could tow them to safety. During this time another tank noticed our position and started shelling us. We left our isba after the fifth or sixth round had hit us. Crying and spitting our blood, we left the building, one of us stumbling over his lowered pants as he was suffering from dysentery. With four or five men, and with no losses,. we were able to put tens of Russian soldiers out of action! But we were not able to enjoy our victory for long. The tanks were resupplied with new ammunition and they started shelling us again with the goal that their infantry would be able to reoccupy our sector. It was the same scenario as with their first attack. It was a violent altercation without name in which particular scenes would take place, impossible to forget by the actors! In the midst of this hell, out of nowhere, a Russian horse was walking around with its mouth half ripped off by an explosion. He had the saddest looking eyes and a little bit of blood was running down from his bit. It seemed that he came to us asking us to release him from its misery but none of us wanted to shoot him in the head. He had to die on his own, twice the victim of the humans, of their barbarism and stupidity. After it had been deathly wounded, we were not capable to see its final prayers.

A medic of the 1st Company was the little Sergeant Volacker, a cocky man and not that pleasant to deal with. It was on his hands that I saw my fur gloves which had disappeared a couple of days ago! He died close to us, crouched while he was trying to help one of our wounded. It would never cross my mind to take my gloves back which could have warmed up my frozen fingers which were full of wounds since this morning. The gloves stayed on the hands of our courageous deceased medic. He earned them more than anyone else! A couple meters away, Ives Lefebvre was yelling at us. A bullet had opened his belly, and it was necessary for someone to rescue him as soon as possible. But who? Every second that we were exposed to the enemy could've been fatal. So Pierre went to rescue him. Ives was holding his hands on his belly to prevent his life flowing out of his body. He was yelling at us, crying, and it was his brother who went to get him. He carried him in his arms and brought him to the infirmary where he died a couple of hours later. He was only 17 years old. Another young man, Legand, fell into the snow next to a corpse that was stretched out on the ground. The corpse was stiff because of death and the freezing temperatures. When he turned over the corpse, he recognized his own father. I knew Marcel from primary school. We were 10 years old at that time, and now we were 19. We had found each other again a few months earlier during basic training. My only friend had his two knees busted and he thought we would leave him there. To the two comrades that wanted to carry him away, he said that it would be better to leave him there to die instead of the three of them dying there. They made it out alive and after a few months of recovery in an infirmary he had full use of his knees again. Our comrade Henry Berghmans died a couple of days later from a piece of grenade shrapnel that went through his heel. Another big corpse was stretched out with its arms crossed; the steel helmet was perforated and covering half of the face with a bit of blood showing from under the helmet. We turned him around and we found out that it was Steenbruggen, a WWI veteran.

When would it be our turn? The same fate certainly awaited us! How come that we were the ones still turning over the dead bodies? "Well what are you thinking about? Shoot in the name of God or do you want to resemble them? No?! Then fight!" It was Adjutant Closset[44], leader of the 3rd Platoon and former Sabena pilot. He was a regular guy, and he was loved by everybody. And he was right, we had better things to do instead of thinking of those from 1914-1918. We had to kill to survive, and so I killed! I killed because I didn't want to die. Next to me the old veteran stood up. His hand coming down from his neck, full of blood. The bullet went through his helmet but only scratched his skull from the front to the back. He died in captivity after the war due to an illness. My comrade Jean Lambert was with me. He had both knees on the ground and calmly he was shooting everything that presented itself in front of him for the last couple of minutes. I did the same thing, but I was more nervous and I shot with less precision. Suddenly I heard "bing!" next to my ear. I looked at Lambert and I saw blood coming

---

[44] Léon Closset was a SS-Frw. Obersturmführer and joined the Legion Wallonie in August 1941. He was initially in charge of the 3rd Platoon of the 1.KP. A former pilot with SABENA - a Belgian Airline company - he engaged in the Legion Wallonie, survived the war, and passed away on February 3, 1954.

from under his helmet. There was a hole in his helmet, around his temple, from which a white/grey matter tinted in red came out. His eyes were fixed to the front and he wasn't moving for a couple of seconds. I looked at him but he was still alive! So we don't die anymore when we lose our brain through our helmet? Suddenly he removed his helmet from his head. His wound was just a scratch on his head and the "brains" were part of the felt liner that came out of the helmet because of the damage that the bullet had created.

Following my marriage in 1953, I heard my mother-in-law talk about a branch of the family in which the last name was Chabot. Never stigmatizing the image and conduct of the young Albert Chabot, a career soldier who had never done anything good in his life according to the family. The shame of the family as we speak. Until the day that I told my mother-in-law, who was a brave lady, that no one in her honorable family had died or was going to die like the young Albert Chabot, who voluntarily, and alone, while the Russians were engaging went to save a wounded Croatian Warrant Officer who was screaming for help on the battlefield. Good for nothing and died for nothing, isn't that remarkable?

Then someone came for me and took me to the last isba in the village, where my father was located. His left leg had been hit by a bullet as well as his left arm; his right foot damaged by a round from a tank. He had already there for more than two hours and temporarily taken care of. Four years without a scratch in WWI, and here wounded after a couple of hours! Unable to move, he was suffering without complaining during my presence. I left him to return to but I would combat find him again later under more dramatic circumstances. Outside the confusion was indescribable. In the 2nd and 4th Company sector, the counter-attack was led by Commander Pauly himself. Dr. Miesse, Commander Buyts had been killed by MG fire. Leutnant Thys who had been one of my comrades during training was killed in action as well. But what could we handful of men do against hundreds of men and tanks? The enemy was too strong and we had already twice lost a large number of men when we counter-attacked with man-to-man assaults. Despite our previous losses, we went in for a third strike! After one day of battle many Walloons fell due to the fire of the tanks and the machine guns. It was 1500h and the short winter afternoon came to its end. The Reds had regrouped, and with their tanks they were going to put a final stop to this battle and throw us out of the village for good. In the remaining ruins we tried to take cover from the constant shelling and continuous MG fire. Above the sounds of battle we could hear the war cry of the Reds: *"Hurrah Pobeda!"* or "Hurrah for victory!" pushed by 1,000 men. They saw that victory was within reach, and they were determined to grab it. It was our last chance because if we were thrown back into the steppe we would be without any possible cover and most likely we wouldn't make it out alive. We were left there to die, and this sentiment was only reinforced when we heard the roaring sound of approaching aircraft. Did they really need this for a handful of Walloons who were fighting tooth and nail? For us it was an honor and we were going to show them; our pride became virtue and we were going to die! They stopped at the last obstacle, succumbing to the unjust fate when from the skies came down the miracle that made death change side.

The airplanes appeared, there were three, and the cry of joy coming from 300 Walloons went above the "Hurrah" from the Reds. Stukas![45] I truly believe that the pilots could hear and see us. It was total delirium, and we were so happy that we were crying, dancing, and rolling in the snow. And then in a couple of minutes, nothing else but the sound of the Stuka engines. The Stukas were getting into combat formation and were setting up at a specific altitude to start their attack. We were in complete silence with our eyes wide open savoring this precious moment. It was like a man who was sentenced to death but the sentence was stayed one minute before the execution. In front of us the tanks and the men were stopped; the men were looking up to the sky muted by the terror that they very well knew from before: the Stukas! The birds of death turned around and then dove down on their targets with wailing sirens. Suddenly all hell broke loose when the Stukas came down releasing their bombs from under their wings while pulling up at the last second. Their deadly cargo came down, making the same noise as the planes while diving down in the ranks of the Reds which caused some serious panic among them. All over the place in the snow we saw corpses, body parts, arms, legs, heads…and the tanks were disintegrated in the midst of the terrible explosions. And the Bourguignons stampeded

---

[45] Stuka (Junker JU-87), German in full Sturzkampfflugzeug ("dive-bomber"), a low-wing, single-engine monoplane dive-bomber used by the German Luftwaffe from 1937 to 1945, with especially telling effect during the first half of World War II. The Stuka was designed to employ the dive-bombing technique. Wind-driven sirens were mounted on the fixed landing gear for psychological effect, and this effect was enhanced by the addition of cardboard sirens to the bombs.

into the irresistible counter-attack. The infernal wave followed the Reds without relief over the terrain, and without anyone firing one single shot we were able to take the survivors as our prisoners. It was easy because the survivors were sitting on their knees thanking the Lord that they had survived this ordeal. This episode only lasted for a couple of minutes, but it lasted for ages for those in front of us. For them this was definitely the end. The Russian offensive stopped at Gromovayabalka. And to affirm the harsh verdict for the Russians, a dozen of German tanks came to finish with a couple rounds the hopeless mess of Reds that were left over. They were accompanied by a German Infantry Battalion who was going to occupy the ruins of the village. We had to hold for 20 minutes to allow them to come to our assistance, but these two units got detached somewhere during the initial movement. When the tanks arrived it was almost 1600h. We had been fighting since 0600h, and we held our positions for 10 hours; one against four crushed by cannons, machine guns, and 14 tanks. The village had only a couple of isbas still standing with big holes in their walls from tank projectiles. The rest of the buildings were going to be used by the German Battalion for their own use and from which to conduct patrols. We regrouped in a couple of isba on the west side of the village and we were finally going to enjoy a good night's sleep. But were we able to sleep? Every one of us saw at least one of his comrades fall and die, maybe it was his brother or father. They were 65 that we wouldn't see again, and we could only find solace in our memories of them; 110 wounded were evacuated.

For several hours the images of that day went through my head multiple times. Dreaming or awake, in which fear would mix itself, the desperation, the horror, the sadness, and the joy of the final victory. Dreams interrupted by a few isolated gun shots fired by patrols and a couple of shells from the Russians to let us know that they were still there. They were certainly still there, only at a couple of hundred meters away from us! Their attacks had grown and were witness of their importance: they had to clear the way to Dnepropetrovsk by a massive Russian winter offensive. But they had failed and on a tactical point of view we delivered a fool's punch by doing the impossible because of the shown courage, persistence, and - please don't laugh - because of heroism. The following day we counted the men at Gromovayabalka, and there were only 301 left of those of August 8, 1941. About 500 Walloon Legionnaires had prevented 2,000 Reds and 14 tanks from having the last point of resistance blown up which blocked their way to the Dnjepr. For the Russians the consequences were severe: material-wise they fought us four against one. The proportion of lives lost also reflected this statistic: 180 of ours against more than 700 Russian corpses on the battlefield. Multiple Russian tanks had been destroyed!

The Russians started a new offensive, and it was still four against one. But the psychological advantage was on our side because we had succeeded in a great performance, a possibility that they were not aware of as they thought they would swipe us away in just a couple of minutes. However they were not the only ones to think this about us, since the German command had ordered us to hold Gromovayabalka for only 20 minutes.

In the early morning of March 1 we were getting ready to leave this village of misery when suddenly the storm broke loose again. They really wanted to get us, the Ivans! And most likely they would've been successful if we were not prepared to fight back. Under the artillery fire and the attack of the infantry, the Germans came to help us out and stopped on our lines. Under an immense artillery barrage the Russians entered the town again because nobody was left there.

Actually, there was one left in the infirmary: my father! Totally forgotten! Is it possible to forget a wounded man in an evacuated village? You better believe it is because it happened. How? Why? But it wasn't the right moment to ask these types of questions. An explanation was given to me a bit later. A classic! The ones that were evacuating the wounded thought that someone else would take care of the rest of the wounded. Nobody did, and it was at that moment when the convoy wanted to leave that not one of us noticed there was one wounded missing. At that moment artillery fire was pounding the Valley of Thunder. Since morning I thought a couple of times about my father, but was persuaded that he had been evacuated and I didn't have to worry about him. His wounds were very painful and relatively serious but not life threatening. Without worrying, I wanted to follow the rest of the company while somebody yelled at me "Lemaire, your father is still in the infirmary!" And I selfishly thought I would attend as a spectator at the last minute. I was held back at the scene to play a certain role and not the nicest one! I could imagine the faces of the Russians when walking in the void of darkness…if they could only see mine under a rain of their projectiles! I was looking at a sled which was called to the scene and waiting for its cargo to be loaded, useless to ask what it would be, and I didn't even ask the question myself. I jumped into the sled and yelled "Dawai Ben-Hur!" but not with a proud voice. The Russian horses have all the qualities and they only ask to gallop. The two in front of me didn't get too excited, and I encouraged them with words while I was observing the village. The bombs were still coming down which was a good sign. This meant that their infantry still hadn't been able to penetrate the village. The infirmary was still safe and I stopped the sled after a sharp turn around the infirmary. I went inside, asking myself the question of what I would find in there. I didn't know if my father was expecting to see the Russians, but he was more than happy to see me! I hurt him for sure when I transported him and sometimes he complained about it. But I do not think I had the time to think about it. It became even worse for him when the horses started running between the holes and bumps on the snow-covered steppe. I really pushed it but the few minutes of suffering equaled the price of our lives. So for that reason it was worth it.

When we arrived at the gathering point, the bombing had stopped and the Russians occupied as good as the entire village now. The Lemaires, father and son, were the last ones to evacuate the village, pushed a little bit by the circumstances of the moment. But we had the chance to remove ourselves from the location, and that was the most important thing at that moment. Then a Russian civilian rushed to recuperate a sled and his horses when he realized they had disappeared. I showed him what was inside the sled and I made him clear that if he proceeded in my direction his career would be terminated immediately. He hesitated for a split second but my MP took a pretty convincing position towards him and he did what I told him to do. He was at 200 m of distance when commander Pauly exited his isba and was looking for his sled. I then understood the short hesitation of the men but nobody reacted, and they all acted as if nothing had happened. Even my platoon commander Warrant Officer Mathieu played the game. Commander Pauly never knew who stole his sled.

In the meantime, the German Battalion started to counter-attack at the moment that the Reds who were out of breath after their run, and totally astonished that they hadn't encountered one single person in the village. The situation had quickly established itself and soon we would occupy our new positions. These new positions were holes dug by hand in the snow, protected by a wall made of ice blocks. We installed ourselves into our new positions around noon until the next day around the same time. We spent the night there in temperatures of -30°C. From one side our positions put us out of enemy sight, and from the other side to get in touch with the German Battalion we only required a minimum of carefulness. Also, two of their observers on the top of the hill, which were relieved every 15 minutes, reassured our safety. The alarm they would have sounded by the slightest suspicious movement would have given us enough time to prepare and occupy our positions since we were not in our positions all the time.

That afternoon and evening within a space of just 20 to 30 meters, we ran more than 10 km because it was the only way not to freeze to death! It wasn't the first time that we had to perform an "exercise" like that, just remember the train ride to Rosa Luxemburg where we spent 10 hours running inside a train car. Obviously, we couldn't keep on running forever, and after a while we were so exhausted. Then we noticed about 100 straw bales that were just sitting in the steppe at a short distance from our positions. With a couple of comrades, I went to grab some of them and we dragged them back to our holes. We slept on them with some blankets under and on top of us with three or four men squeezed together, impossible to move. This was to keep us warm. I don't know how we stood on guard or how they did it, but I remember that I was woken up two or three times at the same time as my comrades by the company platoon chief who was accompanied by Lt. Lippert. I was half asleep when I met this wonderful officer for the second time. He would become the commander of the Legion Wallonie a couple of months later. The entire night he walked around, and every now and then he woke us up to make sure we wouldn't freeze to death while serving us a shot of vodka! He was watching over us until dawn. His name I heard it for the first time a little while ago, as you all know, during a night less terrible than this one. I would never forget him. Most likely he wouldn't have forgotten mine either. Every night when he woke me up he addressed me by my first name.

That particular night I learned the name of a very special human being from which the memory still moves me every day. A memory of a man who would die two years later by a bullet shot through his heart. But let's not anticipate now. We are still in the midst of the night from March 1-2, and we are still in the Valley of Thunder. Some of the men who had dug their holes close to the straw bales in the field heard some movement at the straw bales, of which they had no doubt that it was the Russians. The straw bales were not only attractive to the Walloon legionnaires. The presence of strangers in the sector was a fact! For both sides this was the opportunity to catch some sleep after a couple of horrible days and you never knew what would be next during the war, or when the next opportunity to sleep would again present itself. You could hear the snoring from the Russians and Walloons alike that night. In the morning all returned to their positions as if nothing had happened. With the daylight the reality returned, and the Russian artillery started shelling us again. However their aim was less accurate and the positions of our riflemen allowed us to not worry about it too much. As soon as they started shelling us some silhouettes appeared in the sky, typical for the Stukas! These airplanes were and remained something unique within their species. I always remember the impression they made on the different military attachés during the last international aviation meeting in 1939 in Brussels just before the war.

The roles of these "diplomats" was to precisely inform the government of the new things that were in the hands of their neighbors. It seemed to me that at that time if one neighbor had to worry about something, it was for sure the Junkers 87 or Stuka. All these big shots saw the advantages of this plane which at the same time pointed out the weakness of all the other existing bombers. A small single engine which signified a small action radius and not too much power. But it had a large carrier surface which was its advantage. They even didn't think to put retractable landing gears on it. In my opinion one had not to be a military aviation specialist to know that the accumulation of these defaults was rather suspicious. You just had to reflect about it. It was well known that the Germans were far ahead of the others in regards to engineering and armament. So how was it possible that those who had the fastest fighter plane in the ME-109, the most perfected bomber in the JU-88, the ME-110, the Heinkel HE-111, the Dornier DO-17, and even the transport plane adopted by SABENA, the JU-52, were going to put an airplane into service with old engineering? Really?! There are none so deaf as those who will not listen!

Well we were there. It was to show defeatism to think that those who were already considered by many as the future enemy were a lot stronger and better equipped than they appeared in all aspects. It was this type of blindness that permitted the catastrophe to happen, and those who were (partially) responsible were guiltier than the thousands of men who risked their lives with the belief that they were defending the cause. They also were considered as being traitors and were convicted and imprisoned for years. Others have peacefully contributed their careers with a clear conscience. But this was only a particular piece of the criminal consciousness of certain people. In this case we had to try to understand this anomaly.

The Stuka was a light bomber destined to attack pre-determined objectives which were located not too far away from its base. It wasn't that powerful and it had a short action radius, but the build of the plane allowed it to make steep dives and pull up at just 20 m above the ground. All these elements permitted to destroy its targets with its mall 50 kg bombs. Its real weakness was when it was confronted with fighter planes since it only had an MG mounted in the turret which was operated by a second person on board. Despite what people thought this plane did, and what it was made for, one had to see it to realize they were actually successful. And for the third time in two days we were able to witness their actions. There were six and their objective was the artillery pieces that had been shelling our positions for a while. It was at a couple of hundred meters altitude that the squadron took its combat formation. One by one they dove down on their targets with the distinct sound of the siren. They released their bombs on their objectives which were hidden from our eyes, but we saw the "eggs" being released from under the planes. As soon as the bombs exploded we saw each plane pull up again. But it looked like as if their actions were known by the enemy. When they returned into combat formation we observed half a dozen of Ratas engaging them. These were rather slow Russian fighters compared to other fighter planes, but they were very maneuverable which permitted them to make very sharp turns. When compared to the ME-109 they were absolutely no match, but the Stukas were easy prey for them. During this winter in 1942, with certain exceptions, the German fighter planes were brilliant at not showing up on the battlefield. Actually, I've never seen a Stuka equipped with a MG gunner! This time, like any other time, the pilot was the only one on board. The first two Stukas were fatally hit and they never pulled up again during their dive on their target. It was in kamikaze style that they reached their objective. The ground was shaking under our feet when they crashed and for the Russian pilots it was a welcomed victory. But I fear that the Russian artillery didn't have the time to enjoy this moment. We couldn't see the Russian cannons which were hidden behind a hill, but we certainly could see the lightening and the pieces of equipment flying through the sky and coming back down in the columns of thick dark smoke. Instantly there was a certain silence over the battlefield. On the ground it was quiet now. This vision, which enchanted both sides as if they were hit by a magic wand, petrified all beings on earth. For several seconds the shock had stopped the war. It was like waking up from a deep sleep when we heard the roaring noise of the four Stukas flying away from us. Fleeing from the battlefield was their salute to us and the Ratas were unable to keep up with the Stukas since they were a little bit faster than them. It would have sufficed for one or two ME-109 to come and help the Stukas, and the scenario would've ended differently. In that case the Soviets wouldn't have had the opportunity to talk about their victories in the evening when sitting in the officer's canteen. It was a certain victory for them since two Stukas were shot down and the others fled the scene. But it was not a real victory for the Russian artillery which got hit twice by Stukas and in which two Stukas threw themselves down in real kamikaze style causing a lot of damage and loss of life. Judging by the columns of thick black smoke coming from behind the hill and the sudden stop of the artillery shelling, it meant that the Russians got hit pretty hard.

In the ruins of Gromovayabalka the Soviets were probably wondering why they were being punished like this for the past three days. But they could reassure themselves that these last actions were reactions to their offensives from a couple of days ago. The front line was definitely stabilized now, but most likely the quietness on the battlefield would certainly be succeeded by an infernal rage by the Walloons in which death and glory would found their way. Death and glory, two companions but at the same time so different, and oh so close to each other that many men were called by both of them. They would always be there when the Legion Wallonie would engage in combat until the moment it took its positions and everything would become calm again. The situation was restored and we left the Valley of Thunder in small groups, happy that it was over. We certainly had distinguished ourselves, but we also left with a heavy heart. Sixty five of our men were resting in the snow or in the ruins of the village; 150 others were wounded and spilled their blood there before being evacuated. They were the first we saw falling down on our sides and some of them died in our arms. We were not going to forget them and when nice thoughts would play in our minds the images of our fallen comrades would abruptly be destroyed by the sights of more bodies searching for a place in our memories. Death was chasing death but Gromovayabalka hadn't taken its last victim yet.

We received orders to head to a village name Lubitski[46], located a few kilometers to the rear. With a group of four we went into the steppe, companions of the first hour of August 8, 1941. Paul Mees, Badjou, myself, and I forgot the fourth one's name. I think it was Nissen. One of the infantry weapons which was happily and plentifully used by the Russians was the heavy grenade launcher. These types of tubes mounted on a shield and kept up with a bipod, could launch a bomb to more than 2 km distance. And it happened to be that our group found itself in the field observed by the enemy. So after calculating the distance and the fact that we were already out of sight, the Russians gratified us with a couple of grenades. After one minute it was over and they stopped. We got back up and we noticed that our friend Paul Mees was lying flat out in the snow face down with a big hole in his back. We thought he was dead but after a few seconds he came to and started screaming because of the pain. We placed him on a stretcher made by two rifles and a couple of belts so we could transport him to the village. His position was precarious and our progression through the snow, two in front and one in the rear, was extremely agonizing for him because the way we were walking through the snow was very clumsy. Every moment made him suffer, and after 10 minutes we were only able to walk 200 m. He begged us to shoot him as we would do him a big favor by doing so, but none of us felt it called for it knowing that this would certainly put an end to his suffering. We didn't know how much a human being could take and maybe we would arrive in time so they could take care of him. Even though we hoped he would make it, we knew he wouldn't make it to the village. Slowly his voice weakened until he stopped talking. At that moment we knew we were transporting a corpse. The last victim of the battle of Gromovayabalka, my comrade Paul Mees, is resting in the village of Lubitski.

During these 10 days we all lived without any notion of time or any manifestation of a normal life. Our reactions were conditioned by the exigent circumstances of our existence. We were living on auto-pilot. It was during these 10 days that we saw many of us die, but each individual hoped that luck would be on his side and that his life would be spared. Rapidly we installed

---

[46] The exact location of this town is unknown. The name was written down phonetically, but Lemaire wasn't specific about its location. It is assumed that it's located very close to the Valley of Thunder.

ourselves in this "facility" which was imposed on us by the situation at that moment. For sure a soldier has no idea what is about to happen at tens of meters of distance from his fox hole. He's forced to live in the presented situation and if it would last long enough, he would adapt himself as soon as possible. Luckily one adapts quickly. The lack of experience played a huge role as well since we were so young and we had never experienced real combat before. And all of a sudden, without any form of transition, the last act taught us a new reflex: to kill! Now we knew that another method existed to avoid death, and during the last 12 hours we used it without any interruption. The 700 Russians resting in the ruins of Gromovayabalka are our witnesses. I killed when I was trembling and shaking, I killed when I was singing, I even killed when I was crying, and I threw up when I planted my bayonet into the body of a Mongol. Like most of my companions I started to kill without trembling or shaking, and the stomach could bear the smell of fresh intestines, especially those of Mongols.

Physically we didn't change and we would always be the big boys, timid and a bit shy at the same time and sometimes blushing when looked at. But as soon as the hand caressed the rifle or the grip of a knife our looks became hard. The jaw muscles would contract and then…a complete metamorphosis didn't occur just by the touch of a magic wand. One had to realize what happened, and one had to give his nerves the time to calm down as well. I remember it well that during a couple of days the simple sound of a closing door would make me jump up or when a shot was fired in my vicinity it would make my stomach turn. I was always ready so I would be able to react in a timely manner to any given situation. My family to whom I wrote a couple of letters a few days after the battle certainly would not have recognized my handwriting. But slowly the calmness inside would come back with the sensation of being a human being again. Everything contributed to it because nature itself seemed less savage than us.

The Existence of the Legion Wallonie

The crisis that threatened the existence of the Walloon Legion was beseeched by two factors which had a primordial influence on this garrison: commander Pauly who took command of the Legion, and the battle of Gromovayabalka. Commander Pauly knew that through his authority and dynamism imposed again the indispensable discipline of a military unit. This discipline had deteriorated by the actions of his predecessor which made things more difficult because it's exactly the contrary to how it actually should be. The more difficulties, the more the situation is complicated, the more discipline has to be more rigid. Everything depends on discipline in any given situation. Discipline brings order and order is the organization! If at the top the general staff is able to organize the slightest details of a campaign by mobilizing millions of soldiers, with all its difficulties and implications, it simply wouldn't work when down the ladder two idiots are marching together.

Whoever states that an army is a necessity also has to admit that it has to be equipped with soldiers. And there is only one way to make a soldier. It was the method used by the German Army until 1945, and I'm unsure how it is done today. It's a method that was and still is in effect in the British Army and in any other elite units worthy of this title. Civilians admiring the parades of British soldiers have no idea what methods have been used to get to this point. One had to experience the drill to actually have an idea of how these soldiers got to this point. If they only knew, how I could imagine what a concert of protest it would create nowadays! "That we change these methods, that we end the discipline and end these parades!" because the soldier wouldn't be a soldier anymore. When looking at a marching platoon of British soldiers we see only one arm and one rifle moving knowing that there are 30 or 40 men marching in it. It was the same in the German Army. I have video footage of SS parades in the pre-war period, and it's simply breath taking! On the other hand, I saw 10 American soldiers maneuvering together. There were at least two soldiers that were not in cadence. Aside of that they were clearly capable of juggling their carbines. But war is not a circus or a place for clowns. Unfortunately, it's a fact and we have to take this kind of circumstances into account.

I've heard horrifying stories before the outbreak of the war that the Japanese, during their infantry exercises, used one real bullet out of five. It was to teach the good souls about the savageness of killing. If from time to time an accident occurred where some of the soldiers got wounded or even killed, it meant that thousands of others would have their lives saved during the war because they learned how to take good cover during the exercises. Tens of thousands of soldiers have lost their lives because they neglected such small details like this.

In 1942 the German medical services got worried because many soldiers of the Eastern Front got wounded on their heels or calves. The cause of this could be easily determined: most of the soldiers threw themselves on the ground while coming under enemy fire which always threw one foot up in the air for just one second. I think a lesson like that would be valuable information during exercises. Personally, during these four years with the German Army, I went through basic infantry training, the NCO school, the school for Combat Engineers, and a special session at the officer cadet school. I did many exercises and almost all of them were with live ammunition! Something different than one live bullet out of five. I was aware of two accidents: one was after an exercise and was due to the negligence of a MG gunner; the other one occurred during a night time exercise where a soldier in the darkness had mistaken the ammunition and put a live round in his rifle. The officer cadet who was in charge of the exercise got hit by this bullet in the back. It is only during hard and harsh exercises that one becomes hard and that a soldier becomes capable to kill and to die.

Before Gromovayabalka discipline had failed and we forgot our roles why we were there. The lack of discipline had almost caused the disintegration of the Walloon Legion. But after the spectacular change of power by the new commander, the battle of Gromovayabalka had permitted us to show that the Walloon Legion was as good as any other German unit and that the German Command could rely on us on the battlefield. We passed the "test" with flying colors, with distinction, meaning that 37 Iron Crosses were awarded to the best among us. But in what state was the Walloon Legion at that moment? Well it was in a miserable state! There were only approximately 350 men left. The 2nd Company was disbanded and the remainders were placed in other companies which at the time were also reduced in numbers. It was on March 10 that a contingent of 400 new volunteers had departed from Brussels to join us a few weeks later.

In the meantime, in April 1942, the Walloon Legion was organized and reorganized. Captain Pauly had to leave us for medical reasons and Captain George Tchekoff became our ad interim commander. The battle of the Samara River had decimated the Walloon Legion in all echelons. The only captain that was left was now in charge of the battalion. Three company commanders had left us: Capt. Van Damme - evacuated; Capt. Deprez and Lt Buyts - KIA. The officers were all familiarized with the new contingent and they were placed in command of the new companies. The platoons were led by the Warrant Officers, and all the post-battle promoted Corporals were learning their new jobs as section leaders. Exercises and guard duty were all executed in good spirits. We were men again and our lives had regained a certain regularity.

Spring was here which wiped away all our wounds, but it also had given the signal of the melting of snow and ice. Every pathway or road was transformed into creeks or rivers. In our village there were torrents of water for multiple days. When all this water was gone, the soil which had been frozen to a depth of 1 to1.5 m completely defrosted and changed into a big mud pool impossible to walk through. All over the place we had to put branches and boards on the roads we had to walk on for the needs of the service. Without this precaution the one who dared to adventure would be caught in a thick black treacherous grime. This was called the Rasputitsa[47]. Bit by bit the sun did its work and we could feel the soil hardening up and soon everything would be firm and steady again. But for several days we had the feeling as if we were walking over a thick carpet. Within a couple of weeks we had forgotten all our misery as our pains were chased away by the rays of the sun, rays which penetrated our bodies and regenerated our blood. The horrible cold that we had experienced in the last couple of months was nothing but a subject of laughter now, and its victims were proud to have suffered through it. However, the marvelous sensation to be able to jump into the river didn't wipe away the glory of being the filthiest and flea-ridden a couple of weeks ago. Our occupation left no doubt about us still being

---

[47] The term Rasputitsa refers to the spring season when unpaved roads become virtually impossible to travel in Eastern Europe and Russia. In Russia, these seasons were so intense that they were used as a defense during wartime.

soldiers, however during several weeks nothing reminded us that we were still at war and that we were only a few kilometers away from the front. During this period we didn't hear one shot being fired from a cannon. Not even a skirmish was disturbing the calmness of the front. For both sides the winter had been very harsh and the furious battles like Gromovayabalka, to which we marked the final turning point, had left us and the other side in such a state that neither side wanted to fire another shot with his rifle. However, the birds of bad omen flew over our positions almost every day at a high altitude. These aerial observers had already started this war again and they put us on guard all the time.

At the beginning of May 1942, the Walloon Legion was reattached to a division whose title of glory didn't count anymore. This was the famous 97th Jäger Division of mountain troops (Gebirgsjäger) commanded by General Ernst Johan Rupp[48]. Our emblem became the Edelweiss. Normally a unit of Gebirgsjäger was supposed to fight in the mountains, however the mountains were at more than 1000 km away from the front.

On May 5, 1942 we were en route to the front again, and we told ourselves that we hadn't finished marching yet. In the evening we arrived in Alexandrowka, and at 2200h we relieved a German battalion. We took our places in their positions which consisted of nicely organized and camouflaged trenches and MG nests. Through debris we were able to access our positions which kept us out of enemy sight, an enemy who would occupy a replica of our positions at only 200 m away from us. We had to naturally take all precautions. Frequently we saw multiple Russian soldiers move from one position to the other which permitted us to mark their positions and transmit the information to our heavy weapons. This type of movement was strictly forbidden for us, which was more than logic, because besides the fact it would mark our positions, it would've sufficed a couple of MG bursts to kill a couple of men. But shooting with an automatic gun was also revealing one's position! We let the Russians walk around in their positions since we were all enjoying the sun and it was rare to see a guard dressed only but in his underwear. The war in your underwear! If they would've told us that two months ago... Only a minefield and some barbed wire separated us from

---

[48] A light infantry Division of the Wehrmacht during World War II. It can trace its origins to the 97th Light Infantry Division which was formed in December 1940, it was then renamed to the 97th Jäger Division in July 1942.

them. But since there were always open points in this type of obstacles, there also existed what we called night points. These night points served to prevent the ones in front of us from sliding in between the landmines and barbed wire and causing trouble in our lines. These placements were too close to the enemy, and since it was impossible to camouflage them entirely, one was only protected by the darkness of the night when coming or going.

With lots of precaution and when one thought a position had been overtaken by the others, it sufficed to point our MG at it and shoot a short burst towards the point in question. That moment, on the other side, they would put their heads down. Old straw bales have been used from the year before by them and one could see Russian blood seeping through the bales. There was also a white mark which was impossible for us to identify but which we used as an aiming point or point of observation. This white mark would be the first thing to which we acquainted at the start of the offensive a bit later. One day I had to go on a reconnaissance patrol for the 1.Kp together with my comrade Lucien Gaillard with the objective the white mark. Our commander had said to go and check out the white mark in front of us. But we had two days of rest and sunshine before the day of our reconnaissance patrol. The next offensive was close, and we could feel it. The aerial reconnaissance patrols were more numerous now and every now and then a friendly projectile passed above our heads and exploded amidst the Russian lines. It was to prevent the enemy batteries from regaining strength. However there was one accident which claimed one of my company comrades. One afternoon I was dousing behind my MG when my attention was caught by something that was moving amidst the straw bales. Nobody got excited about it since a couple of Russians were walking around not that far from it. But something was going on there. Somebody was doing something and was crawling on his back and then on his belly. I was unable to see what it was through my infantry issued binoculars, and out of precaution and thinking I was justified in my actions, I fired a burst with my MG. All of a sudden the movement stopped. The MG burst surely disturbed the silence from the previous days and it had its effects for sure. I knew it! After a few minutes of silence, the man in front of me started moving again and I fired a second burst. My second burst was the signal for the other MGs to start shooting. I was able to follow all the bullets because of the tracing ammunition. All bullets went through the straw bales and all movement stopped and never resumed. The "orchestra" stopped a couple of seconds later. A message came down from the company HQ not to shoot at the man who was crawling towards us. It was indispensable for anybody to get close to our lines.

The man who came out alive was actually one of ours! He was an engineer who was dropped in the field in front of us a couple of days ago. He had to stay there and had to mark down what was happening in the Russian sector. During the night his company went back to pick him up, and they had to wait to see if he would show up at the meeting point. It took him several months in the hospital to get his nerves to calm down again. But our actions were justified and one has to know, even the critics, that soon we would have to cross this terrain once the attack was launched. To know the details of the terrain would be a huge advantage for us. On the other hand, an observation from the inside could very well detect defense positions since an observation from the outside wouldn't have the same result. It wasn't a "police secret" anymore, but I don't want to say that one of us didn't know what was happening on the other side. But with this extra information the entire company was on the lookout to observe as much as possible. The movement in our lines could only intrigue the ones in front of us. They too had their observers but even then there was nothing new to see so it was a bit useless for us to remain informed.

Finally, I chose my straw bale in front of which there hadn't been any activity for days. The mission was only a matter of patience and only an accident could disturb it. An accident to which the occupant of a position, one of us of course, had to come out of his cover. That moment he would've been there for 12 hours with another six hours to go. And these hours seemed to last for an eternity. He was done and cramps were taking over his body. He had to come out of his cover to be able to breathe, but on which side would he leave his position? On the Russian side? No, that was out of the question! It would definitely mean a certain death. On our side he had a chance to make it but unfortunately one of his movements caught our attention. I've always had good eyes, but I had to force myself to detect and try to shape the slightest form in the smallest movement or sound. The senses became very sharp at the front. We saw and heard things that we weren't capable of seeing before. But it's also a matter of training. The ones that never understood our rage, our actions, were the Russians who would always question which mosquito had bitten us.

102

Objective: Donets!

After this ordeal we had a period of tranquility until May 17, 1942. That day the Army Corps of Von Mackensen launched a preliminary offensive. The objective was to conquer the important bridgehead of Izyum-Slavyansk, and to push the enemy back to the north of the Donets to ultimately prepare for a major offensive. During the night of May 17 there was a certain tension between all the units at the front. We were in a state of alert, and any moment could've been the moment; we had to be ready to move to the front. We were just a few men keeping company to a young Lieutenant of the artillery observers who was installed in one of our bunkers. His radio channel was in constant listening mode. It was the tenth night that we had again gone through the same scenario. It was identical to all the other nights with the same calmness, the same tranquility, the same silence, only disturbed by the sounds of frogs in a pond close by and by a gentle breeze which seemed like the calm breath of the earth. But this particular night this breath of the earth seemed different. This calmness, this tranquility, this silence seemed to be a lot heavier because we knew that at any moment now the storm could break lose. Around 0230 the horizon in front of us lit up. Dawn was born and the sky was lit up, and in just a couple of minutes all forms and colors would become visible. It was 0255 when far in the east a cuckoo could be heard. In our chests we could feel our hearts beating like crazy.

Then all of a sudden over the radio we heard the message, repetitive like a PTT announcement: "Donets, Donets, Donets!" An innocent word which was pronounced three times which caused the feeling of cold and death among tens of thousands of men. This was the signal for the attack! The last word was not said through the radio when squadrons of Junkers 88 flew over our heads towards the east. The earth was shaking because our artillery, located 100 m behind our lines, started firing at will. In front of us nothing was moving besides the earth that was thrown up into the air because of all the explosions. A bit farther we could see the bombings of the airplanes on the Russian positions which were located in the rear of their lines. The progression in our sector was the occupation of two fortified villages located on our left: Jablenskaya and Nikolayevka. United for the attack were an engineer platoon, a platoon of the 3.Kp, a heavy MG platoon of the 4.Kp, and a German Kp of the 101.Infantry Division. The attack lasted for several hours during which the Walloon Legionnaires which were engaged from the beginning of the attack were showing courage and endurance during this entire ordeal. Both of these factors were present! It was actually an honor to be in front of the German troops amidst the smoking ruins because that was the only thing that was left.

To the front of us were the Reds who wanted to attack us at any given moment, however our artillery with their precision bombings made sure to stop that threat. Systematically they pulverized everything on the ground which could serve as a cover for enemy automatic weapons. During two hours nothing could escape. The Russians sought cover, turned around, and started firing back at us with admirable courage. The Bourguignons were having a difficult time, and we were too far away from the enemy to launch a desperate attack. We would be butchered even before we would arrive at the first Russian positions. We could only notice the enemy by the movements they made through the rubble in which they were stoically hiding and shooting at our men in between barrages, benefitting from every moment of calmness. We had to get out there alive at any cost and patience and cunning were in order. In proximity to the village was a field full of straw bales, and soon it was discovered what kind of temporary cover these could provide. The Warrant Officer of the 1.Kp was leading the Kampfgruppe and we all understood that the objective was a couple of mills at only tens of meters away and that we still had to reach them.

For two hours we progressed millimeter by millimeter which worked negatively on the nerves of our soldiers. Their movement had to be undetectable because the slightest movement could attract the attention of the enemy and their bullets! It was ruthless! When they finally reached the mills while being at the verge of a nervous breakdown and soaked by sweat, they needed several minutes to calm down and to catch their breath again. Physically no efforts were made during that time, and at the end the objective was reached. But at what cost? Seventeen were killed in action and twelve were wounded in action. What would follow was just child's play.

Now we had to move forward under the cover of the artillery, almost invisible, since the ones in front of us were forced to leave their observation posts for a certain amount of time. They doubted that our dirt brothers who were now positioned around the mills had succeeded in their maneuver. They were too high in numbers to be detected, and it couldn't be verified since another artillery barrage hit the Ivans like it did before and for which our observation posts couldn't function properly. The Russians had been played even if they had a certain advantage on the battlefield. But they noticed them again, too late this time, because at the moment they realized that something was happening, 120 enraged and screaming devils entered the village. A little while later, while under our artillery fire, our advanced observers called our batteries.

It's a military rule that says that heavy weapons fire only has to stop when it almost starts hitting friendly troops. This principle was rigorously applied, involuntary for the artillery soldiers, but voluntary by our Bourguignons who felt that it was an excellent way to surprise the others. The striking effects were obvious. Our men endured hours under fire while biting their tongues so they wouldn't be screaming from nervousness. They had endured hours under constant fire knowing that the possibility existed of getting hit by a bullet or shrapnel. Everybody was literally locked on the enemy now by the combination of all these factors and by a unique will power. It was a liberating feeling that the contact with the enemy changed instantly into an unleashing of power. Never in the history of the Walloon Legion would anybody anywhere hold up to 100 Walloons charging into battle, not even here! The Russians who hadn't had the time to flee missed their last opportunity given to them to stay alive. The door of our sector was knocked down. The Russians retreated in masses while our infantry battalion, due to the lack of mobility, had to march as a reserve unit and we had to wait until the afternoon to get on the road again.

Everything was calm now in Jablenskaya and Nikolayevka. Columns of smoke were rising up from the houses that were consumed by fires. The artillery became quiet and was transported to the front following the motorized units who precipitated in the pursuit of the defeated enemy. For kilometers, but invisible at the same time, one was able to follow their progression thanks to the dust clouds they were creating while marching. These dust clouds were at least 50 m high. The airplanes continued to fill the skies to create chaos in the Russian units who were in full retreat now. In our sector in front of the 1.Kp nothing had happened so far. The front line had been evacuated at the same time Jablenskaya and Nikolayevka had fallen. We hadn't seen anything at all but it could have been totally different.

Since the beginning of the attack, these Russian positions had been under an artillery barrage for a short time. They were condemned by the fall of Jablenskaya, and that is the reason why we didn't attack them. In the morning it would've cost us some human lives for sure, while in the afternoon we would just walk with our weapons on our shoulders. There was only one thing to report: before our annexation of Jablenskaya we suddenly observed an artillery piece pulled by six horses appear on top of the hill and drive into the valley parallel to our lines at an infernal tempo. We could clearly hear the cries of the horsemen. Behind us we could hear the shots of the German artillery and the projectiles were whistling over our heads. Suddenly there were four explosions where the horses and the artillery piece were located. Debris of all kinds were thrown in the air to fall down a couple of seconds later. Where the four projectiles exploded a big black hole was the only thing that was left. In a radius of tens of meters everything was black or dark brown with here and there human remains and pieces of the horses. This certainly was an atrocious death; at first you can't imagine the view. Not one man or one horse could've survived one tenth of a second after the explosion. Most likely they didn't feel a thing and it must have been a simple but quick death.

In the afternoon we took off and we walked through the barbed wire barricades and minefields in the safe zone made especially for us so that the infantry could deploy. It was then that Lucien Gaillard and I, as scouts of the 1.Kp, were sent on top of the hill to check out a white spot that had been noticed there. Why take all these precautions? But during the war we were suspicious of everything we saw; the logic was forgone. On the other hand, these useless actions were not the first and not the last ones. Separated by just tens of meters of each other, we were climbing to the top of the hill, about 100 m high in elevation. We were climbing with a finger on the trigger of course. We approached the top of the hill believing that the military logic had been respected, and with the least precaution we reached the top which had drawn the curiosity of all the men for the last couple of days. My companion and I immediately understood that the closer we got the stronger the smell of a corpse became. It was in fact a Russian soldier who had been killed during the winter and who was still dressed in his white camouflage uniform. The corpse was left there all alone, and we clearly noticed that the Russians had no respect for their comrades who had been killed in action. Honestly, and out of respect for our fallen companion-in-arms, we Walloons wouldn't be able to live there with a corpse in our midst. Even for the smell alone. This shapeless mass full of maggots could spread the smell in a radius of 50 m, and when a gentle breeze blew, the entire sector would be affected by it. During years of war I became used to certain disgusting things but I got never used to the smell of a dead body. It was the only thing that would take away my appetite. But it was not about appetite, and Gaillard and I exchanged some less flattering considerations, but energetic enough so that we wouldn't be affected by the current situation.

We were about to signal the company for its progression when our attention was attracted by a noise on our right at about 20 m from us. It was a Russian soldier with his rifle on his soldier and his mess kit was hitting his behind while walking. For us there was no doubt that the good man was happy that the war for him had ended and he had been looking to surrender for a while. However he hadn't found anybody to surrender to. He made enough noise to get noticed and to reveal his intentions. But why did he still have a rifle? Well as a soldier when you're at war, the rifle is not only just the principal object to have. The rifle becomes a part of you! It's something we don't think about of throwing away, not even when you're about to surrender. A soldier in this situation is completely surprised when he had to hand over his rifle. It takes days to get used not carrying a rifle anymore or to use one, simply because it became inaccessible at that time. With this Russian soldier it sufficed that he would approach us and we gently called him out, letting him know that he had finally reached his objective.

But his reaction was one that proved that our reasoning was completely wrong. He was just a few meters away from us when we called out to him in Russian and in French: "Come here friend, the war is over!" He stopped and hesitated since this was the last thing he would've expected. Suddenly he started running away; he was already several meters away when we came back to our senses. Apparently he had no intention of surrender, and he thought he was in a secure sector. How could he have ignored all that happened during the last couple of hours? A burst of MG fire over his head brought him back to reason, and as a soldier he immediately had the reflex to throw himself on the ground and to lay still. We had a good visual on him and with the least suspicious movement we were ready to fill him with lead. He clearly had shown that he didn't want to surrender, so we suspected that he was still going to try to escape. Plus he still had his rifle and a couple of grenades. Carefully we approached him but he didn't move. He was stretched out on the ground with his rifle on his side. When he heard that we were close to him he slowly got up to show us that he was obedient and he put his hands on his head. Gaillard searched him while I kept an eye on him. Subsequently we escorted him to our company where everybody wondered what had happened to us. They were curious to know who had fired some rounds and why. And now they all knew what happened, however we still had no idea what this good man was doing there. Verified that all the Russian positions had been deserted, the companies got on the road again and the battalion made its way to the Donets which was 45 km away from us. The German motorized units had already reached the Donets a while ago.

Walloon Legionnaires - Eastern Front - date unknown

Besides a few points of resistance, which were crushed immediately, nothing got in the way of the offensive between the starting point and its objective. Even if the objective was reached in just a couple of hours, it had everything of a military "walk." The season was gorgeous and the Donets Basin, which left us with some bad memories from the winter months, seemed to be wanting to erase this impression. Trees were blooming and there was this sentiment that the worst had passed here without causing too much damage, without leaving traces of the cataclysm. Villages were abandoned by their inhabitants since they were pushed away by the Russian Army. These good people were made to believe that every German soldier would eat at least one Russian baby for breakfast. Since the early morning, they were on the road with all their possessions mounted on carriages. Even the cows were attached to them. Around noon they were caught up by the Germans. All the troops had stopped by the side of the road, and it was there that these villagers noticed that these German soldiers were not what the Russians said they were. Instead these Germans were friendly, interested in their young women, and friendly towards the kids and babies. Their little world made an about turn, and they all went back to their homes which they had abandoned a couple of hours ago.

Not even on one single face could we see the concern of living under an enemy who was pictured as the most horrible creature. This type of propaganda wouldn't work on these simple farmers; none of them would believe in this type of Soviet ideology, not then and not today. That the mistakes of the German administration had a negative effect on the local population is without a doubt true. But it has to be said that every time we went through a village, we were always welcomed by the locals as liberators. They thought the war would be over soon, and that the old regime would also be wiped out soon. In every family there was at least a father or a son fighting with the Red Army. In every community in the east (Poland, etc...) invaded by the Germans, nobody liked the German soldier. The ones that had interactions with the occupier showed that they were constrained to do so. The interactions were cold and distant. This attitude was all natural for the Russian population since in these eastern countries they had been persuaded that the German aggressors wouldn't be much better than the old regime. However it was different in Russia, and the warm welcome we received anywhere in Russia showed that just a small percentage of Russians had adopted the beliefs of the Bolshevik regime.

By the end of the day we had walked 20 km; the weather was nice and the dust that we created while marching stuck to our sweaty faces. We were marching in happiness and showing all our white teeth when smiling, illuminating our black dust covered faces. We stopped in a wooded area where we were going to spend the night. Suddenly we noticed a magnificent creature walking at a short distance from us. It looked like a wolf but at a certain distance it was difficult to identify. Most likely it was a dog since a wolf would be followed by the rest of the pack. For the two nights we spent there, the horses were always nervous for some reason. Not even the presence of sentinels nor their calming words would calm them down.

But nothing happened during the time we were there. It was impossible to even see a piece of the sky at night since the pine trees were so thick and covering the night sky. At men's height you couldn't see anything at all which added to the confusion and fear of a fight with the Russians. On the other hand we were placed there in the perfect spot. We were staying in little huts which were constructed out of pine branches left there by the Russians after the winter war. The dried pine needles on the ground made an excellent mattress. Since our arrival, we scouted the area as if we had nothing better to do. Around the camp was a junkyard of materials left behind by the Russians. The wild horses even came to check out our camp and pressed their noses through our huts which woke some of us up in real cowboy style. This could've been fatal for these horses since this forest, like many other Russian forests, would serve as cover for partisans which would open fire on our horsemen that wandered off a bit too far. But all the attention and hyper vigilance got drawn away when the rations were distributed around noon. Afterward, a loud snoring sound could be heard coming from our positions. The guard was obviously secured, and this task was not taken lightly. What worried the sentinels the most, who were as good as blind during the night, was that besides the restless horses there was nothing else to report.

The next day on May 19 we were en route again to reach Brashovka which was just a few kilometers from the Donets. In Brashovka we installed ourselves in the village; our combat group was right in the middle of the village. I have to say that it was a magnificent village, and it was there that we were waiting for the arrival of the second contingent of volunteers to arrive which had left Brussels on March 10. The new contingent was about 450 men strong, from which 150 were members of the Jeunesse Rexistes recruited by NCO John Hagemans[49]. He could've easily stayed in Belgium and content himself by recruiting youngsters for the Legion, but he didn't want to! He preferred to undergo the same fate as the recruits that left before him and who for months had given their trust to him. This gesture, flamed by ideals and by honor and loyalty, erased all the other considerations. With

---

[49] John Hagemans (1914- KIA 1942) was the Provost of the Jeunesse Rexistes (Rexist Youth). After the first contingent of volunteers forming the Legion Wallonie had lost so heavily in the fighting in Russia that the Legion was in danger of disbandment, Degrelle called on the Rexist Party for a new contingent. John Hagemans personally led a group of 150 teenage boys from the Jeunesse Rexistes that assembled on the Grand Place in Brussels on March 10, 1942 and volunteered, en masse. John Hagemans, as a former leader of the Rexist Youth, held a special place in the affections of the Bourguignons.

this gesture he would pay with his own life a couple of months later. In the virtues that he professed and his enthusiasm which characterized all his actions, he was able to communicate them all to these youngsters for whom he was a real hero. All demonstrated courage at the Russian front which was very remarkable.

The nice weather continued and the distribution of rations was excellent. A mobile canteen arrived which allowed us to get provisions like toiletry, sowing needles, pencils, and...condoms! All these accessories were absolutely indispensable for a soldier during a campaign. An abundant amount of letter mail and packages from Belgium was distributed as well, for the first time in months because it had followed all the fluctuations of the front. It was a show of force that it had actually survived the Russian counter-offensive. Personally I found numerous letters from my mother, a package from a group of friends who had sent socks, gloves, and a woolen sweater. Further there were cookies, cigarettes, and one liter of cognac! All was mailed out from Brussels in January of that year, but all had been preserved very well during all these months. Then one day I was called in for a second time for mail that had arrived in my name. It was actually a package for my father who had been wounded and evacuated on February 28, and who was currently at the military hospital in Brussels. The mailman explained to me that all the letters were directed back to my home, but he thought to keep the package so he could hand it over to me. He was right to do so, and later I visited him for a drink. His initiative deserved a glass of cognac, and it sufficed to say that the following night we were all drinking and smoking in honor of my father and our friends.

The following days were relaxed, and more time was spent cleaning our weapons and to exercise. Guard duty was lightened as well. However one day this tranquility was disturbed by one of these stupid incidents where one was a bit too careless and which was always at the cost of a human life. In their retreat, the Russians had left a depot of ammunition of all kinds and amidst it they left fragmentation grenades[50]. These grenades had a particular detonation system which required a special movement on the handle,. and they were dangerous due to our ignorance and lack of experience. Each and

---

[50] Russian RGD-33 (Ruchnaya Granata Degtyarev, Model of 1933) - produced from 1933 to 1942 - complicated to use. and used mainly as an offensive grenade. The fragmentation kill radius was approximately 15 m with the sleeve and 10 m without.

every one of us was aware of the danger of these grenades which were sometimes hidden in the piles of ammunition. One of us decided to search the piles of ammunition one afternoon on his own. This ammunition depot was not too far away from my isba, and on that same afternoon I located exactly where a sudden explosion had occurred. Together with some comrades we rushed to the scene where we found our unfortunate comrade laying on his back with his right underarm ripped off as well as the right side of his face. He was moaning and complaining about a headache. While he was moaning, the remaining piece of his severed arm was spraying us with blood. Some of us tried to calm him down while talking to him calmly as if they were talking to a little child. It was the only thing we could do. He died a couple of minutes later while medics were transporting him on a stretcher.

A few kilometers from Brashovka in a forest bearing the same name, the one where we camped a couple of days before, we noticed the presence of partisans. These partisans were groups of regular soldiers cut off from their units, or sometimes purposely left behind to enforce the local resistance. However in all the forests of the occupied countries there were partisans manifesting themselves at the most unexpected moments. They were untraceable with every search party organized by the army. We received the orders to go and search this particular forest, and to find and destroy these groups of resistance, their camps, and their installations. After we had completed our mission we had detected nothing at all, but we spent a magnificent day out in the woods! Full of joy we made our way back following a road at 50 m on the edge of the forest. Lt Lippert and Adjutant Degrelle came towards us on horseback. We looked like a bunch of school kids coming back from a field trip. The only thing missing were the butterflies.

When the "thunder" struck us it only took one tenth of a second to get us down to the ground. We looked up and two Russian planes loomed up above the tree line while their MGs were rattling and bombs were coming down. We didn't hear them coming, they were so quiet! Our two horsemen just had the time to put their head down when the two planes were just two little dots on the horizon. It was when we got up again, furious and astonished at the same time, that a new "storm" unleashed a couple of meters away from us. A third plane was coming! But this time it was one of ours, a ME-109! Not surprised at all, maybe 30 seconds later, we observed two columns of black smoke going coming up on the horizon. This was maybe 2-3 km away from our location. The ME took them down and flew back over our heads signaling its victory by tilting its wings twice. We gave him a well-deserved ovation and we noticed that the two little bombs that each of the Russian planes dropped on us missed us completely. Even their MGs missed us! Now it is impossible for a plane to precisely use its MG on ground troops while being chased by another fighter plane. It would be a suicide mission. If we wouldn't have noticed them coming we certainly wouldn't have moved at all. The pilots, courageous as they were, were just blowing off all their ammunition. We continued our way back without casualties.

On June 4, 1942 the new recruits had arrived from Slavyansk and they understood quickly the circus they had joined. To join us they had to march 65 km in two parts. For everybody their arrival was the main event. The new guys brought us news from the Fatherland. The interest was real and not because it was told to us. News from our parents and friends was always good to hear. They also had a common instructor at Meseritz whom we all knew very well. It left us the best memories and besides a few bad ones which we had in the 1.Kp; NCO Ahnhoff was leading the way. Besides that they were very happy to see us, and they brought us news about their travels which were much more different than ours in regards to the itinerary and the season in which they were deployed. We told them about our adventures in detail; adventures they only knew from the newspapers and personal correspondence. It was our task as seasoned soldiers to instruct the newbies about the tasks of a real warrior which they only knew in theory. We seasoned veterans had already been in Russia for eight months, and we already had two campaigns behind us.

The newbies would get into it pretty fast though. Actually they already were because they were part of a combat unit. And soon they would "savor" it pretty fast. Faster than us, they would get thrown into battle and in totally different conditions too. We walked hundreds of kilometers through snow and ice to finally receive our baptism of fire at -35°C! For them it was a march of hundreds of kilometers through dusty terrain under a scorching sun, finding themselves at an altitude between 500 and 1,000 m with temperatures around +50°C. Because of the latest additions, the Legion Wallonie looked more like a complete unit again. Our total was approximately 850 men with an addition of 100 Russian volunteers, former POWs, which we called *Hiwi*.[51]

The battalion was reformed and reorganized, and we received a new commander: 1st Lt of the Artillery Lucien Lippert. He was 30 years old, and he wasn't really known amongst the men except for those that worked under him at the general staff. He hadn't had a lot of personal contact with the men in the company, but soon he would become the example and idol of the Legion Wallonie. He would be loved by everybody and known by everybody. He knew every man by name and he would stand out for his leadership, his maturity, his courage, his integrity, and his simplicity. Seldom would such a young man unite all these qualities in one leader. For all that have known him, he would remain the nicest figure of the Legion Wallonie. Personally when I think about him it is with the utmost respect to his memory, and a great satisfaction to have had him as my commander.

On June 5, now that the battalion was a combat unit again, we took position on the right bank of the Donets at around 6-8 km from Izyum. Most of our positions were not covered, while on the left bank of the river there was a forested area which gave the Russians good cover and who would shoot at anything that would move. During the day we had to stay low and at night our patrols went out. One night the enemy caught two of our soldiers that were on guard duty, and who were bringing provisions to the front line. One was able to flee, leaving half of his scalp behind with the Reds. We head the other one screaming; he would be wrapped in a blanket and brought to the other side of the river never to be seen again.

However some of the Russian soldiers, knowing that their sentinels were not watching them, crossed the river to surrender. Lots of Russians crossed the river and arrived on our side without weapons and with their hands held high. They were happy to be among us, but the war wasn't limited to these pacifist actions and capturing surrendering enemy soldiers was not the primary task of the Legion Wallonie. Sometimes one of us would notice an enemy soldier hiding in a tree which was followed by a gunshot that almost every time reached its destination. The dead Russian soldier would fall out of the tree, however shortly after that his comrades would take revenge

---

[51] Hilfswilliger is a non-German volunteer in the German Armed forces of WWII on the Eastern Front - lots of Hiwi were Russians.

by opening fire from every tree. We observed lots of corpses floating in the river, but this was the war.

One day we observed a dozen bodies floating by, coloring the water red because of the blood. Immediately we knew what this was all about. The unit north of the Legion was a Romanian battalion. In the morning they were surprised to see a group of surrendering Russian soldiers approaching their positions. Most likely these Russians thought they were dealing with Belgians, but it was an error on their end for which they paid dearly. Without any reason or psychology, the Russians were executed by the Romanian battalion and were thrown into the water so that everybody could admire their work. A big mistake on their part! It was a big mistake to execute a prisoner without a general order of the general staff, and it was certainly not of military conduct. Personally I knew one incident where we were ordered not to take any prisoners, but when a loyal soldier, in uniform, surrendered to the enemy to save his life, then his life belongs to him and no one has the right to take it! The war couldn't justify their actions and the result of it were felt a long time after that. Our prisoners were the last ones taken at the Donets. Because I knew what happened to these Romanian soldiers, I might have an explanation for their behavior. They were all discouraged since they had known only defeat since their first campaign. The last offensive blocked them completely, and the disillusion was enormous. With all the misery they had to go through, they felt that the Donets was again one of those cauldrons where they would be trapped in which none of them would know if he would make it out alive or not. Also preferring to get out alive and as soon as possible, many of them were able to get out alive despite this deplorable incident. This was the front which was the location on subjects of tension and comments of the entire world. Exactly here were the borders of greater Europe, provisionally of course, and behind us were our countries with our traditions, our loved ones, and all our treasures. Up to here reigned those who practically created everything in this world. This fine line, this extreme border of the east, passes through me and I'm its guardian. The entirety of Europe is sleeping behind me. These are just my reflections about the entire situation.

I didn't spend a long time at the Donets, since for a while I had been suffering from an illness we called Russian sores. These sores originated, according to some people, from scratches and little wounds at the front. But this was just speculation since we all had lice and we scratched ourselves to death. Not all of us had the Russian sores, and the ones that had them showed symptoms on their lower legs under the knees. They never appeared anywhere else on the body. Which was certain was that these wounds wouldn't heal as long as I was with my battalion. Regularly I was sent to Brashovka where I received treatment, however it got worse. The funny thing is that it didn't hurt at all. I was evacuated with a couple of other comrades, and one of them had similar symptoms. We left on June 22, 1942, the day of the offensive at the Donets. The Legion Wallonie pushed south of Izyum and participated in the attack of this town. On the other hand, I left under these circumstances and for whatever reason I found myself in Bayreuth for eight days under incomparable circumstances.

I was as good as healed from this "illness", and I found myself in excellent health. My comrade was still with me and he was doing great as well. We had received the same care in the battalion's infirmary, and the food was excellent. The difference, and probably the main reason for our speedy recovery, was that we had time to rest during these eight days. The other thing was that we were in Germany. While we were on our way to Bayreuth, we drove through Poland and the closer we got to Germany the faster our hearts would beat because this meant vacation time. The hospital in Bayreuth consisted of a dozen of buildings in a park. The chief of the hospital was Kesselring, brother of Field Marshall Albert Kesselring. We were treated with the utmost care. The only minor thing was that we were treated in the same wing where the ones were treated with syphilis and other similar diseases. The spectacle we saw there every morning was not one to remember. Because we healed quickly, we got out as soon as possible.

We found ourselves in Bayreuth which was in festival mode, the last festival during the war actually. We only stayed at the hospital to sleep and to have an afternoon nap, but during the day we visited the city and in the evening we went to the opera house. After eight days the chief of the hospital couldn't justify our stay any longer, and we were sent back to our depot in Meseritz. There we received another 15 days of vacation. I arrived home on July 15, and it was with great joy that I saw my family again. My mother had worried for two during all these months that I was at the front, and my father was still in the hospital since our adventure of February 28. But he was in good health and he was definitely going to be dismissed a couple of days later. Considering his age, his service record, and his wounds, he would be assigned to an administrative post of the Legion in Brussels. It's crazy how fast two weeks can fly by and you barely have the time to embrace your family and friends. Before you know it you have to jump back on a train which would take you towards a new adventure.

To the Caucasus: Kuban - Maykop - Tuapse

The papers for my vacation were valid until I returned back at the front, however their validity stopped once you sat down on the bench inside the train. It was my first return from vacation and I was on my own now. There were no other members of the Legion Wallonie on board of the train. In all my life I've never felt as lonely as during those 36 hours on the train to Meseritz. I would leave Brussels another three times during the war, but like all the other times, my demeanor changed completely. It changed because of all that I've been through at the front, and I became cold and insensible which was not what I looked like on the outside where I seemed to be a warm and happy person. Hence the reason why people that don't know me think that I'm a sentimental person. Most likely I was. Napoleon Bonaparte was right when he said that a person aged quickly during a war.

When I left the Legion to get my wounds treated we were part of a mountain division, something that without a doubt would be very effective in the Caucasus. During my absence I followed the movement of the German Army in this area, and since the moment that I left Brussels to come back, my comrades would've marched another 800 km. The train line to the east would pass the town of Taganrog which was at the Sea of Asov. I simply refused to understand the logic of the itineraries of military convoys. It was without surprise that we rode through Bessarabia which became part of Russia after the German-Soviet pact, but was reconquered by Romania in June 1941 and again given back to Russia in 1945. There were 300,000 people in Bessarabia who wanted to have their nationality recognized. I arrived in Moldova where the train stopped for a few hours.

In the region around Iasi I had the pleasure of witnessing a gypsy wedding which was a once in a lifetime event. Everybody was eating and drinking and while these ceremonies were actually prohibited, the people didn't seem to care at all. At a certain moment, the happy couple would retire into a house and a bit later they would appear in the window showing a white blanket with a couple of bloodstains. This was their proof that the marriage was consummated and that both were virgins. It was a beautiful ceremony and I missed my train because of it.

The train I was on turned towards Kiev, and from there it went to Taganrog. Taganrog was under the Stalin regime already; a city on the sea where the big-headed socialists would spend their vacations. The city was beautiful and had many gardens filled with plaster statues like many other places in Russia. To me the city and the sea were an amazing sight. The sun was shining on thousands of little waves that gently rolled on the beaches. The temperature had risen in the last couple of days to +59°C! The sand on the beach burned my feet, but the water was cool and refreshing. I dared to get my feet wet hoping I wouldn't fall into a hole since I couldn't swim. But the view and the beauty were well worth the risk. There were a few girls bathing and playing in the gentle waves, and I'm most certain they saw me trying to keep my balance. But none of them cared and they carried on in all simplicity and so did I. I had another appointment to attend and I knew the war was waiting for me. It was terrible but magnificent at the same time, and it was moments like these that made life worthwhile and which permitted one to enjoy life to the fullest. At the same time it also hurt to be detached from it again, and this is what made men of 19 years of age. I was 19 and I was already a man. I was in Taganrog to get myself on a German supply truck to get back to the Legion. I crossed the Don and drove through Rostov and the magnificent fields of the Kuban, Krasnodar, and Maykop towards the petroleum refineries which were still smoking.

The Legion had left the location two days before. I encountered other Walloons who stayed behind because of illness, and they gave me the latest news of the Legion. There hasn't been any significant fighting since the Donets, however the 1000 km to get here were travelled on foot. I was lucky to drive the distance in the back of a truck. Once again the Legion had surpassed itself and other units by its cadence and its courage. The brave General Rupp never passed one of our columns without saying a well meant "Heil Wallonen!" The sympathetic feelings were mutual and hundreds of "Heil General!" were heard when he drove by. This and the blue waters of Taganrog boosted my morale. It was necessary because the long marches on dusty roads in scorching temperatures that I've experienced myself were long and annoying. I was happy to see my comrades again, and we exchanged stories the entire time. They had been marching for 40 days and now they made sure I would march my part as well. I was happy to be back in the 1.Kp which had been under the command of Lt Dumont since July. I didn't know him at all.

It appeared that the Russians weren't that numerous in the area, and they hadn't accepted the seriousness of combat on open terrain. However they were determined to use the cover of the forests in the Caucasus. Despite a pursuit of six weeks, the enemy resistance started to manifest itself, however it was not consistent. In the foothills of the Caucasus, at an altitude of 200-500 m the 32nd Army Corps had the objective of reaching the hill of Tuapse which was solidly defended by the enemy.

On August 15 the Legion, with an effectiveness reduced to 500 men after 1000 km on foot, became the tactical reserve of the 97th Jäger Division. The battalion left Maykop for a long and agonizing march over Brelaya. On August 16, 17, and 18 we made camp at Abadzekhskaya when the 1.Kp made a stop on a hill; a platoon of the 3.Kp was attached to the command post as a security detail while another platoon of the 3.Kp was tasked to guard the area. The Legion left the camp on the evening of August 18 and made a stop overnight in one of the many forests in the area. The march over the mountains continued on August 19. The heat was almost unbearable until a liberating storm broke loose, pouring down rain like we've never seen before.

The enemy occupied the woods, and one of their battalions cut off one of our battalions isolating the command post of the regiment at Shirvanskaya. Our Walloon battalion was alerted about the situation during a break and came to aid as a reinforcement; the rain was still pouring down. At night we encountered the enemy at Privskaya, and the 1.Kp together with the MGs of the 4.Kp kicked out the Reds in man-to-man combat clearing the way west of the village. The general staff of the regiment could feel the heat of the battle and so did the Russians! Those posted in this sector hadn't met the Bourguignons yet, but now they certainly got a taste of them. In the evening the battalion came down to Shirvanskaya. On August 20-21 the Legion stayed on high alert, still positioned in Shirvanskaya. Violent fights occurred in the valley close to the other regiments. The 97 Jäger Division covered itself by using support points on the mountains dominating the petroleum rich area of Neftegorsk 45 km south of Maykop.

The Legion stopped fighting, and on August 22 continued its way on forestry roads and stopped after 6 km on the heights of Paparotnye. Later we would frequently visit this village for its orchards. Never in my entire life have I seen so much fruit. The 2nd Platoon of the 2.Kp, reinforced by heavy weapons of the 4.Kp, effected a reconnaissance mission at Neftegorsk.

Around 1400h the platoon observed that Cheriakov was heavily occupied and fortified by enemy troops. Well, "heavily fortified" is a big term, but the Bourguignons gave them a sample of their know-how.

Some of them did a more discrete reconnaissance around the village where they picked up the smell of a kitchen. This didn't leave any of the legionnaires indifferent and they all had to know from where the smell came. What they saw astonished them: two kitchens under the cover of a couple of trees in the middle of the village! The two cooks were still unaware that their kitchens would be the objective of a military decision. They had no clue what was going on when they heard the first gun shots. A war cry was heard when we stormed the kitchens to finally seize them. The cooks, clueless what was happening to them, remained quiet and surrendered immediately. Obediently they followed us to our posts, and when we arrived at our battalion they didn't even have to be interrogated. One of them had a complete list on him containing the strength of the Russian forces in the village, plus the amount food supplies. This information couldn't be more accurate and valuable to us.

At Cheriakov there was one Russian battalion and in no time the 1 and 3.Kp supported by the heavy weapons of the 4.Kp engaged the enemy who didn't expect such action from us. The village and the kolkhoz were overrun by our troops and losses were quite low. It was a total surprise to the Russians and we took numerous prisoners. Now about the two cook: what would be better for them than just continuing what they were doing before? Their work was only so briefly interrupted that the food didn't even burn. The food was good and actually of high quality. Of course, it had a particular flavor since it was prepared and offered to us by the enemy!

The Reds were not that far away from our positions and maybe hunger would tempt them to attack us soon. It wasn't that late in the day when they attacked us but we pushed them back in no time. The Walloon Legion occupied Cheriakov and they needed more than one Russian battalion to kick us out! It was there where I rejoined the 1.Kp whose numbers had changed significantly. As a matter of fact, my company was reorganized just like all others, since more than half of the men were missing when I left. When I got back to my unit I didn't know many of my troop mates. But when you're at war one makes friends immediately. The everyday dangers made the men count on each other and friendships were quickly forged. I was welcomed with open arms by my troop from which I only knew one man. I only knew the commander of the troop, Caporal-Chef Albert Orban, a brave Liegeois who was transferred from the 2.Kp at Gromovayabalka. All the others came from the new contingent, however our seniority and camaraderie quickly transformed into solid friendships which would last for the entire time until April 1943, when we were sent back home for a short vacation. After that our functions would separate our ways, but the friendships remained forever. And whenever our service would permit it we would always try to visit each other. Later, from this group, only two of us were NCOs at Cherkassy and we were designated for another session at the military academy. One day Orban's anti-tank cannons prevented the access of the T34 tanks to a bridge with a furious barrage. In the midst of the battle, Orban constantly encouraged his gunners to adjust their pieces and to fire as precisely as possible. Orban died as a true Walloon, as a true Legionnaire, with honor. The price to pay was never too high!

To get from Shirvanskaya to Cheriakov you had to cross a distance of about 15 km through Caucasian forests which had an extraordinary density through which only a couple of difficult roads would grant passage. We had to follow these roads and not divert from them since several enemy units were hiding in these forests waiting to ambush us after the heavy fighting from the days before. The enemy needed to resupply as soon as possible, but without any incidents the supply convoy, of which I was part, arrived in Cheriakov. The village was situated 500 m above sea level and was one of the advanced support points. The population was mostly Armenian and Caucasian and fiercely anti-communist. Many men voluntarily presented themselves to form a militia in support of the German troops. To recognize them they would wear a white armband. They knew the forest like no one else and they accompanied every reconnaissance patrol around the village. But the Reds were quiet and had evacuated the area. As soon as the patrol had passed one of their positions they would resurface and bring their grenade launchers back into position and started shelling the village again.

Many deserters surrendered to us after a 1000 km retreat or because of the propaganda leaflets dropped by the German airplanes. They received a pass to let them behind the German lines. Some of these Russians were given pieces of newspapers, like Le Pays Reel, for their bathroom needs which would actually bring them news from our homeland which was now 3000 km away. But not everything was this simple. One day, between dogs and wolves, the convoy that had joined us from Shirvanskaya escorted by the platoon of Lt Thiessen of the 2.Kp was attacked by a strong detachment of Reds. Literally they just rose out of the ground. It was an incredible action as the enemy was enraged because of hunger. They were chased away with blank weapons, a couple of rifle shots, and some grenades. Several Russians got killed while in our ranks there were no casualties besides a couple of scratches and bruises. Nothing significant to report. But a new attack was already planned by the enemy, however a detachment to go fight them made everybody feel good.

During the month of June, a new contingent of 150 volunteers, all of whom Jeunesse Rexiste, arrived with the Prevost. I admired the Prevost because just like Degrelle he had no obligation to go to the front. But both wanted to set an example. Both could have given a reason not to go to the front where they would be exposed to dangers of war. After all their lives were precious. Not only did these two men want to take all risks, they also didn't want to be treated differently nor accept any favors or benefits that were presented to them. John Hagemans had been a sergeant in the Belgian Army and so was he with the Legion Wallonie. With this rank he commanded the command group of the 3.Kp. On August 26 when the group was gathered to receive their instructions, a Russian grenade exploded right in the middle of the group. There were multiple casualties and one of them was John Hagemans. The Prevost of the Jeunesse Rexiste was dead because he wanted to be with these 150 young men. The shock was terrible for all of them.

We would spend another two days in Cheriakov pushing back some enemy troops. One of these pushes was particularly violent, when the Russians were able to occupy part of the kolkhoz. They were attacked with MGs and mortars and none of them survived the attack! It was a real massacre for them while we had no casualties. 99% of the casualties from the last seven days came from continuous shelling of the Russian grenade launchers. We had 15 KIA and about 60 wounded. During these days something extraordinary had happened with one of these wounded. It's almost surreal but it's true. During a shelling, Jourdain was hit by a piece of shrapnel in his chest. As the nephew of the big boss of La Libre Belgique in Brussels, he was picked up and transported to the infirmary. There he was placed next to three other dead soldiers since they thought he was dead too. They were going to be interred the next day, but in the middle of the night the doctors and medics residing in the next isba, heard some noise coming from the isba next doors. Suddenly their door opened and in the light of their petroleum lamp a silhouette appeared in the door opening, unstable on its feet. What was going on? Who was this? Who's that individual that has nothing better to do but to disturb the sleep of the people that needed it the most? Was this a bad joke? Probably it was one of the men that had too much to drink and who went inside the wrong isba. This silhouette insisted on coming inside and he wanted to know where he was. "You're at the infirmary!" Everybody was away now and they approached the silhouette carefully. It was one of the KIA from the day! What followed was discussions and theories until the early morning. They didn't know what injuries the man exactly had sustained, and an infirmary in the field was not really equipped with the necessary equipment for a thorough examination. The poor guy was laying down with his eyes closed. If they only knew what injuries he had sustained they might have been able to help him. Early in the morning he was evacuated immediately, which was maybe not the least desirable way to do it: in a chariot pulled by a couple of horses. He arrived almost two hours later, having crossed a distance of only 15 km, at a bigger hospital where he felt dead when he jumped off the chariot. In my opinion this is what probably had happened but I'm incapable of judging since I'm not a medic or doctor. At least it's one of the many possibilities. The shrapnel in his chest was embedded in his heart and kept it from bleeding out. During transportation most likely this piece of shrapnel had come loose when he jumped off the chariot. Whatever the real reason was, and even if my opinion is correct, the facts were real and multiple legionnaires can testify to this event.

War is something where strange things happen all the time. On August 28 we were relieved by two motorized Kp of the SS Division Wiking. These Kp were reinforced by PAK 37. I recognized one of the men of the PAK 37; it was Roger Vanhoutte, a good friend of mine from the Saint Pierre Collegiate in Uccle. His brother Jean-Pierre was in my unit. The last time we had seen each other was May 9, 1940, just before the start of the war in Belgium. At that time we didn't know when we would see each other again, and now we meet again three years later at more than 3000 km from home. And under what circumstances! War had separated us under the most unexpected circumstances and now we had to say goodbye again. But we were happy to have seen each other again.

Around 1400h we rejoined the 2.Kp at Kubanoryabyansky, a village located 2 km east of Cheriakov. Simultaneously, the sector became calm but it was a stressful calmness, even vicious one would say. The liaison between the Stützpunkten was done by patrols day and night. Sometimes we would stand nose to nose with a Russian patrol and then all hell would break loose. Sometimes we would notice them from a distance and then we tried to follow them in the hope of finding out where they came from. Where were their camps?

One day one of our patrols was successful in their mission and when the political officer came out of his hiding place, probably hoping that the legionnaires would surrender, he was greeted by multiple rifles pointed at him. Our sector leader was a smart man and the Russians had to observe how their political officer spent the roughest 30 minutes of his life. And there was nothing they could do!

However these people were a lot closer to nature than us. Their needs for food and shelter was not that exigent and luxurious as ours, and they were so much better in finding their way in the Caucasian woods and to disappear in it. We were fighting nature and we were not able to go without proper food or a proper razor. We were complaining about everything and nothing and these barbarians, on the contrary, would survive 72 hours with one carrot in their bag and they would shave with a piece of glass. They didn't care about the discomfort of their current situation.

Even if we didn't see one Russian during one of our patrols, we always felt that they were watching us. With every inspection of the phone lines during our patrols we would find more lines cut than there were any intact lines. In the occupied villages or in the potato fields we always had to be alert and stay in close groups. One day we were caught by surprise; we didn't see this one coming. One of our men distanced himself from the group to get some vegetables from a couple of Russian ladies when he was caught by a couple of Russian soldiers. We heard him yelling and screaming and we knew something happened. Some of the men took cover in the nearby bushes and slowly they approached the enemy. When they finally arrived, they found our comrade stabbed 17 times. The Russians were long gone and he was laying there crying for his mother. Everywhere around the villages were places where the Russians would hide. With every new moon the Russians tempted to enter the villages, and after a couple of failed attempts we started shooting at everything that moved in the field. The slightest movement would be answered with a full volley from one of our MG. One of our horses was able to escape and decided to go for a walk in no-man's land. He took the volley of an MG. The animal was moaning and whining, and it is then that we realized that we had made a mistake but it was too late. Now we had to kill him, but for us this wasn't such a bad thing after all. On the contrary, since it was a young horse it served us well for food. Of course this event would've triggered some ideas with the lovers of fresh meat since they could release a horse or a cow every now and now and then "mistakenly" shoot it. I think each and every one of us had this idea in mind at a certain point. But the idea was set aside quickly because we all knew Commander Lippert, and it would've been very difficult to convince him every time about these types of accidents that would occur every now and then.

The orders about the army's properties and civilians were draconian. Our food supplies were acceptable and fruit and vegetables were somehow abundant. The natural resources were for obvious reasons rigorously protected. Even the European bison which were in possession of a local family in the village were protected by these orders. The people here were friendly Armenians and the relationship with the locals became more and more friendly. One stupid accident endangered this relationship for several days because of the bad judgement of one of our sentinels. However, after a couple of days the incident would settle down and calmness returned. Everything went back to normal.

One day I was on guard duty and monitoring the road that went from the town to the forest. I had to watch every movement since a heavy grenade launcher of the 4.Kp was going to fire at the edge of the forest where the road ended. Ii took place in front of a house where all officers and NCOs of the 4.Kp had assembled together with a "Funker." The order to fire was given, and a few seconds later we heard the distinct whistling of a grenade. The impact of the projectile threw us all on the ground. The heavy grenade went through the roof of the house behind us and exploded on the inside. How it got there I don't know, but the consequences were terrible since there was one casualty. It was the son of the owner, a young man of age

20 and who was ironically a member of the militia that collaborated with the German occupiers. The exercise ended immediately after this unfortunate incident. I don't know what religion these Armenians followed, but for three days and two nights they were sitting with the body of the departed, crying and praying all the time. The day of the interment, the casket was placed on a chariot and the women were walking in front of while crying and chanting. This was the first time in my life I had seen such a ceremony.

For guard duty at night we had made a hole in the roof of our isba where the attic was. There we placed our MG which was covered by the roof and where we would have the advantage to sit at least 2 m higher in elevation. During the day we covered the hole in the roof so it wouldn't raise any suspiciousness. Access to our guard post was gained with a ladder that was fixed on the side of the house.

One night I was on guard duty together with one of my comrades when we heard footsteps around our isba. I took a rifle while pointing towards the ladder and I almost silently asked: "Who's there?" Two individuals halted immediately and I noticed that they were two officers. They were walking around the village but I wasn't sure if they were actually ours. In the darkness of the night you had to be twice as careful and I loaded my rifle. Suddenly I heard a gentle voice: "Keep calm, Lemaire." It was the voice of the commander who had recognized my voice. It was the second time that such an incident took place between us, and it was very clear that he had never forgotten our first encounter since he had recognized my voice. He commended both of us with the position of our guard post and then continued his was.

Earlier I said something about our food supplies from which its quality was pretty good. Until now. The supply units were in Shirvanskaya, and between us and them there was only one road that went through the woods and the mountains for 15 km. This was of course in favor of the bandits along the way. The five wagons of food were accompanied by about 15 men armed to the teeth. On their way to our positions nothing ever happened until they returned to Shirvanskaya. Almost every time that they were attacked it happened not that far from our positions. And in the springtime when the snow melted, there were various landslides and rivers of water coming down the hills and mountains, destroying the only road that connected our positions and Shirvanskaya. The convoy had to go down the hills to take an alternate route and all the men had to help guiding the wagons downhill.

At the same time some of the men had to fire their weapons in all directions to prevent the enemy from attacking or ambushing the convoy. When the convoy was back on the road, they made sure to be out of the forest as soon as they could. It was almost like in a cowboy movie where the cowboys would be attacked by the Indians. I experienced several of these attacks and ambushes multiple times during my time on the Eastern Front. And when the convoy finally had arrived at its destination, it seemed to have come out of a giant dust cloud while the men were screaming war cries.

Every day our patrols would go through the forest ensuring the liaison between the Stützpunkten, while the Russians were trying to break any form of communication between two enemy points while securing their own positions. One of the main points was the village of Ismailovka, situated at 640 m above sea level. This position was attacked twice by platoons of the 2.Kp and 3.Kp who were able to seize many weapons and take many prisoners without suffering any casualties. There were maybe two or three lightly wounded men, but none worth being evacuated.

Our morale remained good even when we constantly had to be on high alert and that we were never able to take a break. The platoons were always at the ready and they had to move out for several missions that were deemed necessary. We were in excellent physical condition since we were exercising a lot especially because the season was great. Even rations remained excellent even with the difficulties that arose during transport. The long distances and the endless roads through the mountains were just a few difficulties we had to deal with. But every move we made was always well organized. And besides the food, a large amount of vodka was distributed to us through the distilleries at Maykop. This vodka was a well-refined spirit with 65% alcohol by volume. We had an abundance of fruits, particularly very delicious grapes which were so tasty that they were incomparable to the ones from France where I was in 1940. Here every isba had its own wine press and when we pressed the grapes the juice that came from them almost tasted like wine. Mixed with vodka it became an explosive drink, but in this way we were able to kill some time.

Every now and then a Russian plane would fly over chased by one of our fighter planes since they were continuously patrolling the skies.

128

Furthermore, there were our observation planes flying towards the Black Sea and back. One of these planes was baptized "Father Joseph" and the reason why was because of its asymmetric form (Blohm & Voss BV-141 reconnaissance plane). A similar model was the Fieseler Storch. This name was given to the plane because its large wing surface. It was a slow flying airplane, but it could take off and land on any terrain. These planes were slow and vulnerable, but the Fieseler that was flying over our village was a truly skilled pilot. One day he gave us an airshow which we've never seen before. He flew over us while being attacked by a Russian fighter plane. And like any other fighter plane it was its task to appear when unexpected. We sounded the alarm in the hope to help the unlucky pilot in the Fieseler. He tried to climb to a higher altitude in the hope to get rid of the fighter plane but the Russian kept on following him. When the Fieseler came down in a steep dive we could hear the MGs from the Russian fighter. The Fieseler almost came down vertically and stalled its engine. The MG fire missed him and the Russian fighter attempted another shot at it, however because of the steep diving angles of the Fieseler he wasn't able to follow him. Every time the Fieseler took a steep dive, the Russian fighter had to fly around to put itself in a favorable position again, but at the same time the Fieseler gained altitude and performed the same maneuver again. We really admired the skills of the Fieseler's pilot and we applauded and cheered for him every time he shook off the Russian fighter. After the third time, the Russian fighter left the area most likely disgusted due to the fact that he was outrun by a small reconnaissance plane!

In October the weather started to change and the Germans wanted to reach Tuapse before winter. The offensive was started in the "Abshish Valley", and the artillery and airplanes were very active during this time. On October 6 the Germans initiated a violent attack to the southeast of Shadyrovskaya but without success. On the evening of the 7th the Legion Wallonie, located at Kubanskaya, was ready to participate in the movement of the 97 Gebirgsjäger Division offensive. The next day we rejoined the hospital center at Travaleva Balka (5 km west of Kalinia) since our company was hit by enemy artillery which caused several casualties. After a couple of hours of rest we regrouped and received new ammunition. Along with approximately 100 comrades, I received my Ost Medaille, awarded to those that fought in a combat unit the entire winter campaign of 1941-1942. This ribbon on our uniform would remind us of the suffering of many unknown soldiers during those terrible months in the Ukraine and Donets basin with the coldest temperatures for the region in 60 years! For us it concluded with the battle of Gromovayabalka after seven months of hardship. There the temperature difference between the coldest period during that winter and the hottest temperature in the summer was 106°C. While reflecting on this period of my life I have to say that the human body is actually able to endure a lot of misery.

On October 9 around 1600h the Legion Wallonie was on high alert. A Turkistan unit fighting for the Germans had betrayed us and switched camps. This wouldn't be the only time that this would happen with a foreign unit in the German Army, and the same would happen in the ranks of the Legion Wallonie. These incidents were due to the grotesque errors which consisted of enrolling volunteers and letting them fight against their compatriots in their own country. These volunteers were ready to do anything except fight against their brothers, so we couldn't really blame them for what they did.

We continued our march during the night of October 9-10 and we set up camp in the forest, reassuring the occupation and protection of the *Stützpunkten* and ammunition depots until October 19. I was 20 years old at that time, the age of all dreams and the age of hope, the age where one would think of being a man. But I didn't have the time to dream or think. My only hope was to stay alive since I was already a man.

Until the 22nd we occupied a defensive position on a mountain south of Navaginskaya. During the long marches in the mountains the food supplies had more difficulties reaching us and the food quality was poor. Half molded bread and canned meat was on the menu now. No more potatoes, vegetables, or fruits; water was scarce too, and the natural streams' levels were still below average due to the draught from the last couple of months. In the almost inaccessible areas, there were only small streams of water and one had to wait 45 minutes to fill one water bottle! These areas were fiercely guarded and protected and it was out of the question that an unwanted individual could go fill his canteen there. And it would've been impossible anyways since wagons loaded with cisterns would run on and off day and night to collect this precious liquid. In other locations these wagons were substituted by thousands of prisoners each carrying a water jug. Every now and then a man or a horse would lose its balance and slip, suffering a fall of

200-300 m down the mountain. On October 23 we left the thunder mountain and we reached the railway which was going in the direction of Tuapse, the paradise of the Black Sea and objective of the division.

Since October 28 the Legion Wallonie was positioned at the front after numerous days of marching over mountainous terrain. As the crow flies, we only moved maybe 10 km forward, however the landscape made the distance count times three. We were now located at an altitude of 900 m, but we couldn't complain since we were part of a mountain division.

The only benefit we contributed to the mountain division was our endurance and our willingness to move forward. It took more than just a pair of mountain boots and a Gebirgsjäger hat to be a mountain climber though. We also had a specific insignia on our uniform which was the Edelweiss, already famous because of the 97 Gebirgsjäger Division, and we certainly wanted to show that we were worthy of carrying this insignia on our uniform. None of us wanted to look weaker than our German comrades. After all we had a reputation to maintain! No matter what we had to go through, whether it was training or the hard times in the Donets or here in the Caucasus, we always seemed to impress the Germans. We were doing things better than them and that was all that mattered to us! Our goal was to show them that even if they conquered Europe there would still be these Belgians that were at least as good as them if we were given the proper equipment of course. We had already reached this objective a long time ago, as we impressed the general staffs of other units and other soldiers that had observed us during battle. Even with the civilian population in Germany, the Legion Wallonie had made its name, and for us this was the most glorious moment.

The last days of October were also the last days of the nice weather which permitted the Luftwaffe to deploy their planes at its fullest. During the day we observed the light bombers of the type ME-110 flying through over the mountains and diving in the valleys to drop their bombs on the Russian positions. Because no one knew their exact positions in this dense forest with zero visibility, the Germans obtained their intelligence through the reconnaissance troops on the ground. All the information from the ground troops would be transmitted to the Luftwaffe who would then bomb the marked locations. The success of these bombings was rather doubtful though. The noise of the plane engines and the impact of the bombs could be heard all day long. The artillery started to be more active as well when the visibility became poorer for the planes. Again, it was doubtful if these planes were actually that effective on the Russian infantry. One thing was certain: with the presence of the planes the Russian artillery wouldn't fire. It was difficult for a plane to find the Russian infantry in the woods, but it was easy to see an artillery position that was firing. When the weather got better and the ME-109s were not present in the skies, the Russian artillery would take advantage of the situation and shell our infantry with an unseen precision. The war here changed to a show of force between the belligerent parties' artilleries since the atmospheric conditions wouldn't allow any infantry movement or aerial activities. The fog made it rather dangerous for the infantry to move since they could've ended up in the enemy camp. This was the case for one of our patrols on November 1 who by chance was able to escape from the Russians just because they retreated in the right direction.

Beginning November 4 all offensive activities were stopped. Life in our current positions was harsh because the rain was pouring down, striking the ground with such a force that it transformed the soil in a big puddle of mud. Our bunkers were transformed into giant frog pools and it was impossible to stay dry or to keep anything dry. We tried to make a fire in every possible way, but the only thing that we made was smoke which only caused ophthalmia. It was also impossible to eat anything besides canned meat...cold of course. The lack of proper food caused jaundice and for a couple of days I was feeling weak and I had difficulties in swallowing. Just a single drop of water would make me throw up, and the color of my vomit was literally brown in color which was obviously a sign of jaundice. One day a medic that I knew stopped for a chat and he observed my symptoms. Immediately he sent me to the doctor and not even 10 minutes later I received my leave papers, and I presented myself at Commander Lippert's quarters and informed him of my medical leave. He laughed with me just like all the others did, and said that I already had an ugly face and that he would've never suspected the jaundice. I already had a tanned face as I still have today. I was happy to leave this hellhole for a while, not that I lacked camaraderie, but the situation presented itself and I was forced to leave. For eight days I suffered and refused to see a medic because I knew this would result in a stay at the hospital. I was finally forced to leave, but my conscience was clean since I had endured the jaundice as long as possible. I did what I could to stay but I had no choice but to leave at the end, leaving my comrades behind at the front. Five weeks later when I returned to the front, only half of my comrades were still there. Luckily this "decimation" of manpower was not due to a catastrophe, but was rather due to illness. On November 15 the Legion Wallonie was relieved of its duties at the front by two German Engineer Companies. After three weeks of holding the front lines at only 26 km from Tuapse, with reduced our manpower to 400, the Legion had distinguished itself in this European Army.

The battalion arrived on November 19, the same day as the Soviet counter-offensive at Stalingrad, in the village of Dondukovskaya, located 35 km northeast of Maykop. On November 29, 200 veterans embarked in a return to Belgium where they would spend their first vacation back home since August 8, 1941. Fifteen men stayed behind under the command of Lieutenant Léon Closset. It was in Dondukovskaya that I rejoined the troops on December 8 after spending three weeks at the hospital in Rossov. It was then that the German forces started their retreat in the northern Caucasus. At Dondukovskaya time flew by like in any other place where we were able to take a break. We were tasked with light duties, guard duties, and maintenance of our weapons. The snow and the cold temperatures made their first appearance, however compared to last winter temperatures were much more bearable this time. For the entirety of Europe the season wasn't that harsh compared to the one of 1941-1942. Our location at the eastern border of Europe was at the same latitude as the French Riviera (Cote d'Azur). Not once did the temperature drop under -10°C.

We celebrated Christmas and the New Year under these circumstances. A couple of bottles of French liquor were distributed a few days before Christmas, as well as toiletries and repair kits for our uniforms. The abundant supply of razors, soap, shaving cream, toothpaste, floss, and stationary would last us for a while. The rations were equally as good, and the local market in the village would help us to make our meals a little bit more exquisite. We had fruits, vegetables, potatoes, cheese, poultry, and even pork and veal. My comrade Albert Orban and I were living together in a house of very friendly people whose daughter was 17 years of age and very charming of course. Since my comrade had already been there for three weeks, the hunt for the girls was over, however I enjoyed her presence nonetheless. She was very attentive and friendly and she always took good care of us. For sure she was a brilliant cook and she surprised us every time with her deliciously cooked meals. Her name was Vera and her older sister was married and lived with her husband on the other side of the street. Her husband worked in a steel factory; one week dayshifts and one week nightshifts. Her sister was also very friendly and helpful, and during my time in this village my uniform was always impeccable thanks to her! For Christmas Orban and I invited the whole family to come and celebrate with us. We were able to get a nice meal together: we bought a nice fat goose, not with money because it had no value at that time, but with a couple of tubes of shaving cream and razors. We had lots of food and we were taking care of this Christmas dinner! Through keeping ourselves busy with cooking, it pushed away a bit of the nostalgia of celebrating Christmas at home. It wasn't easy though since we were so far away from home and even for the toughest guys among us it was hard. I've seen a lot during the war, but I've known only one who was that sensitive for such events.

As the war continued, combat units of the Wehrmacht secured 70 km of railroad from here to Berezenskaya, located north of Maykop. Our mission was to patrol this railroad which ran through Dondukovskaya where it crossed a ravine just outside of the town over a huge bridge several hundred meters in length. Needless to say that this bridge was our biggest concern. On January 5, 1943 my platoon was detached to Labinskaya where we again had to take care of our own things; remember that in Dondukovskaya the locals took care of our basic needs. This was war and worse things could've happened, so one would adapt himself quickly to a new situation.

At Labinskaya our group of 10 soldiers under the command of a Sergeant was sent to a larger village named Ismailovka, a place from which the memories would never leave me. It was located about 30 km from Labinskaya, and it was the end point of the railroad. A hundred kilometers south of Ismailovka was Mount Elbrus with an altitude of about 5,600 m. Normally in Europe one would see the Alps or Pyrenees from a distance of 20 to 25 km as a chain of mountains, but from our location we could only see Mount Elbrus on the horizon. It was a magnificent sight upon which I could stare to for hours and hours. Most likely we were the only ones of the Legion Wallonie who've ever seen the highest point of Europe. Actually we were 10 soldiers posted there, but only three of us made it back home after the battles fought at Cherkasy, in Estonia, in Pomerania, and at the Oder front.

It is very sad knowing that most men never came back. In January the water level in the rivers was pretty low, but in April the rivers would double or triple in size because of the snow melt and rain. At the railway we stayed in an abandoned house, and we were dependent on the Kommandantur, but we were well fed. One convoy crossed the bridge to Ismailovka at 0900h, and around 1400h I went back in the direction of Labinskaya.

One day the Sergeant and I, both acting as translators, were waiting to see an officer in the Kommandantur building when a big woman entered the building. I think she must've been at least 50 years old, her face was nice and fresh, but her posture was a real killer. We both looked at each other and we were about to exchange some thoughts about her that were not so nice. But what was holding us back was that we were most likely the only ones speaking French here in this region close to the gates of Asia. So we started talking about something else and to our surprise this woman was all over us explaining in French, most likely better than ours, that she hadn't spoken the language for such a long time with strangers since 1917. She was very emotional, and we were happy that we never made a comment on her physical appearance. We were actually ashamed that we had such thoughts about her earlier. While we were waiting for the officer, we had to promise her to pay her a visit the next day in her house where she lived with her mother. The next day we went to her house and we were welcomed there in a manner that only true aristocrats would be welcomed. The mother, who was over 80 years of age, had during WWI followed her daughter along with a diplomatic officer of the Czar whom she had met in Paris. Just before 1914 she married this young aristocrat in Paris but he was called back to Russia after 1917, and obviously he obeyed this order while accompanied by his wife and mother-in-law. Unfortunately he would die a few years later and the two women were deported to Ust-Labinsk (20 km northeast of Krasnodar). They showed us large photographs which they luckily had preserved, photographs of their wedding and of the big partisan wedding afterwards. The bride in the photos was a very beautiful 20-year-old, maybe the most beautiful I've ever seen. It was incredible. We visited them every now and then, but for us it was more like a chore. But how could we refuse their hospitality? In the end it would cost us nothing at all except some of our patience.

On January 24 the Kommandantur let us know that the railroad bridge would be abandoned by our troops. The retreating troops used another point on their way back, so the railroad bridge became useless to the Army. At this point the partisans could have their go at it, but the chances were slim to none since the bridge would be put to good use by the Russian Army a bit later. The staff of the Kommandantur evacuated their location a couple of days later, and we were convinced that nothing would happen to us since the Kommandantur left the area so late. For that reason we directed ourselves towards Labinskaya at a very slow pace but still on time for battle the next day in the afternoon. In the meantime, we said our goodbyes to our acquaintances in Ismailovka which were not limited to the two French ladies.

Just before 1400h the next day we were in the guardroom waiting for the train to take us back to Labinskaya. It was around 1500h that we started to get worried when the train started moving very slowly; we were already running an hour late. However, the slow pace of the train was normal, but the absence of the locomotive's smoke made us wonder what was pulling our three rail cars. To our biggest surprise we discovered that there was no locomotive, but that the three rail cars were being pushed by tens of Russians and their families. The locomotive that had left us in the morning never came back, but we never knew that since we were still in Ismailovka at that time. There was no doubt that this was not the only railroad in the region going to Labinskaya. What was also surprising was that the tracks were free until we got to our final destination. We didn't see any convoys going to other way. The Russians that were pushing our train were surprisingly in a good mood and never did we have to put our boots on the ground to help them even a little bit. It took us approximately two hours to travel 30 km, and in the early evening we arrived at our destination. All the way we were going at a speed of 15 km/h but when we were almost at our destination, the tracks seemed to go in a small descent and we started to pick up some speed. Now we were doing 30 km/h but we had no idea how the brakes would work. Embarking the train was no problem nor was getting off since our travelling speed was still reasonable. But we had to act fast because we were getting closer to the station. We all jumped off and the only thing that was missing was a camera to put this on film. It looked almost like a gangster movie and we could almost pass for professional stunt men. Besides a couple of scratches and bruises there were no major injuries. Most likely the consequences would've been a lot worse if we had stayed on board the train. Because it was getting dark, we noticed that we were actually closer to the station than we initially thought. Not even 20 seconds after we got off the train it crashed into something. The silence of the evening was disturbed by the loud noise of the train crashing. At this point we let the Russian civilians know that our ways would split here. Our groups parted ways and they left making a lot of noise while we were silent and always on alert. It looked like the train station was farther away than we thought, and the train had hit another train.

Now we were moving in the darkness of the night, a darkness which would permit us to enter a building through a window without being seen or heard. When we were inside the building, we heard voices in the main room, voices speaking German! So, we entered the room and there were three soldiers with their rifles pointed towards the door. As soon as they saw our uniforms they lowered their weapons and continued drinking coffee and smoking cigarettes. They told us they were waiting for orders by phone to blow up the entire station. Their slow fuses allowed them to take the time to calmly leave the station and to get into a vehicle that was waiting for them. When the Adjutant explained to us what the plans were, we started thinking about what could've happened if the order to blow up the station had come in five minutes earlier. We certainly would've been disintegrated! This event could've ended in a massacre if our rail cars wouldn't have crashed just outside the trains station. Together with the three German soldiers, we stayed at the location waiting for the phone call to come in. We slept in the waiting room of the station, but I can assure you that we were not 100% relaxed. In the morning we started marching towards Dondukovskaya in two to three stages. During our march nothing significantly happened, and the entire region seemed to be calm. Sometimes it seemed we were the only soldiers in the area. Most likely over a distance of 75 km in between the retreating troops and the rear lines there were comrades like us out in the field waiting for orders or on their way to regroup with other units.

The Legion Wallonie had already left Dondukovskaya on January 20 and only three men stayed behind, a Sergeant and two soldiers. Lt Closet had ordered them to stay behind and to wait for our arrival. As soon as we met up with these three men, we had to join the battalion as soon as possible.

The Legion had left a couple of horses and some wagons behind as well. Since January 20 the majority of the troops were retreating, and most of them had been evacuated by planes and gliders. The Junker 52 was capable of transporting 20 soldiers, fully equipped with backpacks and firearms. Combat planes like the Dornier 17 and the ME-110 pulled the gliders and were also able to carry up to 20 men on board with all their equipment. It was said that about 300,000 men had been evacuated, but I'm not sure if that number is actually correct. But I can say that during 15 days I've seen thousands of planes in the sky. Like I said before, the climate and temperature of this winter were more bearable then the previous winter, so this time we didn't suffer that much.

We rejoined the battalion at a certain point in time, but when and where I can't remember. Most likely it was in Krasnodar as we went through Gianginskaya, Velikovechnoye, Ust-Labinsk - direction of the Kuban - Niskaya, Novotitarovskaya, and Mededovskaya. It was during one of these marches that I assisted a Luftwaffe pilot. A ME-110 passed on top of us pulling a glider when he was chased by a Russian fighter. The task was easy, and the infantry Corporal knew what he had to do: shoot with an MG at the Russian fighter until it would come down in flames. The pilot of the ME-110, aware of the Russian fighter, was thinking about detaching the glider and then making a U-turn to engage the Russian fighter. After all the glider would land on the steppe without any problems. But to his biggest surprise the ME pilot saw the Russian plane shot down, however now he had to land which wasn't an easy task due to the terrain conditions. He had to look for a piece of hard and flat terrain which was not covered in snow otherwise the plane would skid and crash. One possibility was to use the tracks left on the road by vehicles and foot soldiers. In the blink of an eye all traffic was stopped and soldiers would place themselves on the edge of the "runway" to make it easier for the pilot to land. After a couple of attempts the ME and the glider were able to land safely thanks to the experience and boldness of a German pilot.

From February 4 to February 8 the battalion was at Krasnodar where we guarded different installations, bridges, parks, and equipment. We stayed with four in a local isba at the edge of the city. One night I was on guard duty from 2200h to 2400h. When I left for my post my companions told me that they would wait for my return so we all could eat crepes! At 2330h the city center was bombed by a violent air raid, and just before midnight I noticed one airplane approach our sector. Listening to the sound of the engine, I think it must have been a bomber and this could only mean one thing: a Russian bomber! My conclusion was rapidly confirmed when I heard a particular whistling made by objects coming down from the skies. I was in the middle of a parking lot and I threw myself under one of the parked wagons. The bomb impacted at about 50 m away from me. Luckily it was a small bomb, however more would come down in the next couple of minutes. The other bombs came down 300 m away from me and they seemed to approach my isba! When I ran back to my isba I noticed that many nearby houses had been hit, and that there were a lot of civilian casualties. The last bomb came down just 3 m away from our isba and caused some significant damage: one window and one wall had collapsed towards the outside, and I was upset to learn that debris fell into the dough of our crepes. Better luck next time!

Between February 9 and February 12, the battalion regrouped at Slavyansk-Na-Bubani, and during these two days we burned everything except for what was necessary to us. We thought we would be evacuated by air so all equipment had to be destroyed. Whatever was left as far as chariots and heavy weapons moved out under the command of officer-candidate Genray. This small column would head towards the Crimea through the Strait of Kerch. On February 14 we entered the airfield where we were met by 10 JU-52s which an hour later would land us 350 km farther in Simferopol in the Crimea.

Three days later we travelled another 300 km by rail and we arrived in Kherson at the Dnjepr delta. We stayed there for the better part of a month until March 14. Our stay in Kherson was, I have to say, very pleasant. The winter was mild and our 24 hour guard rotation was followed by 48 hours of rest! Like at most of the other locations, we stayed with the locals, two soldiers per house, and the rations were excellent. Even in the local restaurants there was no shortage of caviar and vodka. In Kherson we were reunited with Genray's column. We were privileged and honored as the 97 Gebirgsjäger Division was defending the Kuban bridgehead which allowed the evacuation of troops and equipment in that area. During the many and sometimes violent battles, our greatly admired General Rupp was killed in action. On March 14 we left Kherson to rejoin our barracks at Meseritz where the March 30 we were reunited with our comrades who had returned from their vacation. They were accompanied by an impressive number of new recruits, and our Commander Lippert was promoted to Captain.

Entry into the Waffen SS

After a well-deserved three weeks of vacation we rejoined our military camp where 2,000 legionnaires formed an infantry regiment with two battalions. Amongst them were many new recruits, former NCOs and officers of the Belgian Army, and former POWs. The staff was filled by veterans who had been promoted and I became a Caporal-Chef of Master Corporal, and I spent six weeks in a special training platoon where I received my new NCO shoulder boards. In the meantime we received an unexpected visit by the Reichsführer-S, and on June 3 all the foreign legions, considered as political formations, became part of the Waffen SS. Commander Lippert was promoted to Major, and on June 27 the Legion Wallonie was transported to Wildflecken. Now we were SS and this enraged our opponents even more who had seen us as traitors since August 1941. But I don't want to express my opinion on that as numerous books have objectively been written about what happened and what didn't happen on the topic of the SS or Waffen SS. But for many ignorant people this transition to the Waffen SS still ignites a lot of hate. For us legionnaires the transition from the Wehrmacht to the Waffen SS changed absolutely nothing to the cause we had joined in the first place. The only thing that changed was the salute and the insignia on the uniform, specifically the SS runes on the tunic collar and the death's head on our headgear. Also, the motto on our belt buckle changed from *"Gott Mit Uns"* to *"Meine Ehre Heißt Treue."* The fighting unit that would come out of this regiment was no longer an infantry regiment, but became a motorized assault brigade (*Sturmbrigade Mot.*) Personally I think this was the most beautiful unit I've ever known in the Legion Wallonie and in any other conventional ground army. An assault brigade of this model had enormous fire power and a huge variety of firearms. Such a unit was able to do anything considering its composition. The motorized infantry brigade consisted of: 1,000 men, a battery of 14 medium-sized tanks, an anti-aircraft battery of four 88 mm guns, an anti-tank battery of twelve 75 mm cannons, a battery of field artillery consisting of two 105 mm and two 75 mm cannons, a battery of two rapid firing 20 mm light anti-aircraft guns, one signals platoon, one motorcycle platoon, and one platoon of combat engineers. There was one general staff at company level and one at brigade level. Furthermore, we had a repair and maintenance unit. A true assault force that could be used in the campaign at Cherkasy with all the success that we had predicted.

From all these units the infantry battalion had its training on location. All the other units were part of the special weapons and received their training in different schools between July to October 1943. All the units of the newly formed brigade were wearing the name and insignia specifically for their unit and their mission, except for one: the platoon of assault pioneers. This platoon consisted of a troop of 60 men, all volunteers from which their specialties were anti-tank and close combat in which a man could singlehandedly destroy a tank by jumping on top of it, of course equipped with the proper weaponry. Other specialties were man-to-man combat with blank weapons or martial arts (karate and ju-jitsu); shock troops (*Stoßtruppen*), capable of destroying bunkers with explosives and flame throwers. Additional special units trained on assault boats/rafts capable of engaging waterfront positions and fortifications, creating mine fields and mine detecting, and the construction of bridges and temporary roads. I was an NCO with the assault pioneers in the Sturmbrigade Wallonie. We were sent to the school in Dresden - *SS-Pionier-Schule Dresden* - where for 12 weeks we were subjected to an intense training night and day, with the highest form of discipline and sometimes the most dangerous exercises. Responsible for the training was Adjutant Schumann, a Dresden native who knew everybody and who was known by everybody. The most difficult exercises were those with the pontoons, and the most dangerous was the close combat with tanks. By the end of our training all the ammunition used during exercises was real ammunition and not blanks! So it's well worth explaining its details and that our final exercise was the most precise operation in which an excellent homogeneity of the troops was demonstrated. We had simulated the operation at least 20 times and we had to execute it flawlessly eight days before our departure.

We made a promise to impress everybody at the school including our instructors, the school commander, and any other people that would be present. But it didn't suffice to show our capabilities to the instructors, specialists, and other military personnel. We had to perform our exercise in front of hundreds of people, including the commanding General of Dresden and party dignitaries with their families. The person in charge was the German Adjutant who provided our training and who persuaded the school commander to show this event to the public. The invitees had accepted that the exercise was executed by these Walloons who had fought during the winter campaign and in the Caucasus. During these 12 weeks in Dresden, the

Walloon assault pioneers showed themselves capable of many things, and our reputation had quickly reached the city limits. So when people received the invitation for this exercise they didn't hesitate to come and watch.

The weather was nice and the spectators were placed on higher ground with the terrain for the exercise laid out in front of them. Our terrain looked as follows: a little bush of pine trees with 200 m in front of it a small concrete fortification. In between the trees and the bunker there was sandy terrain, and 50 m in front of the bunker there was a barbed wire fence. Towards the bunker the terrain went into a slight elevation. Suddenly there was a little bit of panic amidst our spectators when a military ambulance approached the terrain. The person in charge calmed them down and explained that such exercises would always result in a couple of lightly injured soldiers and that the ambulance was just a precaution. The last casualty during such an exercise had been two years before.

The exercise started with the infantry coming out of the bushes supported by heavy MGs and heavy grenade launchers. Everything was directed towards the bunker. From another bunker, just outside the terrain, four soldiers were firing blanks at us, simulating enemy resistance. To cover our progress, smoke grenades were constantly fired in front of us. Up to this point during the exercise, this was the push forward of the regular infantry until we reached the barbed wire. While we were moving forward we were constantly firing at the enemy. But the enemy also had its artillery. About 60 anti-tank mines buried at approximately 70 cm in the ground were detonated by some of our instructors using a wire system. These mines exploded in groups of 10 with a 0.10 second interval between them. This had to simulate an enemy artillery barrage. We knew exactly where these mines would detonate since we ourselves had placed them there earlier. The spectators however ignored all of these details and they found the effect incredible.

The storm unleashed its power! At the same time we were lying flat on the ground keeping our mouths open to prevent ear damage and counting the detonations. When the storm was over, a smoke grenade was launched to cover the work at the barbed wire, and a small team slid under the wire, equipped with explosives to create a breach in the barricade. This type of work needed a certain calmness, accuracy, and synchronization to have the explosives occur simultaneously. When the signal was given to the team, they removed themselves from the area under the wire, and the explosives were detonated. Two men ran through the newly-created breach while the bunker got pounded by our artillery. More smoke grenades were launched to cover the activities at the barbed wire. When we crossed the last obstacle we found ourselves at 30 m away from our objective. Since we were too close to get hit by friendly fire, only the MGs were allowed to fire at the bunker. For the same reason, the bunker was only allowed to use its light weapons. Now it was time for two teams to approach the bunker with 5 kg explosives which was even more dangerous than the work executed at the barbed wire. The men had to stay in the dead corners of the structure to prevent the enemy from seeing them, and the most dangerous thing was the possibility of being hit by a flame thrower - and that stuff would stick to everything! The explosives were strategically placed, after which the men immediately fled and the signal was given for detonation. What followed was an enormous explosion and pieces of concrete were flying around, making this the most dangerous part of the exercise.

In the meantime, twenty-four enraged soldiers would storm the enemy positions with a war cry that would make the last of the Mohicans jealous! While we took our positions in the bunker, or what was left of it, we threw some live grenades into the back of the structure to cease all resistance. This was the end of the exercise which lasted for about 40 minutes. For the spectators this was money well spent! It was very impressive to observe such an exercise of this magnitude, and I had the privilege of observing the performance of two such exercises, executed by new recruits that I had trained. The publicity of this exercise performed by the Walloons had reached its objective, and the next day every newspaper in Dresden reported on this event and that there was only one wounded soldier who had to be evacuated from the scene but who was in good health. The severity of the wounds was only noticed at the infirmary while the papers were lying about it. This was a true example that this type of exercise wasn't without risks.

Within a couple of weeks the Walloons became very popular in the city, and the ladies especially liked us very much. We were a group of only 60 men, and we were spending our last days in this magnificent city. One day we had an anti-tank exercise, and we had to dig an anti-tank hole: 1 m long, 1.2 m deep, and 0.4 m wide. One had to go sit inside the hole on his knees while waiting for the tank which would drive over the hole with one of its tracks. Then a grenade would be attached to the track and the rest is history. The hole had to resist the pressure of the weight of the tank. This was perfectly possible in Russia where the ground was very hard. On our exercise terrain the ground was rather soft and we all had to dig a hole in it. Once we were done we had to get inside while the instructor started the engine of an old WWI Renault tank. He drove over the first hole and made a turn on it. When the tank was gone, the hole was gone as well, and our comrade was buried alive and had to be dug out.

The Germans were magnificent soldiers, but sometimes there was no logic in their way of thinking. Adjutant Schumann said that these holes had to be able to resist the pressure of the tank, but we tried to explain to him that the soil was too soft. According to him the instructor's manual stated that the hole would resist the pressure so it had to work. Again we tried to explain to him that the terrain couldn't sustain the pressure of the tank, not even the pressure of a light vehicle, but he wouldn't listen and jumped into one of the holes as he wanted to demonstrate that he was right. One of the other instructors jumped into the tank and repeated the exercise. We were all ready to intervene, and once the tank drove over the hole, we were even quicker to get the Adjutant out. After we dug him out he was still not convinced, and now two other NCOs had to place themselves in a hole and try to maintain their positions while the tank ran over them. Once the tank had run over the holes there was nothing left but sand and a flat surface. Suddenly Schumann's attitude changed, and now he was telling that in such terrain these holes wouldn't last and that they were worthless.

Within seconds he noticed that the situation provided him with a new method of proving us Walloons wrong. He looked around and asked the platoon for volunteers for the continuation of the exercise. After some hesitation the entire platoon stood up to volunteer, and the Adjutant understood our motivation and the exercise stopped right there. Looking at the situation of this exercise, we have to realize that the damage was caused by a light tank and not by a T34 (28t) or a Stalin tank (52t). If one of those would run over a hole like that it wouldn't be necessary to dig the person out. It would suffice to plant a wooden cross on top of it to finish the work!

During these exercises we would use dummy explosives and when we placed the explosives on a track and arm it, 6.5 seconds later it would go off, that is the firecracker inside the dummy. This way we were able to simulate explosions. But one had to be able to actually arm the grenade so it would explode, so staying calm was paramount. Calmness was a word or a state of mind that a few of my comrades didn't know. They already failed with the dummy grenades, and they completely lost it when they were given a live one. So every now and then they threw a live grenade into the exercise so that everybody learned to take appropriate cover while waiting for the explosion. Our training, which was commando training, also comprised man-to-man combat with numerous methods of attack and defense, with and without weapons. The obstacle course was run at least once a day, and the anti-tank exercises were the ones with direct contact with the tanks since the long-distance projectiles like the *Panzerfaust* and *Panzerschreck* were non-existent at that time. Until their appearance in the war, one had to jump on a tank to destroy it while knowing how much time it would take for the charge to detonate. Simply said, you had to know that when a 20-30t tank was coming your way that you had to jump out of the way, then onto the tank, place the explosive on it and jump back off it as soon as possible.

All our assault pioneers were volunteers and we were seen as tough soldiers from the start, and it was true. In our platoon of 65 men there were about a dozen NCOs who had endured a thorough infantry training with one and a half years of front-line experience where they had learned to cope with the most difficult situations. The remaining 55 soldiers were all new recruits who had to go quickly thought their infantry training because of the war situation. The pontoon exercises took place at least once a week on a reserved spot on the Elbe River. Our resources were limited, but we had to learn how to build pontoons and bridges with rubber rafts, etc. Sometimes the beams we had to carry to build the bridge were 25 kg each, resting on our shoulders. Two men were carrying two beams and everything as to move quickly. We exercised with real materials and we were able to build two pontoons in one morning, capable of carrying a tank. This was the minimum requirement, and in our case it had to be able to support a tank accompanied by 20 men over a distance of 2 km down the river. In the middle of the exercise we were allowed to take a break and to smoke a cigarette, but then we had to return to our starting point which meant going against the flow. Back at our starting point we had to dismantle the pontoons and then go back to the barracks which would take at least an hour. We marched back singing, but we arrived at our barracks on the verge of complete exhaustion, our shoulders bleeding and our backs aching. After a good meal we went to our rooms where we laid down to get some well-deserved rest.

The next day wasn't a day off though! At night we had permission to leave the barracks until 2200h, and the NCOs had to be back at midnight. The girls in Dresden were irresistible for sure, but before we left the barracks we had to present ourselves at the duty NCO. This meant that we had to have an immaculate uniform, belt buckles shining like mirrors, finger nails clean, and our faces clean shaven. We also needed a handkerchief of some sort in our pocket all the time, and we were given prophylactics for our own good. It was hammered in our heads that we had to be safe all the time, and if one would come back with a sexual transmittable disease, he would pay dearly for this mistake since one was given the necessary equipment to protect himself. A good friend of mine in the Legion Wallonie, this is when I attended the officer cadet school in 1944, was given permission to go visit his fiancé when she was travelling through Prague. He came back two days later with a sexually transmitted disease, and he was sent back to the front. Even if he had stayed for another 10 years in the German Army and pass all the tests for promotion, he would have never become an officer because of this. The rules were very strict and had to be followed at all times. During one afternoon, my friend Coppé and I met two girls in a local bakery. First we went out together, but after a while each went his own way with his girl. My friend's name was Irmgard and I very much enjoyed my time with her. Every night I also took the tram to the Postplatz, a place where one had to go if he didn't want to spend the evening alone, even after a day of pontoon exercises.

We never thought we would rejoin the Legion after these 12 hellish weeks but the end of our training was near. The reputation of the Walloons in Dresden was impeccable, but the last night of our training we partied like we never did before! There were a lot of emotions that night, but Irmgard was not one of the many girls with a broken heart. I had already broken her heart a couple of days before, but she was still happy to see me again on my last night in Dresden. We were both 20 years old and I was a soldier so I had to be realistic. I had dinner with her and her parents a couple of times, and I knew this relationship was special. I was going back to the front and there was a chance I wouldn't come back, or even worse that I would come back mutilated. This was the risk of a volunteer and I didn't want her to be worried about a lifestyle that I chose; the life of a soldier. We were both very young and we had lots of time for things to return back to normal. I told her my intentions and what I had chosen in this life to which she replied that she loved me. She remained quiet and kissed me for a couple of minutes. She clearly showed her feelings that she had for me, but after she left I thought it would be best for both of us to go our own separate ways. It was hard for both of us but it was better to end it this way than ending it later due to a catastrophe.

We rejoined the Brigade Wallonie again after some intense training. Our new tanks, artillery, etc. were all waiting for us to be used in battle. The Walloons had finished their training with flying colors and showed the rest that they were masters in each discipline that was taught to them. Every time during competitions, whether it was anti-tank, artillery, anti-aircraft...the Walloons always ended up in first place, beating the Germans. We had already showed them what we were capable of during the last 18 months of campaigning in Russia. They saw us marching from Dnepropetrovsk to the Caucasus, and on many future occasions and locations we would show them again what we were made of. The only shadow on our reputation was our driving skills. We had to send 200 men to the driving school to get their driver's license even though many already had some driving experience. Most of them had already driven a car, and some of them had seen a truck from a distance, but in an assault brigade the limo services are pretty rare to non-existent. However, driving a 10t truck versus driving a tractor resulted in the fact that certain candidates managed to return to the unit without a driver's license. It had nothing to do with their attendance and engagement, but more with the instructors. Like in any army in the world, the rules for a motorized unit were very strict, however the Belgians, the Walloons in particular, were more easy going and more relaxed because it wouldn't take that long to cross Belgium by car. We all knew that the driving conditions in Russia would be totally different from what was taught during driving school.

Everything was set to go now, but the most important thing was to stay together. During the next couple of weeks there would be exercises in which all units would participate. With the Legion up front of the group we drove 300 km with all our vehicles to Wildflecken; thank God everything went smoothly. We had exceptional vehicles and the morale was high; any area we would drive through the people would recognize the Walloons since we had been mentioned in different German newspapers regarding our adventures at the front and from training. We were proud of this, but it also made us a bit cockier. Some people thought that we went to fight in Russia for the Germans, which didn't bother us at all. There was always a sense of camaraderie between us and the Germans, but we were never treated differently than any other units. Our spirit and temperament were in fact completely the opposite than that of the Germans at any level, and every side had to compromise a bit to avoid certain frictions. It wasn't always easy and sometimes it seemed to be impossible. At Wildflecken, the camp was under the command of veterans, some of them were disabled from the war and who were living in the camp with their families. We shared our barracks with a signal's unit and some tank drivers, and we all shared the same canteen.

One night an old friend of mine, Adjutant Touriste, was drinking a glass of wine in the canteen when he overheard some Germans talking about the Walloons. Little did they know that he was fluent in German, and what they said about us wasn't very flattering. Our Adjutant's reaction and facial expression was all but friendly, and he left the canteen to come back with 12 Bourguignons who wiped the floor with these Germans. As soon as they were done, the Walloons left and went back to sleep. These Germans had already alerted their security but they had no clue who the suspects were since they had no time to look at their assailants during the fight in the canteen. The following day, the entire brigade had to march in columns of three in front of the victims but none of them was able to identify the culprits. Obviously this news spread like a wildfire around the camp, and the German authorities were absolutely not impressed. Adjutant Touriste had to explain himself to the commander since he was the only one that was recognized from the group, however our officers, knowing the reason behind the fight didn't pursue the complaint. On the contrary, the entire case put a big smile on our faces, except for one because when Degrelle seemed visibly amused, our commander Lippert was not impressed at all. These types of punitive actions away from the front were not his kind of thing at all. And because he was the commander of the unit, everything came down on him while he had an impeccable reputation and he tried to keep it that way. There were no sanctions that followed, but try to put yourself in Lippert's shoes for just one moment. Since the culprits were all unknown, the entire unit had to pay the damages totaling 4,000 Reichsmark. So with the next pay, every legionnaire had 2.5 Reichsmark deducted from his pay, something that we gladly paid with a big smile on our face. The incident was closed after this and we all moved on.

It was already October and we were bored, and the monotonous exercises and the air raid alarm going off every now and then didn't do the morale any good. There was nothing to do in the region, and there were only three bars close to the camp. When I was on patrol with two Corporals, we spent more time catching men returning to the camp late after a night out.

It was at Wildflecken when we received our tattoo, which was a practice only with the Waffen SS. This mark made sure that after the war not too many could escape persecution and imprisonment. In every country after the war it sufficed to let a man lift his left arm to identify him as a legionnaire of the Waffen SS. Many thought that this mark would represent affiliation with the Nazi qualities or qualifications. Even today people think that, while in reality it meant something totally different. In every army soldiers would wear dog tags containing their unit' information, their regimental number, and their blood type. In case anything would happen to the soldier, the family could be notified or a blood transfusion could be performed. In the German Army we had a tag that was worn around the neck, but lots of soldiers put it in their pocket since it was easier to carry it that way. The result was that a tag was easily lost. Others would lose it because the string around their neck would break after a while. In lots of cases a heavily wounded soldier had no tag on him, so they would have to analyze his blood first before they could do a transfusion. Because of all these problems with the tags, they thought a soldier to carry his blood type on him all the time where it would be visible, easily accessible, and protected. So here you have the mystery of the blood type tattoo explained. For whatever reason, I was never tattooed though.

One day a General came to visit us and the entire brigade had to parade for him. Usually a General would be there around 1100h, but we were already all dressed up and ready at 0700h! That particular day I was the duty NCO since the new officer of the general staff from Brussels hadn't arrived yet.

I had received a letter from my father not that long ago, informing me that this new officer would be Captain Anthonissen. He was the brother-in-law of a good friend of my father, and the three of them were mobilized together during WWI. Obviously my father and the Captain talked about me, and my new commander promised my father to look after me. I wasn't sure if this would've been good for me, but there was no way to escape from this

150

situation. The day of his arrival I was called to his office but I didn't know if this was an official introduction of just a friendly meeting. I opted for the official introduction and I dressed up in my tunic, boots, helmet, and service pistol on the side. The way I presented myself impressed the Captain, and he told me to take my helmet off. This meant that the official part was over and until the moment I would put my helmet back on, there were no more ranks or uniforms between us. The Captain was about 50 years old, tall but with a slim build. He always expressed himself calmly and his eyes were blue with a soft friendly expression. Just like my father said, this man was honest and correct in all things he did. And later on he would certainly prove his leadership during battle. I think our meeting lasted more than 30 minutes, and we spoke about my parents, common friends we had, and our return to Russia. His intention was, if I would come back from the next campaign, to send me to the military academy. But he wanted to see me in action first to reassure himself I was worth it. When I returned to my room, 12 men were waiting for me to hear about the new Captain. If you were correct in the things you did and your uniform was always nice and clean you wouldn't have to worry about him.

The future would prove me right. In a troop of 2,500 men you always find those that don't know why they joined, those that lack discipline, and of course deserters. The last couple of months there had been a few deserters, and some of them were caught and incarcerated. Others were sent as a volunteer to the platoon of the assault pioneers. The ones that were incarcerated were given the choice to stay in prison or to go to the front, which in exchange would make their sentence disappear. All of them chose for the front and they were placed into a disciplinary unit. In the Legion this unit was the assault pioneers, and they had to be treated as any other soldier and member of the unit. The one who dared to say anything about the mistake they made would be severely punished. Basically these men were in some kind of way adopted by us. Legionnaire Dewilde wasn't that lucky, but he deserved his punishment. He was on his third desertion and he was used as an example for the others. He was sentenced to death like every other military force would do and he would be shot by a firing squad. This firing squad were all Walloons commanded by one of its officers and in presence of the entire Legion. In the morning of his execution he was brought to the guard room where he was given a last meal and a bottle of excellent wine. He shared the bottle with a comrade that he had asked to stay with him for the night. Dewilde was very calm and the Legion was already waiting outside in square formation. The Germans were obviously present as well. Two days before, one of their own was actually executed at the same location, but I don't know the exact reason. The poor guy had to be brought to the execution pole since he was not ready for this. Dewilde was brought there by truck with him sitting on his coffin while he was joking and laughing with his guards. At his arrival he marched all alone to the execution pole where he faced the execution squad. He took off his shirt and commander Lippert ordered everybody at attention when he read Dewilde's sentence. As soon as he finished reading, he ordered the men to stand easy while he presented Dewilde a cigarette. I can't say that this was an act of humanity but rather a sinister one. The moment he was finished smoking would be the signal for the firing squad to shoot him. He took the time to smoke his cigarette, and after a couple of minutes he took his last drag, held his breath for a moment and exhaled. He threw the cigarette on the ground, crushed it with his boot, and faced the commander and the firing squad while saying "Gentlemen, now it is your turn!" This was a moment where it seemed that time stood still and that everything became silent, even nature. I'm convinced that most of the men from which 85% were new recruits, wouldn't have lasted for another five minutes. The tension was broken when Dewilde threw his cigarette on the ground and when the rifles were being loaded. The officer of justice approached Dewilde and tied his hands behind the execution pole, but Dewilde refused being blindfolded. He looked straight in front of him while keeping his head held high against the pole. Commander Lippert placed himself behind the firing squad and ordered the men at attention and to bring the rifles at the ready. After that, the execution officer took over command of the firing squad, and from that moment everything went very fast. "Attention! Make ready! Fire!" Twelve rifles fired at Dewilde, but just a second before that one could hear a cry of "Viv la Legion!" Dewilde's head titled forwards and his legs slowly collapsed. His torso remained straight up as if his proudness was still present. After the officer of justice gave him the coup de grace, the entire Legion paraded in front of the dead body. Some of the bullets hit him in the chest, some of them in his arms which caused one of his arms almost to come off. There was blood all over his body and blood drops fell on the green grass. A vague smell of gun powder was still in the air. I've seen many men die during the last two years, both friends and foes under different conditions. Dewilde deserved his sentence, but he was still one of us. Somewhere between September 1944 and 1947, 200 Belgians were executed like this by other Belgians for collaborating with the Germans. I'm not here to judge, but my opinion is that these executioners were simply driven by hate and instinct. I call them cowards.

Korsun - Cherkasy Kessel

The weeks that we stayed at Wildflecken started to bother us since we didn't move out and we didn't know what they were waiting for. Our training had wrapped up a little while ago and the evenings were very monotonous. On October 13, the day of my birthday, I unexpectedly received a card from Dresden. Since we had separated weeks before, Irmgard had said nothing at all and we hadn't sent any letters to each other. I already had accepted that she wouldn't hear back from me, but when I received this card from her, I considered it as a sign proving me wrong. Apart from this I was sincerely hoping that she would write me. It seemed that these weeks after our separation hadn't changed our feelings for each other. On the contrary, and now I had something to do every night. At the beginning of November rumors went around that we would be leaving soon, but most of us didn't believe these rumors at all. It was through a stupid incident that I got conformation that we were about to leave for the front pretty soon.

We had two defective landmine detectors that needed to be brought to Dresden and I volunteered for this "mission" while I would be accompanied by a soldier. Captain Anthonissen wondered why I wanted to go to Dresden so badly, so I explained him the reason why and because I spoke German. A car dropped us off at the station where a train would take us to our destination. It was November 7. The following day I dropped off my detectors at the station and from there I took a tram to Freital, a suburb of Dresden where Irmgard lived and worked. I called her office, and 30 minutes later we were together, just the two of us.

Early in the morning on November 9 I was back at the station in Wildflecken where a car picked me up. The Legion was still there and ready to go! They almost left without their best NCO! The departure was set for November 11, but I had other things to think about. I laid down in my bed after two sleepless nights and I slept until the day after. November 10 was the big day of the inspection of all equipment, and on November 11, 1943 in the pouring rain the Legion moved out and went to the train station where six trains were waiting for us. On these trains they also loaded 350 vehicles, 46 artillery pieces, 12 grenade launchers, 18 flame throwers, a heavy MG, 90 light MGs, and 2,500 men. In the evening we were on our way, once more, to a destination unknown to us.

Only a few of the officers knew exactly where we were going and we could just speculate. Looking at the train stations we passed we were clearly going in the south east direction. We passed Lemberg, Iasi, Kishinev, Tiraspol…however even if we were moving towards the Black Sea, the weather became colder. But this time we came prepared! At the next stop we were given winter gear that would make an Eskimo jealous! All our uniforms and headgear had fur, even our boots. And the outside of our uniforms were all white serving as a snow/winter camouflage. First we thought we would go to Kherson again, a place where I spent quite a bit of time together with some other veterans about nine months ago. But now in the month of November of 1943 there were heavy battles raging down there and our train deviated from its course going northbound. Not too long though, and finally we arrived in Korsun at 2200h where we unloaded all our equipment.

Normally we wouldn't unload our equipment at night however the situation changed since the Russian Air Force, which was still pretty weak, was already active in the region. So here we are for another campaign in Russia, and for 200 of us it would be the third one in this war. For the rest of the Legion this would be their baptism of fire, but under what circumstances? What would our mission be? What is the situation in the east in general, and in particular in our sector? Where are we?

During the fall of 1943 the Russian Armies confronted the Germans east of the Dnjepr and started with the recapturing of the Ukraine. The Russian Army was able to take strategic points on the other side of the river in the region of Kiev and at an important bridgehead just a couple of kilometers west of Kremenchuk and Dnjepropejansk. The width of the river which flowed between these two cities was between 2,000 and 2,500 m. The river was very shallow, and the water stream was very slow. Many of the sand banks divided the river into smaller streams and meanders. In the region of the lower Dnjepr, the Ukraine had a very picturesque presence and was relatively flat, the highest region being somewhere between 100 and 200 m in altitude. It had low rolling hills and the valleys were covered by thick pine forests. During the spring the water of the Dnjepr would flow sometimes 15-20 km outside its natural borders, making other rivers and streams swell significantly. Even in the wintertime when temperatures reached -40°C, the river rarely would freeze. There were always big chunks of ice floating in the river though. Winters were harsh in this region, but there were also periods of unexplained thaw which made most movements between locations almost impossible. At the end of January and beginning of February 1942, I had already experienced this type of winter.

The locals were open and independent, but they were not in favor of the communist regime. In 1941 the German Army was welcomed as a liberator and received unconditional collaboration from the population. But in 1943 things had changed due to the rigorous Russian propaganda. It very well explained the difficulties of life under the German occupation which according to them made the local economy suffer. By the end of 1943 many locals had fled into the woods and became dangerously active as partisans. Their anger and passion to fight only got ignited by the Russian Army who provided them with weapons and ammunition. They organized their military actions fast, disciplined, and effective. The people that stayed behind in the villages feared the repercussions from both sides, and they had no choice but to continue with their lives under the current circumstances. With a typical Slavic attitude, they showed no hostility towards the occupier. They were very apprehensive upon the return of the Red Army and the communist politics. The Russian front in the Dnjepr region was very similar to that of the Germans from 1942, and consisted of many support and defense points.

It is true that after Stalingrad some of the officers of the Wehrmacht joined the Red Army under the leadership of Von Paulus who was teaching at the academy in Moscow. In October 1943 the German High Command noticed the difficulty of a successful offensive in the Dnjepr region between Kiev and Kremenchuk where the Russians occupied strategic bridgeheads. But they tried to keep the enemy forces pinned in their current locations, knowing that they wouldn't be able to engage on other points of the front. This would give the German High Command the time to prepare other defensive lines in the rear and to evacuate material, weapons, and ammunition, and to destroy military facilities which were under the threat of the Russians. Later I personally heard from General Wöhler of the 8th Army at Cherkasy that there was a third reason to maintain our positions at all costs by order of the Führer.

At the time, Germany entered into political and diplomatic conversations with Turkey, but until now Turkey had maintained a neutral position and many of the German allies saw the chances of Germany winning the war become smaller and smaller. When we look at the map we see that Turkey has a border with the Soviet Union, and it was of major importance that Turkey stayed neutral despite of the pressure of the belligerent parties. They also wanted to prevent a new front against Germany if Turkey would support the Allies. Even with the situation being in favor of the Russians, the German Armies were still present in the Dnjepr region and were maintaining their positions. And there was also the argument that the troops in and around Cherkasy would maintain their positions until the end. General Wöhler already mentioned that it would be impossible to hold our positions for a couple of weeks, let alone for a couple of months. At that time we were still not encircled by the enemy, and by the time he received permission to move out of the region the encirclement was a fact. This explains the many useless tactics to maintain positions at the cost of many young lives with no positive outcome at the end. Simply explained, there was a very strong Russian Army in the Dnjepr region who had pushed back the Germans to Zhytomyr at 130 km west of Kiev, and was pushing them towards Uman. This resulted in the German divisions being forced to abandon their posts and to reposition between Berdichev, Bielaja, Kharkov, and Tannev. About 10 divisions were engaged in this operation which translated to about 120,000 men. In the southern part of the Dnjepr, the German High Command tried to establish different defensive points to prevent the Russian Army from entering the Ukraine from the direction of Romania.

One of these positions, 160 km from Kiev, was an industrial center and covered one of the only strategic access points towards the western Ukraine: Cherkasy. Cherkasy was occupied by the German forces, however communications from there with other units was very difficult. Apart from that, Soviet forces already had settled east of the Dnjepr and were able to anchor strong offensive points which they tactically exploited. The 5.SS-Panzer-Division Wiking, comprised of the Regiments Germania, Narva, Westland, and Nordland under the command of SS Gruppenführer Gille, had the task of engaging the enemy forces in the region in a 20 km radius and in particular the forests between the rivers Olshanka and Fosa. Heavy fighting took place for the only two supply routes to Cherkasy by Shpola and Gorobich-Korsun. Korsun was the place where we arrived on November 19 around 2200h and where the Legion was going to deliver appreciated and favorable support to the 5.SS-Panzer-Division Wiking.

After a couple of hours of rest the Legion received the orders to occupy a sector of 17 km on the Olshanka, downstream of the confluence with the Fosa. The Olshanka was approximately 35 m at its widest and 15 m at its narrowest point; deep in certain areas, but mostly shallow. It was a fast-flowing river so it would never freeze entirely, not even in this new winter season which was not comparable to the winter of 1941-1942. The positions by the river were occupied by the infantry battalion, and in certain areas we had an anti-tank and anti-aircraft set up as well. The other cannons like the 105mm, the 88 FlaK, and the tanks would only be used for specific missions. The assault pioneers which operated all over the sector were posted at Baibuzy, 20 km west of Cherkasy, a large village from which the eastern point was used by the command post, the 3.Kp, and the rest of the men that were not placed in one of the positions along the sector. Our positions were located 40 m from the river bank and 1 km from the village. The assault pioneers had the task of building shelters and covers for the infantry for when they were resting, and also for their protection against enemy artillery. Since we were located so close to the enemy, the construction of these shelters occurred only during the night. Every shelter had the same dimensions and they were all built from the same materials. There was an abundance of pine trees and we made good use of them. The prep work was done during the day, and in just a couple of hours we took down more than 10 trees and cut them in the appropriate size according to their use. All were loaded on trucks and transported by night, close to the front lines where they would be unloaded. While the men were at work the truck would get a new load to keep the flow of materials going. The clayey soil was easy to dig, and by the early morning the men were able to seek shelter in 12 structures, and especially now the cold started to come in. The skies became gray and soon it would be snowing again. It was just a matter of one week and everybody had their own shelter.

Every now and then a small Russian plane would throw a bomb on one of the German occupied villages but without causing any significant damage. We were also ordered to build roads before the first snowfall, and since we were on guard duty at night we built extra covers for our sentinels in case it started snowing. One night I was making my rounds and to my surprise I didn't find a sentinel there where he was supposed to be. The explanation was simple: my soldier was sleeping! He was sleeping next to his rifle which I slowly removed from him. Then I took my jacket and put it over his head while yelling at him in Russian. The sentinel was a rookie, but he had his heart in the right place. I think this would've been the scariest moment of his life, and most likely this would've been the last time he would sleep while on guard duty. Fatigue was a common thing and it happened to me before as well, so why would I report him and have him locked up? In the meantime, somewhere else a dozen sentinels most likely did the same thing while they wouldn't be punished for it. I believe the way I scared him was more effective.

Since the Legion was comprised of one infantry battalion, one could easily imagine life in this unit. The battalion stayed for the most part always in one group, and it was posted in one village or support point. Even if a platoon was detached from it for a particular mission, this wouldn't be for too long. We all lived through the same misery and adventures.

In a motorized assault brigade life was different. There were many specialized units which were deployed in their area of specialty. These specialized units had, because of their expertise and engagement at the front, a life on their own. The occupied sector was more stretched out and was 17 km wide at the beginning of December 1943, and it reached 25 km by January 1944. By the end of the month the platoon of assault pioneers occupied some of the infantry positions to fill the gaps in the defense lines. When 10 men left from the battalion for a patrol, then everybody waited for their return. Everybody knew that they were out in the field and where they were. In the brigade we remained sometimes in the unknown, and when a platoon had helped us out with a reconnaissance patrol, we wouldn't even know that two comrades were killed in action. Some of the companies had an easy time in their positions while others would fight for several days in a row. In the battalion the mission was the mission for every member; when one died then all the others died a little as well. In the brigade each man had his own mission and once this mission was completed, he would simply return to his unit. Whatever happened after one had left was none of the other men's business. When a soldier died the assault pioneers or artillery had other and better things to do than to think about the deceased. We didn't know many of the other men outside our unit except for the 200 veterans and some NCOs, however we didn't see each other that often.

It was seldom that one would meet another soldier who would be wearing the Osmedaille ribbon on his uniform. To give you an example, I was notified about the death of my comrade from the Caucasus Albert Orban; I had not seen him since last April. We were in the same sector though: where he had the command of an anti-tank cannon and where he was killed in action. Because of these events it is impossible for me to give you an overview of what happened in the entire brigade, and I can mostly speak only about my own unit.

The snow accumulation during this winter was about 50-60 cm with temperatures as low as -20°C, but this was no match for our exceptional equipment. Rations were in abundance and they always arrived to us with some French liquor or Cote d'Or chocolate. Mail was being delivered on a regular basis and the morale was excellent.

At Baibuzy where we were posted everything was calm. Sometimes a bomb would fall somewhere in the village, and one of them exploded in an isba where a Sergeant was resting his eyes for a couple of hours. Unfortunately he died there on the spot. Another day I was in my isba on the other side of the village when a bomb shattered all the windows and made the entire structure tremble on its foundation. When I ran outside I noticed a cow, not hit by the bomb, but which was disoriented and was walking around as if she jugged down 1 liter of vodka.

I was staying with a young woman but I never knew if she was married. Maybe her husband was somewhere in the forest with the rest of the partisans? Her 5-year-old son loved the candy we gave him, and I gave him candy in tubes which I got from the canteen. On the other hand, we received tubes with pills which had no flavor at all but who would help against fatigue since we had many sleepless nights. Of course we were to use them with moderation but when I was gone the kid had found one of these tubes, still half full, in my drawer. There were also a couple of bottles of Remy Martin and Negrita, but he wasn't interested in those. Unfortunately he was more out for the "candy", and upon my return we had to put him in a restraining jacket to go see a doctor. There was nothing they could do but to give him an injection to make him sleep and then to wait patiently for a couple of hours to see how he was recovering. Then the boy woke up a couple of hours later, and he was completely disoriented for which we had to give him a second ration. After that he returned back to normal. It was only two days later that I noticed that my drugs were gone, but now I understood why he was acting so crazy. From now on I would be more careful when I was around the boy.

During the month of December my platoon had to accomplish two tasks for which it was split into two groups. One group would be working during the day, and the other group during the night. During the day we had to build a bridge of 25t over the Fosa at about 100 m from its confluence with the Olshanka. The road was located approximately 4 km from Baibuzy. During the night we had to set up the barbed wire between the Olshanka and the infantry. The bridge, being 5 m wide and 15 m long was supposed to allow our tanks to cross the river to the east into Russian occupied territory. The terrain there was rough and almost impenetrable. Every now and then we noticed through our binoculars some Russian soldiers looking at us from the hill, curious about the progress of our work. They didn't bother us due to some unexpected interventions, and we would continue our work without interruption. However the cold made it difficult to work. Our materials consisted of pine tree trunks which were cut 50 m upstream. The cut trunks and assembled pieces were transported over the water, and men in rubber rafts would intercept them and put them into their positions. Every now and then one unfortunate fell into the ice cold water and had to be rescued. Once out of the water he would be stripped naked and covered with snow, then covered in warm blankets and transported to the camp. There he was given a big glass of rum or cognac with some aspirin and after which he was sent to bed. The next day he would be back to work!

After 15 days of hard work our bridge was inaugurated by our commander who crossed the bridge for the first time on board a tank. We baptized our work *"Pont Van Eyser"* or Van Eyser Bridge in memory of a good comrade of mine from August 8, 1941 and former commander of the 1.Kp. He became a platoon commander and therefore he received the order on December 13 to take 30 men and infiltrate the woods in front of us for about 15 km, just east of Kom Kuom. It was suspected that there would be a battalion of partisans in that area, and they had to go and investigate the situation. Before dawn a group of assault pioneers helped Van Eyser's patrol cross the Olshanka in rubber rafts; after that the Van Eyser patrol had to advance until they reached the buildings at Kom Kuom. However, there they would be encircled by more than 100 partisans, but the Walloons fought back like demons. Outnumbered, the Walloons were almost all massacred by the Russians, and only six of them were able to escape by crawling their way back to our lines. When they finally arrived at the Olshanka river, the assault pioneers had actually no hope at all to see any of them back alive. Most of the Van Eyser men were rookies, and this was their first engagement at the front and first real contact with the enemy. One of the survivors was Freddy Geetz who now lives in Austria, and Andre Poulet, an old faithful of our group. Totally exhausted they told us what happened. They explained how the second in command, Corporal Lemay - also a veteran of August 8, 1941 - after Van Eyser was killed in action, defended the body of his commander. He fell on top of him, mortally wounded while firing his last bullets which gave him no protection at all. He died there with his commander. I wasn't part of the Van Eyser patrol, but in memory of my old commander Lieutenant Van Eyser and out of friendship for those of August 8, 1941 who were killed in action, and out of gratitude for my other comrades Andre Poulet and Freddy Geetz, I wanted to tell you about this dramatic event. The following story was told to me by my good friend Andre Poulet.

Moshny, December 13. For about three or four weeks, our group of the 2nd Platoon 1.Kp was positioned between the villages of Moshny (left) and Baibuzy (right); approximately 1,500-2,000 m in front of us was the somber line of the Cherkasy Forest. In between us and the Cherkasy Forest was the Olshanka, a small river barely noticeable from our positions. The group was comprised of 12 men, and we were on a relay 24/7 - six men holding the positions while the other six were resting in Moshny. Around 1800h we were about to finish our patrol and the six of us were looking forward to our relief and to get some rest. It had been snowing for a couple of days, and a white blanket covered the landscape. Soon we would see dark figures popping up out of the snow which were our comrades who were about to start their shift. As soon as they arrived, Sergeant Phillipait, our section leader, approached me and told me that the next day we would leave for a patrol and that we had to report to the command post of Lieutenant Van Eyser immediately. First we would be supplied with four magazines for our MG, and four boxes of regular ammunition and grenades. In our quarters we ate and we checked our equipment, and after saying goodbye to our comrades, we left during the night. Loaded with our MG, ammunition, and grenades, we arrived at Van Eyser's bunker where we met Sergeant Decamps, our patrol leader, Corporal-Chef Bataille, and some other corporals. Descamps and Bataille were also veterans of August 8, 1941. We installed ourselves inside the bunker as well as we could because space was limited. There were many of us and we were all fully equipped.

The entire night we discussed our mission, and around 2300h there was a phone call. Suddenly everybody became silent as Van Eyser answered the phone, replying with a yes or a no without showing any signs of emotion nor enthusiasm. As soon as he hung up the phone he communicated that from this moment on he was the patrol leader. Everybody applauded because Van Eyser was highly praised by his men. Van Eyser asked us to be silent and to listen to the new orders that he had received. All light MGs had to be brought back and eight of us left the bunker. Thil and I were on our way back to Moshny, and on our way back we picked up some boots the Lieutenant had ordered. We arrived back at his bunker when it was already late at night and we could feel the fatigue coming on. Inside the bunker everybody was asleep except for Van Eyser. The fire was out and the cold had slowly crept inside the bunker. We looked for a spot inside the bunker and we fell into a deep sleep. I had the feeling that I didn't sleep at all, and I didn't feel that great when I woke up. Other comrades had woken up as well now and cigarettes were lit. A cigarette would at least warm you up a little bit.

Van Eyser hung up the phone; apparently it was the Adjutant of the 3.Kp that warned us about an enemy patrol approaching our positions. There was a lot of commotion in the bunker, and I couldn't really understand what was going on. The only thing I heard was that one of the men was asked what time it was: 0400h. Descamps stood up and ordered us to be quiet. He also ordered us to check our weapons and ammunition. Only six light machine guns would leave: Van Eyser, Descamps, Bataille, and the three Corporals. The rest of us had 9 mm pistols, our rifles, and grenades. Van Eyser asked one of the men who wasn't going to participate in the patrol to leave the bunker. As soon as the soldier left, Van Eyser addressed his men and said that we would only go on a reconnaissance patrol, and that strict discipline was required from each patrol member. No cigarettes, no loud talking, no clicking of weapons, and no firing of weapons without permission. He really insisted that we would follow his orders. One of us asked a stupid question when he asked what he should do when he would find himself nose to nose with a Ruski. One of the men answered in his dialect: "you put your finger in front of his mouth and tell him to shut up!" This answer made the rigid atmosphere go away a little bit. Van Eyser added that if we would be confronted by the enemy we would be fucked, and in case of great danger the Adjutant will fire a red flare in the air so that help could eventually come to our location. Van Eyser gave us more details about our mission just before we moved out. First of all we had to penetrate the forest for 4-5 km and hope to discover a partisan camp at point X. Secondly we had to march 3 km away from point X in a slight deviation towards point Y and hopefully spot a concentration of tanks and recognize the types of tanks. Upon our return we would use an alternate route to point Z and take a couple of prisoners if possible. Van Eyser asked if we had all understood the plan and the importance of the three capital points X, Y and Z. Then he turned towards Descamps and Bataille and repeated the path we had to follow. We checked each other's equipment and Descamps gave the orders on how the patrol had to leave. Descamps and two NCOs would form the vanguard of the patrol, and Bataille and two soldiers would be placed in the rear with the rest of the men lined up between them according to the weapons they were carrying. Van Eyser checked his watch and he gave us permission to have a cigarette.

At the last moment we learned that the *Propaganda Kompanie* or PK had a *Kriegsberichter* (war correspondent) of the Leibstandarte ready to take pictures of us. We were just waiting for his arrival. Outside we could hear footsteps approaching and a tall man with glasses entered the bunker and saluted us all with a Heil Hitler. He presented himself as SS Sturmmann Ausha of the Leibstandarte Adolf Hitler - Propaganda Kompanie. On his belt there was a holstered pistol, and around his neck hung a camera. Some words were exchanged between him and the NCOs, and then the order was given to get ready to move out.

We all went outside in the cold of the early morning, and I ended up just in front of the rear guard close to my friend Thil. I think Descamps, who knew us both very well, intentionally placed us close together. We marched towards the river and the assault pioneers transported us across the river on rubber rafts. When I landed on the other side of the river, the patrol had started to move in a single line. The assault pioneers wished us good luck, and Descamps waited for the last man to pass before he would return to the front of the group. The operation was executed in silence and lasted about 30 minutes. Without any encounters, we arrived at the edge of the forest which formed a dark screen on the snow. It was still dark but the sky started to clear in the east. Soon it'll be day.

Van Eyser and Descamps had us all take a place in a hole just at the edge of the forest, while the scouts penetrated the forest in front of us. For most of us it was our first engagement at the front and one of our comrades cramped up and started coughing like crazy. The echo of the coughing sounded even louder. A multitude of swear words followed from all sides, and he was told to keep quiet. Everything became calm again and we observed the shadows of our scouts coming back to us. One by one they went to Van Eyser to report what they had seen. Anxiously we were waiting to hear from Van Eyser, but the only thing that was said was that there was nothing to report.

We started marching again, following a path that would take us to the left flank of a hill. It became daylight and now I could clearly see the shadows of the men in front of me. The environment made me think of my Ardennes back home. We went higher up the hill, but suddenly a flash lit up the sky. We found ourselves with our faces in the snow, but it was nothing but a lighter that Bataille used to light up the compass and the map for Van Eyser. Now we were able to see all the men and we all got back up again. Since it was light now we could clearly see the route we had been walking and what was still in front of us. We could clearly feel some sort of tension in the air since the cover of darkness was gone now. We continued our way but it seemed that the map that we had was not 10% accurate. Every now and then Van Eyser and the two NCOs would stop and we saw them discussing points on the map while holding their compasses in their hand and their heads turning to all directions. There were our scouts again, but they still had nothing suspicious to report. When we arrived at on the top of the hill, everything cleared up around us. In front of me I could see the open space where there used to be a forest. Now it was just tree stumps and branches laying all over the place.

Suddenly Van Eyser ordered the men to lay down, and we were all waiting for something to happen. Sometimes a head would pop up in the hope of seeing something. With lowered voices the questions like "What's going on?" or "Do you see something?" went around. I looked at my friend Thil who was 10 m behind me, and I noticed he was passing his lighter to others so they could have a smoke. Another comrade made a sign to them that they were crazy, but with the shoulder gestures the other men were making a point that everything was calm and that the spirit of the Bourguignons had taken over again. We were unable to see what was going on in front of the patrol because of how the path was going. Then Descamps came to us and gestured to carefully move forward. In front of us was an open field covered with 5 foot tall bushes with a road in the middle, almost invisible. We advanced and we regrouped just before the intersection. The scouts and Van Eyser were discussing the map while I observed about 10 columns of smoke in the distance. We whispered to each other that this would be the partisan camp. With the help of Descamps, Van Eyser let us advance in groups of five: two pistols and three rifles, and we received orders to hide ourselves in the bushes. Whether you were laying down or sitting on your knees, these bushes would give us zero visibility. We could barely see the group in front of us! The only thing I knew was that I was in the last group of five with Thil, D.H., and Geetz. I forgot who the fifth one was. I tried to see what was going on in front of me by slowly getting up. I noticed that the NCOs were agitated and I could see one of them crossing the road with one of the men and disappearing. Two others disappeared at the same time to the right of them. I went down on my knees again and I was waiting patiently for some news to come in. Almost everybody was smoking now and there was total silence. Sometimes this silence was broken by one of the men coughing but that was it.

Suddenly the calmness of this morning was interrupted when we heard two shots being fired followed by the crying of injured dogs; a crying that slowly degraded and disappeared. My blood stopped flowing and I felt ice cold to the bone. I looked at my comrades but we remained silent. Thil was the first one to relax again after this incident and lit a cigarette. Time went by and we heard footsteps running towards Van Eyser's position. I stuck my head out of the bushes and the others did the same thing. It was two of our soldiers that came back; both seemed very excited and they didn't even bother to speak with a lowered voice. I could hear everything they said and it seemed that there were bunkers all over the place, and that one of them went inside one and that he had to kill a partisan. "There are many submachine guns to take to the Lieutenant!" Lots of veterans had a thing for these Russian submachine guns since they were easy to use and very accurate.

166

I couldn't hear the reply of Van Eyser, however the orders he gave were executed and several groups marched into the unknown right in front of us. Bataille moved us forward for about 20 m, still under the cover of the bushes. We learned that PK Ausha left with a couple of the men that went on a reconnaissance. We had nothing else to do but to wait in the vicinity of the Corporal and the Lieutenant. It was calm for a couple of minutes, and then it seemed that there were multiple shots fired in the distance. I heard Van Eyser say "What the hell are they doing out there?" Time seemed to have stopped and nobody was talking. Even if the situation didn't seem to be tragic, it was certainly not solid. I was very nervous and finally a couple of men came back. Van Eyser and Bataille ran towards them and now they were all standing up in a covered space. I could tell by them arguing and gesticulating that something was going on. They all looked very excited, but then they all became calm again.

A little bit later Van Eyser summoned me to come to him. He was standing there all alone, Bataille wasn't there, and around his neck and in his hand he had two Russian submachine guns. To my biggest surprise I saw two partisans standing behind him dressed in uniform with fur hats; one was very tall while the other one was rather small. Van Eyser ordered us to take position on the elevation behind him. Without thinking I asked Van Eyser "Are we taking prisoners Lieutenant?" He replied "Yes, but these idiots let a couple of them escape!" "And what about these two?" while I pointed with my pistol at the two Russians behind Van Eyser. "What? Which Russians?" said Van Eyser while he turned around. The two partisans, surprised by our presence, ran away and Van Eyser fired his submachine gun but without success. Van Eyser grabbed Geetz' rifle and fired three more times but the partisans were running crisscross through the landscape and disappeared on the horizon.

On the horizon I could still see the smoke columns. Personally I think these two Russians were part of an unarmed patrol. "Where is Corporal Bataille?" asked one of the men. "He went to get the others," answered Van Eyser. "It looks like we've been discovered and we have to act fast now!" Thil and I were ordered to hide on the elevation and to observe the horizon. "If something happens then let me know immediately." We took cover in an undisturbed space, and Van Eyser went back to the others who were 100 m behind us now. I looked behind me and I saw different groups arguing with Van Eyser while in front of me there was no movement at all.

Then I heard several shots being fired and I could hear bullets whistling; I had no idea where they came from. Behind me they were all gathered together, but they didn't seem to worry at all. Thil pointed out that there was a woman in the group. Later I figured out that she had approached Bataille and Descamps. I was watching the group arguing and smoking cigarettes and I felt assured that everything was OK. "Don't you think they have forgotten about us?" asked Thil while he got up. Then he pointed at something on my left. I got up and with oblivion I observed at 150 m from us an endless column of men with weapons in their hands. We could clearly see them and we knew they were going to cut us off and attack us from the rear. We sprinted down to Van Eyser and alarmed him immediately, however he seemed to doubt our observations. "But Lieutenant, we both saw them and they should be very close now!" The group became agitated and Descamps said that we should deploy immediately but "she" wasn't back yet. Bataille replied "What the hell is this bitch doing?" In between the nervousness of the group the PK man addressed us all in German: *"Das sind nur Partizanen, Mensch!"* The contempt of the Waffen SS for partisans was well known. The NCOs were discussing tactics while everyone else was down on the ground with their weapons at the ready. It was agreed that "she" and her men would be back soon. Van Eyser remained silent, and Bataille suggested to go to the right and then straight ahead back to our positions. Van Eyser raised his shoulders and he was visibly unhappy with her being late as were many of the other men.

A couple of minutes went by, and in the distance the gunshots were multiplying. Finally she arrived with some of her men; she was excited and enthusiastic, and at that moment she totally ignored the situation. They were gesticulating and explaining to Van Eyser that they had found a village full of partisans, and that they had to fight their way back. When Van Eyser understood what they had done, he became worried. He got up and ordered all of us to be ready and to sleep with the eyes wide open. He sent a couple of men to scout the road that we had taken to get here, and as soon as the men left the vanguard fired a couple of shots. Bullets were flying very close now and you could hear them whistle. "These surely are partisans Lieutenant!" yelled some of the men. The entire group retreated and we found ourselves back at the intersection of the two roads where we were earlier that day.

The Russians were now at only 50 m and hiding behind the trees. In our ranks there was total disappointment, and everybody was giving his advice since the NCOs gave no precise orders for the troops. One of the men yelled "Let's go on the hill!" We all started running through the bushes and I was right behind Van Eyser. Thil was not behind me and when we arrived on the top, Descamps explained to Van Eyser that there was a forested area with pine trees close by at just 300 m from us. The female prisoner explained that we just had to follow the road to get there and that we would find a concentration of tanks close to the woods.

We arrived in the woods and when I turned around I saw a group of men, at least 20 coming towards us. To my biggest surprise and despite the distance, Descamps took his submachine gun and fired at them. A rifleman fired back and the group launched an attack on us. There was no reaction from Van Eyser, and suddenly we heard yelling. This time it came from our left flank. "Be careful, they're here!" and all hell broke loose. I threw myself into the snow, and I wanted to cover myself with snow; only my eyes would move. Bullets were flying over my head and grenades were exploding all around me. From every direction, men were yelling but in front of me I saw nothing at all. Everything seemed to happen on the left flank since we were the right flank of our patrol. Thil was laying down 2 m in front of me and that was it. Nobody else was in front of us. Van Eyser was on my left and a bit farther was the PK man with his camera at the ready.

The Russians, just like their Walloon counterparts, were yelling like crazy. The atmosphere was a mix of yelling, shots being fired, grenades exploding, death. Thil signaled me that there were partisans on the other side as well, and I saw him throw a grenade. Van Eyser asked us to carefully use the grenades we had since the supplies were limited. Descamps came back and nervously explained that the partisans are there in great numbers and that they are armed with submachine guns. He also mentioned that there was another group of partisans attacking us from the left. Then Thil suddenly yelled "What about the flares Lieutenant?" to which Van Eyser replied "It's useless!" Descamps however fired two red flares in the sky, after which he left. Bataille approached Van Eyser while his chest was covered in blood. He yelled "They all have submachine guns Lieutenant!" Before Van Eyser could reply Bataille left like a raging bull. Moments later one of the men yelled that Bataille had blown himself up with a grenade. Poor Bataille. He had been an NCO for a while and a very good friend of mine. He had always told me that he'd rather blow himself up than to be taken prisoner. At that moment I got to know how real fear feels. If Bataille killed himself he knew that the situation was without any hope. I looked at Van Eyser, but he remained quiet; he gave me no orders at all.

The battle was still raging on our left flank but in front of us there was still nothing going on. "The Lieutenant has been hit!" I heard someone yelling. I turned towards Van Eyser and I saw him unsteady on his feet, his forage cap laying in the snow. His head was moving back and forth as if he was nodding. A red spot was visible on his chest and blood came out of his mouth. I wanted to go help him but that moment the PK man ran towards us; he still had his camera around his neck. He placed himself behind Van Eyser. I turned towards Thil, but he signaled me to stay down.

In the meantime the bullets seemed to come closer and closer. I stayed low and I put my jacket on top of me. Only my eyes were moving. Then on our left, just in front of us, Lemmens appeared out of the bushes. He was completely covered in blood and looked at Van Eyser whose head was still moving and he saw the PK man. We yelled at him "Stay down Corporal!" He seemed to only notice us, and he said "five times, Poulet!" Then he went down in the bushes in front of us and most likely these were his last words.

The cries of the wounded were taking over the battlefield. I wanted to get close to Thil, but fear kept me pinned to the ground. "Things are looking bad eh, ma Poule?" He called me *ma Poule* to make fun of my name. I made a gesture with my hand as no sound was coming out of my mouth because I saw a Russian appearing behind him. In vain I tried to stop him, but everything happened so fast. He didn't see the Russian and I grabbed my pistol, pointed at him and fired three rounds. Too late! A flame was coming out of the barrel of this submachine gun, and Thil made a long and terrible cry. He tried to get up but he fell down again in the snow. The Russian was already gone. Did I hit him? I found myself alone, the only survivor on our side.

Suddenly a shadow appeared in front of me and I remembered the words of Descamps and Bataille to never let yourself get caught alive by the

Russians. My fear now was to be taken prisoner, and there was only one thought in my mind: suicide. All my thoughts came together and my blood seemed to freeze. To die at the age of 20…I hesitated and hesitated…especially when thinking how to die: to shoot a bullet in my temple or through my mouth? But suddenly I heard footsteps running through the bushes, and to my surprise it was other Bourguignons just 4 or 5 m away from me. One of them noticed me and signaled to follow him. Immediately I was back to reality and I was able to move again. We were running, more like galloping down the hill. I've heard some cries, and at the bottom of the hill there I noticed we were only five or six.

Then there was Demoulin, he was sitting on his knees holding his stomach. He seemed to be severely wounded and he said: "Give me your weapon comrade." Neither did he wanted to be taken alive. He was leaning against a tree with his eyes looking into infinity. The others were already moving away and I started running again not granting him his wish. I turned back one more time and I won't ever forget how he looked.

I caught up with the others and we disappeared into the bushes. Behind us shots were still being fired, and the group stopped after a while when the shots seemed to be more in the distance. Anxiously we were listening to see if the Russians were still following us. When we came out of the forest in sight of our positions, calmness came back to our group since we knew that the fight was over for us. This was the story of my friend Poulet.

It took us a lot of time to build the bridge over the Olshanka, but it would only take 30 seconds to destroy the entire thing. It was two and a half months later that two of my comrades had to destroy the bridge. They did it with a lot of courage and discipline, and that when the Reds were already on the other side. They installed all explosives and then retreated making sure that the circuit of wires was properly set and functional. The others arrived, and a few seconds seemed to last forever. And then the end of the world, especially for the Russians who were already on the other side of the river. Our men were not waiting until the debris of the bridge came down, and some Russians would fall down after the explosion, but our guys ran as fast as they could and rejoined their platoon. They certainly earned their iron cross!

Setting up barbed wire fences was another problem. The wooden posts were cut beforehand and transported by truck at night. But to jam these posts 30 cm deep into the frozen ground was another story. We used a metal peg and some explosives, and Bengal fire to make holes in the ground. We installed a kilometer of fence per night which meant 200 poles and the equivalent explosives and 40 fuses. This could've been done during the day as well since at this time we were not constantly under enemy fire. The Russian sector close to the river bank was calm and deserted, but some things made us not trust this calmness and silence since our patrols had noticed a lot of footsteps in the snow. During one night in the sector of the 3.Kp close to Baibuzy, the sentinels heard some agitation on the river; two or three grenades and a couple of rifle shots made everything return to calm again.

The next morning however, a small boat was found on the river shore. With rubber rafts a comrade and I went to inspect the vessel, and without a doubt the intentions of this night patrol on the river were clear. I found many long charges which would've been used to destroy the barbed wire fence. I recuperated all the explosives, and I let the vessel float away on the river. I put a couple of grenades in it and a couple of meters away, in the middle of the river the vessel exploded and it disappeared in the water. This vessel was most likely going to be used to attack our positions and it was certainly an action from the enemy to show us that they were still there and that they would be capable of destroying some of our positions. Even if their mission was aborted, it was a clear warning for us that next time things could be a lot worse.

One night we had to go back to the 3.Kp sector, and we had to deliver a big truck with materials in it close to the river where a small footbridge was located. As per usual, I reported to the company commander so he would brief his men that the assault pioneers were working in front of them so that they wouldn't be alarmed by our activities and wouldn't "defrost" their MGs on us. The commander informed me that his men noticed a lot of activities on the other side at night, and that there was a possibility of the presence of a heavy weapon, possibly a big cannon. Every now and then a shot was fired in the direction of where they thought there was some movement, but with the forest in the background it was almost impossible to distinguish the shadows in the darkness. I told the commander

I didn't believe one bit of this and neither did he, but he just wanted to warn me of how his men thought and behaved at this location where we had to work. Better to be safe than sorry! But I wasn't going to drive a 3 km detour with tons of materials to get to the footbridge when it was easier to drive straight to it. Of course we would have to drive in front of the supposed cannon, but I didn't believe it was there.

When I was talking to the commander, the truck driver was in the room next door and he overheard our entire conversation. Once I returned to the men outside, he approached me saying he didn't want to be used as a target for that cannon. I couldn't convince him about the non-existence of it, and there weren't just 36 other solutions available. So I let him walk with the others and I got behind the wheel of the truck. Ten minutes later I was driving towards the footbridge, and two minutes later I arrived there, proving that I was right. I was breathing heavily though and I was happy that nothing happened. The truck was unloaded and I left again to pick up some more materials, this time with its original driver behind the wheel, and we worked the entire night without any incidents. In the morning those in front of us noticed that another kilometer of fence was put up, but this was not the only thing that happened in our sector.

On December 18, five days after the Van Eyser massacre, a platoon of the 3.Kp, educated by experience, infiltrated about 10 km east of Komuna Komitern, and noticed several entrenched armored units. At about 7 km from our positions there was a heavily fortified enemy position, and it appeared like it would be difficult to get through. On December 22, a platoon of the 2.Kp and 3.Kp, accompanied by six assault pioneers armed with flame throwers, approached the village without being discovered. Their goal was to push the occupants into the forest. The soldiers had to keep them in the forest while the assault pioneers would burn everything down to the ground. This was most likely the easiest part of the program. The walk back to our lines would be a nice and gentle stroll if everything would turn out the way we planned it. The first shots were fired, and 80 yelling and raging Walloons took the Russians by surprise. Stupid as they are, they didn't know what was going on and they quickly disappeared into the forest, a bit faster than we had expected. From there they launched a vigorous counter-attack, and that while the assault pioneers had only done half of their work. The situation's outcome was not as expected, and we had to leave as soon as possible while we were carrying three of our men that were killed in action in addition to the seven wounded men. This was done in all calmness and with the highest discipline which prevented the entire situation, which seemed an easy operation at the beginning, from turning into a disaster. The footbridge of Baibuzy would be mentioned one more time because soon it would lose its planks.

The Olshanka entered Baibuzy from the southeast; southwest of Baibuzy was the confluence with the Fosa over which we built the Van Eyser bridge. Before the Olshanka passed this point it went through a village named Bolshoistavosivye which was occupied by the 2.Kp. The positions of the 2.Kp were located on the right river bank on a road which went through the village and into the forest of Zagrevka. Part of this forest was taken down to make place for a barbed wire fence and a mine field.

One night, for an unknown reason, two German trucks drove through Bolshoistavosivye and passed the positions of the 2.Kp. They drove into enemy territory without being stopped by one of our sentinels. The driver and their companions thought that they were still in friendly territory believe it or not, but it's those impossible actions that seem to be the easiest ones. Nobody was expecting it and it was merely impossible that two German trucks went for a ride in Russian occupied territory. Even the Russians most likely thought that these were their trucks. The truck drivers, not seeing any familiar locations, continued to drive on the road thinking that it would take them to one of our positions. They passed Agrevka without making any of the Russians suspicious of their presence. The incomprehensible part is that these two trucks were able to pass our positions without being stopped by a sentinel. From the command post it was communicated that two trucks were headed towards Moshny and that there was no reason for them to go there. This story was totally incomprehensible. In the meantime, after 8 km the two trucks arrived in Moshny and it was there that shit hit the fan when they got stopped by a Russian sentinel. Both parties were flabbergasted and before the sentinel could react, both trucks made an impossible U-turn and made their way back. They were already far away from the sentinel when they heard some gun shots, and now the situation became clear to them: if the enemy is on one side of the river the friendly troops must be on the other side. Now they just had to take the same road back and cross the first bridge they would encounter. The first bridge they encountered was the footbridge at Baibuzy. They were approaching the location at the highest speed possible while driving through the darkness and snow. On our end we knew what was going on now, and if the Russians were shooting at some vehicles, then these vehicles were certainly not theirs. But they weren't shooting that much, most likely they thought that it would be useless to destroy two vehicles that would end up in their hands. For them it sufficed to alarm Zagrevka through which the two trucks would be driving back anyway. However before Zagrevka there was the footbridge which the truck drivers mistakenly had seen as a bridge. The first truck just drove over it and got stuck in the water with its nose a meter under water. The second truck had stopped, and its occupants jumped out to help out the first truck. Everybody was safe and they all told us about their adventure in enemy territory. They also informed us what they were transporting: the first truck had anti-aircraft ammunition, caliber 88mm, which the Russians couldn't use after all; the second truck had 3,000 liters of fuel on board in barrels of 200 liters. That would be a great catch for the Russians who were coming closer to look at the two trucks; for sure they would've wanted to salvage the truck full of fuel. They only had to put the truck into gear and drive away and disappear into the forest which was 50 m away. During the night this would've been very easy to do and to prevent the trucks from falling into Russian hands, our commander proposed destroying both of them.

The following day, somewhere late at night, I went back to the footbridge accompanied by my Lieutenant and 10 other men to destroy both trucks. By looking at their cargo it was going to be a nice spectacle of fireworks. The entire day the two trucks drew the attention of the men of the 3.Kp, but on the other side they were interested too. When we crossed the footbridge we could clearly see silhouettes on the other side. Some of our men armed with submachine guns prevented some nasty surprises, and it took us only 10 minutes to carefully place the explosives on the trucks so that they would detonate simultaneously. This type of work in the darkness isn't easy at all, and if a detonator was handled the wrong way it could light up the entire thing. Plus we were not the only ones there so we had to work quickly and stay calm at the same time, knowing that we were sitting on 3,000 liters of fuel and 88 mm ammunition. The silence around us was horrifying, and the only thing you could hear were the light clicks of the charges being placed on the trucks. We heard men approaching our positions, but we were ready and it just sufficed to light the candles. Even with the temperatures standing at -10°C, we were perspiring like crazy. And we had absolutely no idea what the others were doing as soon as we left. Maybe they figured out what we were about to do, and they stayed behind cover which was a very wise thing to do. Suddenly there was a very loud explosion producing a flame that was at least 10 m high, igniting all the 88 mm shells which detonated one by one. The sky was lit up as if it was day, and after a couple minutes we would only hear the sound of the fire eating away whatever was left. After that we went back to our positions, and the day after I went to have a look at the footbridge or whatever was left of it. The bridge was gone and all the snow around it had melted; the ground was black in color and full of debris.

Now before we arrived at our positions everything was already prepared by the Germans, who were there longer than us, with the necessary placement of mine fields around our positions. One day I received orders from my platoon commander to go into one of these fields to replace one of the mines that had detonated. These mines were called *Stock Minen* which were anti-personnel mines placed about 40 cm above the ground while they were anchored in the ground with a wooden stick. All these mines were interconnected with a very sensitive trip wire; just the slightest touch would detonate the mine. These mines were placed in a corn field from which they still harvested the crops. At the same time, the corn stalks were ideal camouflaging the mines. My commander had notified me that an NCO of the 2.Kp and a couple of his men went into the field and when they were leaving, one of the men hit one of the wires, detonating a mine. One soldier was wounded, and I questioned the actions of that particular NCO.

Many years later after the war, I met another veteran of the Legion, another one from August 8, 1941, whom I really got to know in 1944. He became an officer and commanded an infantry company on the Oder front in Pomerania where he brilliantly had led his men and where he had sustained his eighth battle wound. From that moment we became really good friends, and since we hadn't seen each other for about 20 years, we were recollecting old memories from our time in Russia during the war. I told him about the episode of the mines of Cherkasy and the stupidity of that NCO that walked into the minefield with a couple of his men. Lieutenant Regibeaux looked at me with a big smile on his face, and then he told me that he was that stupid NCO. We both started laughing and it was then than he told me the rest of the story of the minefield. A patrol ended up in the minefield and one of the men got hurt. The NCO wanted to go after them to actually guide them back to safety.

The month of December slowly came to an end, and Christmas and the New Year were now just around the corner. Both holidays were celebrated where we were posted. Close to our positions, just across the river there was a little town named Zagrevka. It was located in the woods, and actually not that far away from the destroyed bridge over the Olshanka. Zagrevka was heavily occupied by the Russians and every patrol became acquainted with the intentions of the enemy forces. We had never been able to take any prisoners, but we needed one at all costs. On January 1, 1944 a platoon of the 3.Kp attempted an attack on Zagrevka without suffering any losses. The next day another platoon attempted another attack, but this time with one severely wounded. The others were just too stubborn, and it was decided to go there with a huge force. A storm troop that comprised a platoon of the 2.Kp, a platoon of the 3.Kp, one group of assault pioneers, and 10 tanks under the command of Lieutenant Derricks of the 2.Kp attacked Zagrevka at the break of dawn. They moved through the forest northeast of Starosillya. A second detachment with Lieutenant Denis of the 3.Kp attacked with a platoon of the 1.Kp, and one of the 3.Kp crossed the river on rubber rafts and executed a movement from the north, joining the 1st detachment at the rear of the village. From the edge of the forest the tanks were providing cover for the infantry.

At night I went with a group of assault pioneers to the forest of Starosillya to be at the disposition of the commander of the 2.Kp. There we spent the night with men of the 3.Kp. At 0500h everybody mounted the tanks, and the column of tanks started moving on the same road where the two German trucks had been driving on a couple of days ago. But our intentions were not that pure like theirs. We arrived at our location where the tanks stayed under cover and we got into our positions. All of this happened in silence which was very impressive. During that time the other detachment made contact with us, and everything was executed as planned. At 0600h we initiated our attack; the Russians were completely surprised and had absolutely no time to organize a proper defense. Only one hour later, the resistance at Zagrevka was completely destroyed. Sixty deaths stayed with the ruins of the village, and we took 85 prisoners and were able to capture four anti-tank cannons. On our side there were three casualties, five wounded, and five missing in action. Two tanks lost a track because of landmines, but other than that they suffered no damage. If the enemy had placed themselves on more strategic positions, then they could've easily predicted our attack.

The Russians had the goal of bringing down the defensive forces and lines in the lower Dnjepr and to threaten the armies in the rear who attempted to join the front lines. The activity of the dissimilated forces in the woods around Cherkasy lead to numerous local actions which prevented the Russians from establishing a stronghold. Because of this, in the first days of January, two Soviet Engineer Regiments had established themselves east of Teklino in a triangle shaped forest which was of a high tactical importance. This menacing push threatened direct communication with Cherkasy and the Korsun airfield, and because of that the German High Command couldn't leave the situation just like it was.

On January 8 units participated in a counter-attack to conquer this strategic position after a heavy artillery barrage. But the Russian engineers had already prepared very strong fortifications so it wasn't easy at all. The losses were relatively noticeable. On January 11 and 12, units of the Regiments Germania and Narva of the 5.SS Panzer-Division Wiking to which the Brigade Wallonie was attached, initiated the attack without success.

Léon Degrelle took advantage of the occasion and easily convinced the General that the Walloons could succeed there where the Germans and Danish had failed already three times. This was easier said than done! To execute this attack, the Legion had to move all its men to the same location. To relieve the 4.Kp located at Moshny and Starosillya, they used men of the reserve company which was located 4 km away from the front lines. Our infantry battalion arrived at Orlovets on January 13, and it immediately took the front positions close to the forest. The assault pioneers were posted with the locals and only had to intervene when necessary. In military terms one would say we were the reserves. The arrival of the Walloons at Orlovets was certainly noticed by the Wiking who was after all one of the most famous divisions of the Waffen SS and commanded by General Gille. They were hardened fighters, while the Walloons consisted of 80% rookies who had never been in an important battle like the one which we were about to enter. The Wikinger never ceased to make comments about us, but the Walloons were not shy about speaking their mind as well. In the village there was a placard which announced the following: *"Hier Circus Wallonien - Morgen Vorstellung 6 bis 8 Uhr - Eingang Frei!"* This was too much, and the "Fritz" would be shown what we were capable of.

Everything was prepared to the slightest detail by the liaison officer Lt-Colonel Wegner with the commander of the artillery. In just a few days the enemy had significantly reinforced their position,. and they were determined to take advantage of the situation. According to our intelligence the forest was occupied by an infantry regiment, a grenade launchers regiment, and a group of light artillery. It was freezing (-25°C) and the soil was covered with 30 cm of snow and was very slippery. In the following days the German artillery had fired 6,000 projectiles which had transformed the forest in an indescribable pile of trees which were covering the Russian positions. After another artillery barrage of 800 projectiles, the Legion attacked under a heavy Russian artillery barrage. The 1.Kp was the spearhead, the 4.Kp the reserve, and the 2.Kp and 3.Kp formed the other points of the diamond formation. In the rear a couple of tanks supported the attack with direct fire. The progression of our infantry was fast and seemed to be perfect for the first hundred meters. From there the Russians rigorously defended themselves with such tenacity which made it an indescribable man-to-man combat just to conquer small pieces of land. This demanded furious actions from all the soldiers involved. In the conquered positions we discovered several mutilated German corpses. It was 0800h when two platoons of the 2.Kp and 3.Kp, after running on a slight elevation on the terrain, found themselves only 20 m away from the enemy's light grenade launchers. Obviously the cannons opened fire as soon as they noticed us coming, and a violent barrage of grenade launchers swept the 1.Kp back to its starting point. It was not the first time that we were confronted with the accuracy of this Russian weapon.

At 0900h the Russians initiated a counter-attack and shook our infantry companies who were already scattered all over the place. There was confusion everywhere. A platoon of the 3.Kp placed on the extreme right flank lost its liaison with the rest of Legion; the 3.Kp on the left flank was completely isolated, and they had a deep ravine in front of them. It would take two hours to regroup and reestablish the liaison through a motorcycle unit. The attack was initiated again at 1300h after another artillery barrage. The position of the Russian light artillery had been damaged after the brutal man-to-man fights. On both sides the losses were very high. And these man-to-man fights always resulted in the isolation of troops and broken communication. So we had to stand our ground at all costs. It was during the night around 0300h that the 4.Kp closed all the gaps, and we reestablished the liaison between the different units in the field. On January 15 during the day, barbed wire and landmines were placed on the front lines. The Russian artillery however claimed numerous victims in our ranks during that time.

The following day another enemy attack occurred, and the 1.Kp and 2.Kp were pushed back to the edges of the forest and the triangle was occupied again by force by a Russian battalion and light artillery. Commander Lippert remained calm under the situation and he was determined to reach the objective. And we would be successful! A quick resupply of the troops and then all went back to their positions ready to attack again. During the last three days our men had to endure a lot: 80 killed in action and about 200 wounded in action. After three days of combat the survivors were exhausted, and the 72 hours in the snow at -25°C didn't do us any good. However the morale was intact and the will to fight was more alive than ever. Actually the men were going to show their comrades of the Wiking what the "Circus Wallonien" was capable of, and that what had happened until now was just a general repetition.

For three days the assault pioneers assisted with the interment of death at Orlovets. The wounded were taken care of and some had the honor of returning to the front lines immediately while others had the privilege to be a spectator. In the evening we arrived at the forest, armed to the teeth, however it wasn't the right time to attack. During the night we approached one of the Russian flanks to reduce their effectiveness, and accompanied by a platoon of the 1.Kp, we helped a German platoon placing landmines in front of the positions of the Narva Battalion on the right flank of our sector. The situation was delicate, and in the woods it was pitch black; every step you took in these woods could've been one onto a Russian bunker. After two hours of moving forward, we advanced one kilometer and landmines were placed at 800 m which seemed to be an unexpected success. But the nervousness of the German pioneers became more and more noticeable, and our men of the 1.Kp were genuinely worried. However we were able to stay calm and we kept our ears open for the slightest or suspicious noises.

About half a second before the "Hurrah!" of the Reds, we heard absolutely nothing. In a matter of seconds the German pioneers all disappeared as well as the 1.Kp. It was nothing tragic, and even the Reds had to be careful in their progression in the darkness of the woods and to not to throw themselves in front of our guns. For us it was not a battle until the end. It was approximately 2300h when we retreated to the edge of the forest; all Walloon assault pioneers were already in a covert position, and I found myself with the company commander and a couple of NCOs in a ditch. For the last time, we fired our submachine guns while we were walking away. The Reds didn't risk it to advance towards us because of that teamed with the poor visibility.

A few hundred meters to the rear and out of sight of the enemy, we took a small break to catch our breath again before joining the rest of the men on the southside of the forest. Our other comrades were already far away, and we thought that this would be the end of the mission when suddenly we heard a shot coming from the friendly side. It was commander Lippert, Léon Degrelle, and a couple of men who were happy to have found us.

But the happiness didn't last that long since our mission was far from over. All men were ready except for one NCO who thought he had sprained his ankle. A little later he noticed that it was actually a piece of shrapnel that hit him. We rejoined the southern point of the forest and we took our positions. At the break of dawn our artillery came into action, and a few minutes later about 60 yelling assault pioneers advanced like a pack of wild men hitting the Russians on their way, Russians that were fighting back with an energy that seemed to go forever. Soon the advance would slow down and again the man-to-man fights started. But this time we didn't have to worry about our flanks since these were covered by a platoon of the 1.Kp and one of the 2.Kp. Our mission was to create a breach in the Russian lines and open the way for the infantry battalion. We were able to create the breach, but I was the only uninjured NCO left.

My friend, Sergeant Damiani, threw himself upon a bunker with a grenade in his hand when he got hit by an explosive round in his private parts. He would leave the hospital a few months later fully recovered, but what happened changed him forever. He wasn't a man anymore, and a few months later he would get killed in action in Breslau at the banks of the Order. He would blow himself up while he was in an ammunition depot.

Many other assault pioneers were wounded, but we were holding our positions. During our advance we found the body of a Wikinger whose private part had had been cut off and stuffed in his mouth. A bit farther we saw a German who had been crucified between two trees. We hadn't taken any prisoners, but most likely our enemies had no intention to put their hands up for us. Everything had to go fast, and by 0830h the breach was big enough so that the infantry battalion could initiate their attack. On the battlefield one could hear the cry *"Bourguignons, en avant!"* and the north side of the forest was reached where it was bordering Male Starosillya. It was there where we found two young women in uniform, most likely victims of our artillery, both with their chests naked. But weapons and ammunition were important to us and these Russians knew damn well how to adapt themselves to their environment. It was truly amazing how they did it. It was clear that they were much closer to nature than us, and that they were able to adapt to any situation and use it for their own protection. On demand of the commander of the 1.Kp, I remained at his disposition with a group of assault pioneers. The rest of the platoon had completed their mission and regrouped. Not a lot later the commander of the 1.Kp sent me on a reconnaissance mission to Male Starosillya.

After a few hundred meters I was at the front of the group when I heard someone yelling from the rear. I turned around and there was a Colonel who was yelling at me, asking why I was going into the wolf's lair. I reported to the commander of the 1.Kp about what happened, and the incident was closed. After two days in these positions I was able to return to my men. Some alcohol and chocolate had been delivered, and my commander made sure he put a double portion aside for us. Useless to say that the victory of the Bourguignons was being celebrated, and again the Walloons had proven the others wrong. However this victory was paid with a high price: 100 killed in action and more than 200 wounded in action. These were the sad witnesses of the battle. On January 20 our victorious units went back to their positions along the Olshanka. Now the Teklino Forest was occupied by the Regiment Narva who would lose it a few days later; this was also part of the tragic story of Cherkasy.

At that time the situation on the lower Dnjepr had become critical. The Russian offensive towards the north had damaged our defense point, making it able to make an encircling movement. Another offensive push in the west had cut the entire army of the lower Dnjepr from the rest of the troops. Furious battles enraged to prevent this strategic move by the Russians, and a new front had established itself at 100 m from the Dnjepr. The goal of the German command was to fiercely resist the Russian attacks and immobilize them, then take advantage of their maneuvers followed by a well-prepared offensive. The order was given to the troops in the pocket to maintain their positions and to cover all flanks. The Luftwaffe assured the supplies and urgent evacuations.

On January 25 the Battalion Narva who was in position on the left side of the Brigade Wallonie, received orders to rejoin their regiment in the region of Teklino. The sector of the brigade therefore became a lot bigger, approximately 25-28 km. It was the 2.Kp, which had been reduced to 80 men and who occupied Starosillya, who had to fill the gap. They would be replaced at Starosillya by a platoon of assault pioneers - approximately four men - from which I was the highest NCO. For a couple of days the platoon commander had been bed ridden due to rheumatism.

In the afternoon of January 27 we occupied the positions at Starosillya, which was the main road that would take you to the forest of Zagrevka. The village bordered the forest, but for safety reason all houses close to the forest were taken down, and a safety zone of 50 m was created. At 20 m from our positions we ran a barbed wire fence with a minefield in front of it. These mines were all linked to the barbed wire and by the slightest touch it would trigger one of the mines projecting it 1 m above the ground and then detonate. These mines had a 2 kg TNT charge that would fire deadly projectiles in all directions.

For the first time since their arrival in November the assault pioneer had to play infantry. Since we lost about 50 men there was no time and place anymore for specialty units. Everybody had to contribute to the main cause. The motorcycle unit was also at the front, and the heavy weapons filled up the gaps here and there. For me this was nothing new; we were at the beginning of 1944, and in the last two years I had already occupied many positions from the Ukraine to the Caucasus and back.

Adjutant Sapin, an old comrade of August 8, 1941, invited me to stay with him in his isba and informed us that we were going to be in the calmest sector of the front. After that I briefed my men and I said goodbye to my old comrade and wished him good luck, just like the old Generals did to Napoleon Bonaparte just before the battle of Waterloo. We would see each other again six months later. My neighbor in the village was a Sergeant from March 10 of the 2.Kp. He had to stay there for a few days because of health reasons. I met him in the Caucasus, and I was very happy to spend the long night with him. In reality we only spent two nights in each other's company, and after that I would never see him again. He became an officer, and Lieutenant Wouters would be killed in action at the Oder front during a counter-attack on April 20, 1945.

It was at Starosillya that we heard on January 28 that the Russians had already encircled the entire 8th Army since January 21, meaning 50,000 to 60,000 men and 10,000 vehicles were trapped in an area of 60x40 km. We had been encircled for a week, and we didn't even notice it! But now that we knew, we realized that the enemy wouldn't take long to attack the *"Kessel"* bit by bit. When and where would they start their attack? When it would happen, that was the big question, and where it would happen was a given: the calmest sector at the front. It was the second time we spent the winter in the Ukraine, and this time the melt started early and temperatures in January went from -20°C to +2°C. In just a couple of days we would be standing up to our knees in the water.

After two days without incident, I was in my isba on the night of January 29, sharing the company of Sergeant Wouters and two charming ladies. We had a nice dinner and listened to a couple of Russian records which were playing on a very old record player. It was around 2300h that we were all shaken by an explosion close by. This ended our quiet evening together, and I went to check on our positions. My men hadn't noticed the explosion, and since it was close to the barbed wire it had to be one of the landmines that had detonated. Most likely a dog or a rabbit touched the wire. I had a plan of the entire minefield, and the next day I would go and check it out because I wanted to replace the detonated mine. It was just a routine job, however I didn't sleep that well that night and I checked on my men a couple of times.

Early in the morning and accompanied by *Caporal-Chef* Courtain - also a veteran of August 8, 1941 - I went to the minefield with my plan in my hand. The temperature was nice outside and I was dressed in a light jacket with my hat on my head; I was unarmed and I didn't even have my belt on. Courtain however had his submachine gun and his magazines, and he was the one that was right to bring his weapons. It took us only 10 minutes to figure out the location of the detonated mine. It was just 30 m away from my isba. I returned to my quarters and I completed a report to have the mine replaced when I heard MG fire. It was normal to check your MG after a frosty night just to make sure it was still working. But this wasn't done at our positions because of the risk of being discovered by the enemy. This time the MG fire came from the front lines, and I wanted to send Courtain to check out what was going on. However he was usually out there when he suddenly ran inside my isba: "Quick, it's an attack!" I knew what time it was and needed no explanation.

The Reds were in front of the barbed wire exactly in that place where we were not that long ago to check for the detonated mine. One didn't have to be a sniper to shoot the two of us, and I wondered why the Russians never shot us while we were checking the minefield. It was a mystery to me, but maybe they were respecting their time to initiate the attack. In just a few seconds I put the rest of my uniform on and grabbed my submachine gun and magazines. I joined the rest of the assault pioneers, and quickly I did a blitz inspection and gave some orders on how to treat the situation. The enemy's progress towards the minefield and barbed wire fence was fast, but once they arrived there things got complicated for them. Some of them wanted to cut the barbed wire and triggered the landmines and were blown to pieces. While observing the situation I estimated approximately 100 men in front of the barbed wire fence. Some of them were running around and seemed to be looking for a breach in the fence. They were able to advance 5 m, however they were unable to move back to their previous positions. They were in a tricky situation and they surely knew it. The Russians tried to shoot at us but it had no effect since our assault pioneers were dug in in their bunkers. Disadvantage: due to the terrain they were unable to see everything in front of them and one almost had to stand up straight to see what was happening. From my isba I had a better view, but then I would be a better target too since I was exposed from all sides. But what could I do? It was just like in a theater where the best seats come at a higher price. I checked the edge of the forest for tanks or cannons when suddenly an explosive bullet went through my hat and exploded in the wall behind me. I didn't have the time to put my helmet on, which was a big mistake, but luckily this time I had my hat on. I ordered some rifles to be set up in the neighboring houses while I installed myself in the attic of my isba, accompanied by one of my men. The effects were clearly visible and we were able to distinguish the silhouettes in front of us. Through my binoculars I noticed that there were different women armed with submachine guns going through the minefield. They remained there like all the others, and during the next 15 minutes it was a real massacre.

I noticed that several smaller explosions took place around me in the attic especially there where my barrel would stick out of the roof. Most likely somebody on the other side must have noticed me and started shooting at me with something different than a regular rifle. It could've been a special rifle shooting 20 mm projectiles? We had one back in 1941 which was used to shoot at armored vehicles. Or maybe it was a rifle with a grenade launcher? Anyway. The projectiles exploded on impact, and I couldn't locate the shooter. The training I gave to others and the training I had received told me to change my position, however the only way to keep a visual on the enemy was to stay in the attic. The alternative was clear to me, and I had to find the shooter. I told my companion to go to the rear and I remained in the attic, but I stayed away from the most dangerous points. Then I observed a man coming closer; he was just a couple of meters away from my isba. Maybe he was the one I was looking for? I shot him and he fell down on the ground.

Suddenly I was laying on my back with my legs in the air. I tried to get up and I was wondering what had happened. I tried to go to the ladder to go to the main floor. With the help of my companion I was able to reach the main floo, but there again I found myself on the floor laying on my back. The others who were alerted by my fall entered the room and got me to another room. They laid me flat out on the ground and removed my boots which turned out to be a delicate operation. I can't say I was in heavy pain, and many times I didn't bother about my physical suffering. Outside there were still shots being fired, and I think it was around 0900h that the entire affair had been dealt with except for my visible shooter. Once my boots were off I was able to assess the damage. Nothing broken so that was good, but judging by the blood coming down from my legs I noticed several wounds in my left leg and foot and a couple of wounds in my right leg. Nothing too serious, but I wasn't able to walk. Not that much later I was getting a fever and the pain became more noticeable. Having nothing else in the house, the farmer brought some gasoline to clean my wounds. It was strange that they still had some gasoline in their house especially during the third year of the war because all types of fuel were very scarce by then. Some important villages and Kolkhozes had electricity, but for most of the houses they used gasoline to have a little bit of light. For a Ruski it was a sacrifice to use a good bottle of fuel to treat an enemy soldier, but because of this gesture it was clear that the Ukrainian farmer didn't see the Germans as his enemies, especially the *Belgiskis*.

At that moment Lieutenant Renier, the commander of a motorcycle platoon had arrived; they were occupying the sector on our right. He was also a veteran of August 8, 1941, and he had been seriously wounded at Gromovayabalka. He came to get some information, and I explained briefly what happened. Then he ordered his *Sanka* to come over and a couple of assault pioneers carried me to it and placed me on it. Amidst our ranks we had a 19-year-old who was there because of disciplinary reasons. He had just joined us, and even with just my 21 years of age I was already a veteran in his eyes. He had taken my submachine gun and he asked me to give me my magazines. Apparently he had the intention of taking my place in the attic and I told him to be very careful and to certainly take out that shooter.

After that I left my comrades and I was transported to the other side of the village to get some medical attention. I was accompanied by Sergeant Wouters who was sitting on the luggage rack of the motorcycle. Three months later I learned that my rookie had been killed, and that he was found dead in the attic with a big hole in his chest. At the infirmary I found Dr. Poekels whom I'd known from Uccle from before the war when he was still at med school in Louvain. He joined the Legion as soon as he was done with school. With the aid of a Russian nurse, he was trying to reconstruct the jaw of a legionnaire who had been hit by a projectile. While the nurse was looking after me, Wouters went back to look for transportation that would take me to Korsun where I would be treated at the field hospital and from where I could be airlifted as well. Supplies were now only delivered by air and vehicles were scarce. Devoted as Sergeant Wouters was, he was able to stop a column of trucks, and 30 minutes later right in front of the infirmary. With my legs covered by a blanket they put me next to the driver and the column of vehicles started moving again.

Now I had definitely left the Walloons, and knowing about the situation, I made illusions to myself about the troops that were encircled in Cherkasy. Of course there was the 1.Panzer-Division Leibstandarte Adolf Hitler which arrived from the southwest to help us out. In case the operation would succeed it would take several days though. But the weather wasn't in our favor with the defrosting of the ice followed by frost a day later, and this wasn't calculated in our plans. I've said it before that in Russia the weather conditions are never normal for Europeans, however we already managed to get out of different desperate situations, so why not this time? All these thoughts were running through my feverish head while the terrain made the truck bounce up and down causing me a lot of pain in my legs. It was around noon now and I hadn't eaten since last night. I left everything on the table of my isba last night: tobacco, a lighter, a pen and paper, toiletry, etc. I really wanted a nice bottle of vodka and I wanted to smoke. I thought about so many things of which I hadn't thought about for the last three months: my comrades, my family, my fiancé,... Most likely I didn't look that good and the truck driver passed me his pack of cigarettes without saying one word. Then he gave me his matches, I thanked him and I started smoking like a chimney.

The field hospital was located at the entrance of Korsun, and the airfield was on the other side of the village. Two medics came to get me and carried me through a couple of rooms where I saw hundreds of wounded men laying on the ground. They put me on a primitive operation table, and a surgeon of the Wiking gave me a tetanus shot to begin with. When he heard the sound of airplane engines he said to hurry up to take me to the airfield before the planes would leave again. He took his scalpel and quickly popped out most of the fragments that were stuck in my legs, but he didn't notice that I had two pieces stuck in my left foot. One came out by itself a few days later, but the other one is still in there. After 10 minutes my legs were all wrapped in bandages and I was put in a room with 10 other wounded, ready for transport to the airfield. Eight of us were put into a vehicle which was normally equipped to transport only four people. Luckily the distance to the airfield was short. There were many others that had much more severe wounds than mine, so I had to bite my tongue every now and then when one would lay down on my legs. Finally we arrived at the airfield when a dozen JU-52s started their engines and rolled to the runway. We had to wait for the next squadron to arrive since we were just too late. All the ambulances had to wait there at the airfield, and by some miracle no air raids occurred during that time. Then a new squadron of JU-52 landed and within 15 minutes the planes were unloaded. Immediately after that the ambulances rushed to the planes and the wounded soldiers were put inside the planes as soon as possible. Some of the wounded had to be carried in on a gurney, while others like me were carried inside with the help of two men. I was safe, well almost. The entire operation was executed under the watchful eyes of three ME-109 who were constantly flying around the airfield. They had accompanied the JU-52s, and once the planes were airborne three new ME-109 would take off and escort the planes out. The other ME-109 would land and wait for the next squadron to come in. The squad commander who was flying the plane I was in immediately noticed that I was able to use my arms and hands. He made me move to the rear of the plane where I found a seat and a double machine gun. He showed me how things worked, and he said that I would definitely know how to use and MG.

The airplane finally took off and it was the second time that I was airlifted out of an encirclement. The first time was after the campaign in the Caucasus where I was in good health and in perfect physical condition. This time was a lot different because of my wounds. I didn't feel well and as soon as we were airborne, I almost had to throw up, even with nothing in my stomach which made it even worse. I was in very bad shape, and I'm not sure if I would've been able to repel an enemy attack. Luckily there were the ME-109s that accompanied us. Despite the escort of ME-109 fighters, our plane took a couple of hits while we were flying over Russian occupied territory. There was only minor damage to the plane and we were still able to fly. The slow JU-52s were flying at an altitude of 300 m at 250 km/h which made them an easy target for rapid firing anti-aircraft guns. The bullets penetrated the fuselage through the floor and exited the top, hitting some of the wounded that were laying down. Some of the projectiles exploded in the air outside the plane but their shrapnel also penetrated the fuselage in different places hitting more people inside. When we landed in Uman after a long flight, I can't remember exactly how long, we had several casualties on board.

I on the other hand was OK and my stomach settled as soon as we hit the ground.

In Uman everything had to move even faster than at the Korsun airfield; several ambulances and a bus were waiting on the airfield. They were all set up for embarkment of wounded soldiers as soon as the airplanes came to a stop. A selection of wounded was quickly done: the ones laying down went into the ambulances and the others, like me, who were able to sit went into the busses. When the bus took off I became myself again. It must have been around 1600h and it started to become dark. When the bus stopped 200 m down the field next to a JU-52, I clearly understood that this adventure wasn't over yet. We were boarding again and there we were flying at low altitude again all packed together like our old train car. However my stomach was OK now since I knew this was going to be an easy flight which would take us to Kamenetz-Podolsk. There the transport was arranged by ambulance, and two hours later I was cleaned up, bathed, shaven, etc., and I found myself laying down in a real bed surrounded by many young and beautiful nurses. For me the Cherkasy campaign was over.

A few weeks later I learned the tragic epilogue of the Legion Wallonie. The day after my evacuation, in the sector of the assault pioneers at Starosillya, the Russians executed an attack that could've signified the end for all encircled troops. It was their final goal which was never completed, but at what price? The Leibstandarte, already in trouble because of the severe weather changes, had to fight in violent battles in the area of Lysyanka. In this area the destruction of the bridge over the Hnylyi Tikych definitely slowed them down. Between the encircled troops and the ones coming to their aid there was a gap of about 15 km. Two days after my departure the melting of the ice and snow made the Korsun airfield inoperable. The supplies had to be delivered by parachute and the wounded couldn't be evacuated anymore. My wounds were not that bad, but it could've cost me my life if I had to stay in Korsun. And all the others that stayed behind, unable to walk, died in the burning vehicles ignited by Russian tank projectiles.

For 15 days the nightmare of the Walloon legionnaires was dreadful. The radio transmissions at the front encouraged the encircled troops to surrender, however the high command had its reasons to reject the invitations from the Russians. If we surrendered, then from the 50,000 prisoners only 500 would make it back, but if the men fought back they would probably save 2/3 of the men. To obtain this number they had to assemble all the troops in one point and push through these 15 km that stood between them and liberty. The Sturmbrigade Wallonie fought continuously without supplies for 17 days in temperatures of -20°C against a superior enemy who outnumbered them by thousands. They fought under the continuous bombings of the enemy airplanes, heavy artillery, and grenade launchers in an area that was shrinking in size every day. The breakthrough was on February 17 around 0500h in a corridor not even 500 m wide between the Russian tanks. Luckily the first Panzerfäuste made their debut at the front thanks to the parachuted supplies. These weapons were terrible weapons against isolated tanks, but they were very effective.

Another catastrophe occurred at the last moment in Cherkasy. At just 3 km from freedom, the corridor was abruptly cut in half by the Hnylyi Tikych, and the Tiger tanks of the Leibstandarte were unable to cross the water since the bridge had been destroyed. All the men had to cross the river with enemy tanks on their tail. Many of the men drowned by pulmonary congestion. At Lysyanka the Leibstandarte welcomed 35,000 men out of the 50,000 that were encircled. The survivors of the Legion Wallonie were regrouped around February 20 at Jegelovskaya, and only 647 survived the pocket of Cherkasy. Not counting the already evacuated wounded men at the beginning of February, I can say that about 1,100 men were killed in action since November 1943 in the area of Cherkasy. In Novo Buda on February 13 one of the best men of the Legion Wallonie was killed in action, our Commander Lieutenant-Colonel Lippert who took a direct hit in the heart by a Russian sniper. Commander Lippert was 32 years old and he was admired and respected by all the men. His loss was a terrible blow for the entire Legion, and the ones that have known him would certainly never forget him. Many times I still think of him, and when I do so it is with the greatest respect! Another officer of high valor was lost during this campaign, my company commander Anthonissen. He was reported missing in action on February 10 when he was out on a patrol at Derenkovets. He never came back from that patrol and they never found his body. His wife, whom I've known for years, always hoped that he would return one day after being held captive for so many years by the Russians. Unfortunately he never came back.

Cherkasy was the most horrible campaign in Russia for the Legion Wallonie. After I woke up on January 31 after having a couple of sleeping pills I wondered where I was. Immediately I was brought back to reality when I wanted to move my legs. The good thing was that I wasn't suffering anymore.

I was forbidden from getting out of bed, but at the same time it was impossible for me to get up anyways. A nurse had to help me to go to the washroom, and I had to borrow a razor from one of my comrades. After breakfast I answered the questions my companions had who were actually a bunch of German Wehrmacht officers. It was the first time they saw a Walloon legionnaire and I wasn't leaving the hospital any time soon, so I was able to tell them about the Legion Wallonie. In total I had to stay for four weeks at the hospital with my leg completely immobilized. Luckily my stay was without suffering except for the third night when one of the pieces of shrapnel came out of my foot. The next day they found it when they changed my bandages. On my right leg they removed the bandages after a couple of days.

Since February 15 I ignored everything that happened at Cherkasy, but I was capable to imagine what would've happened there after I left. I would get the entire story by the end of March around Easter, and in the meantime life at the hospital was very monotonous. One day at the end of February in the early evening a doctor came into the room checking all the patient cards; he marked the ones that would go back west to Germany for a medical leave. And as long as we were in Russia, close to the border with Poland and Romania this medical leave wasn't guaranteed at all. The bridge over the Dniester had been destroyed, but never reconstructed. It used to be a bridge of a couple of hundred meters in length, but the Germans thought it would be better to let the trains make a detour towards the east (Uman) and then make them come back to the west. This type of reasoning was acceptable and understandable as long as the army occupied most of the country.

But this wasn't the case anymore by the end of February 1944. The Russians were only 50 km from Uman but the detour was still possible. I wasn't put on the list for medical leave and those that were selected were put on the next train. It was the next day that we would hear what had happened to them. During the night, about 50 km from Kamenetz Podolsk, the tracks were blown up and the train became immobilized. The train was under partisan attack and only the protection detachment and the medics were able to stand their ground and fight back. Reinforcements arrived a couple of hours later and it was only during the day that a new convoy could be arranged to transport the survivors to the hospital. After this unfortunate experience all wounded convoys going in the direction of Uman were suspended indefinitely.

The weeks went by and we were now at the beginning of March. My left leg was getting much better and the bandages came off; no worries about that anymore. At night a Russian troupe played at the local theatre, and I asked the doctor if I could go. He made the remark that this was the first time I would get up on my own after a very long time, and that I would have to put on my boots and walk for 1 km. I insisted and I told him this would be good exercise for me. He finally agreed and gave me permission with a grin on his face. Later on I would discover the reason behind that grin on his face. A walking cane and a nurse to accompany me was required though, and I was lucky because the *Schwester* that accompanied me that night was young and very charming. After dinner I put my clothes on and for the first time in five weeks I had a nice and clean uniform. I felt like a man again. Putting on my boots was a little bit difficult and standing up was even more difficult, however *Schwester* Ilse, that was her name, showed up and nothing could stop me anymore. I put my arm around her and on my other side I was leaning on my cane. I was able to walk the 1 km to the theatre where we made quite an entry since I seemed to radiate a condescending attitude in the eyes of the other less privileged soldiers. *Schwester* Ilse seemed very proud to be on the side of a Walloon volunteer; Walloon volunteers that were known for more than two years, and that have been mentioned in many news feeds. It became a nice evening accompanied by the music of Johan Strauss. Needless to say that the impressive applause at the end of the night in March of 1944 was not recorded in the theatre of the army at Kamenetz-Podolsk. The artists weren't world famous, but an opera from Strauss was always a joyful distraction and the ensemble was very talented. It was also the first time in seven months that I saw something different than camps, barracks, hospital bedrooms, and war. Everything was perfect and my company was very attentive and attractive. During the first *entre acte* my left leg started to feel very heavy and at the end of the second act my calf muscles made me suffer so much that it was impossible for me to follow the music. My early return to the hospital was very painful I must say. *Schwester* Ilse had to drag me into the hospital where my entry was as dramatic as the one in the theatre but less glorious.

My roommates liked the story, except for me, and maybe *Schwester* Ilse neither. But the funniest moment for the others was yet to come. I had to take off my boot and I wasn't able to do that on my own. While standing up it didn't work and neither did it work in the sitting position. Finally when I laid down the boot came off when one of the men pressed on my leg while another one pulled my boot. It hurt like hell and the two men apologized to me while I was cursing like a pirate. But finally I was liberated and for a second I thought my foot would've stayed inside my boot. Obviously the blood was running down my leg and I was so angry at myself that I had interrupted such a nice evening. While the nurse was taking care of me I apologized to her for ruining her evening. Totally exhausted I fell asleep. The next morning I felt a lot better and like any other soldier I would forget about the pain from last night and I was laughing and joking with my comrades. When the doctor came to see me he had the same grin on his face as the night before when I asked him for permission to go to the theatre. He asked me if I had a good time last night. That jackass! He knew very well what happened last night, but I had to tell him that it didn't go as planned. I knew that inside he was thinking that he was right and that the little Walloon got taught a lesson. But I wouldn't have been a good team player if I were mad at him because he was the one that was right after all. But it seemed they didn't tell him about my open wound on my leg because when he saw the blood he wasn't smiling anymore. His demeanor changed and he strictly forbade me to get out of bed until he said so. *"Jawohl Doctor!"* The others however found the situation very amusing.

Everything went well until mid-March when Kamenetz Podolsk found itself in the operational zone. Our *Kriegslazarett* became a *Feldlazarett* and it wouldn't have any more female nurses. All female nurses were transported to the rear the next day. Wounded men like me that had to stay for at least another 15 days received marching orders to join a *Genesungskompanie* where wounded soldiers would go and do light duties until they were fit again for combat duty. The wounded that couldn't be mobilized were evacuated within a couple of hours after the state of alert was announced. Luckily I was able to escape the hell of Cherkasy because of my wounds, but I sincerely doubted that the rest of the brigade would be in

Belgium before me. I arrived in my Genesungskompanie after two days of travel through Poland.

I completely forgot where it was located, but it was there that around Easter, at the beginning of April, I received the first news from the Legion Wallonie. On the other side of the station there was a pub where they served some very good vodka, and one day I was drinking there in company of an Adjutant of a tank unit when a military convoy stopped at the station. A couple of minutes later three men of the Wiking entered the pub and they approached me as soon as they saw the tri-color shield on my sleeve. They shook my hand while petting me on the shoulder, taking my drinking buddy and I completely off guard. We had both had already two big glasses of vodka and the Wikinger started talking about the Sturmbrigade Wallonien and that they had been sent back to Belgium for a couple of weeks of vacation. Normally a vacation from the front wouldn't last that long, but for the Cherkasy *Kämpfer* the high command had a lot of respect and were treated differently. When a little while later I would travel back to Brussels through Poland and Germany, I would notice that my arm shield of the Legion Wallonie functioned as an "open Sesame" on many occasions. The wounded badge that I received from the doctor at the hospital made people look at me as well and I would earn their respect.

My Lieutenant at the Genesungskompanie asked me how long ago I had been on a vacation. It was about a year ago and not even an hour later I was called to the commander's office who told me that I would leave on a vacation tomorrow. Since most of the convoys were going towards the east, and to not interfere with those operations this good officer gave me a marching order to go to Berlin where I would be given papers for my vacation. From there I'd be in Brussels after one night of travel. Everything went like planned, even better I have to say since the SS officer in Berlin, where I arrived two days later, gave me some blank paperwork. The date on these documents would be put on there by an officer of the Legion Wallonie in Brussels. It was my very good friend Lieutenant Jacobs who put the next day date on my paperwork when I arrived in Brussels.

In April 1944 Degrelle held his speech at the Palais des Sports in Brussels, and obviously the press had published his speech. It was astonishing that in the occupied territories the speech would be published word by word. One can actually look it up even today and believe me that it wasn't some sort of propaganda since the Legion Wallonie had lost more than half of its effective in these last 2½ months. More than 1,000 were killed in action, and more than 500 were wounded in action. For this, one had to be engaged in battle and deliver a hard fight which was proof of an immense courage. One simply had to be a hero! However long after the capitulation there were those that kept on insulting these heroes, these Walloon legionnaires, these heroes of Cherkasy and everything that Degrelle had given us after the campaign. These sad individuals, fueled by hate didn't know that the courage of a soldier is not measured by the color of the flag he's dying for. Our flag was Belgian, and on our uniform we had the Belgian tri-color and the Burgundy cross. Never did one of us walk into death by yelling Heil Hitler. You would never find a soldier who would do that. And every year English and German veterans from both wars would gather together; they fought in a war and if they fought each other they did it without fear or hate. Of course there was the hate amongst those that went nowhere when others around them went to die in battle.

There was a Russian Major named Krampov who said that the Walloon volunteers were villains, and that most of them were the worst adventurers ever. That Russian Major takes these insulting words in his mouth about young men who went to fight, who killed, or were about to get killed. They were leading a different way of life than other young men that were timid and afraid to step into the real world. So I have to prove you wrong Major, and most likely you are making these stupid comments since you were never ready to face these Walloons. You are simply an idiot or you had to see them from close up to describe them the way you did, but to me it seems that you're just using some sort of propaganda that is not from this time anymore. Even the most retarded of mongoloids wouldn't buy this rubbish anymore. However I've seen the horrors you're men had committed in the forests of Teklino: they crucified our men, cut their genitals and stuffed them in their mouth! Or do I have to mention the others that cut off the fingers of the dead, just so they could steal their rings? But my apologies again, I didn't mean to touch your civilization. Despite what the haters say I still consider my comrades and I as the heroes of Cherkasy!

Recuperation and Return to Active Duty

Thanks to Lieutenant Jacobs I arrived in Brussels with an extra day of vacation. And due to some other circumstances, I got another two days extra. Three days of extra vacation! I wasn't complaining at all, and these extra days were more than welcome because three weeks of military leave went by too fast. Especially when I spent a week in Dresden where I visited Irmgard and her parents. We were engaged now, and we would get married as soon as I graduated from the military academy. Since I had already missed one week at the academy due to my stay in the hospital, I had to start classes in September.

In the month of April, the Legion Wallonie was transferred from its temporary posting in Casteau (Belgium) to Heidelager in Debica (Poland), about 80 km east of Krakow. In order to make this trip I needed to be in possession of a marching order and a uniform. To join the camp I had to take the military train from Brussels to Tilsit, get off in Berlin, and from there take the train to Krakow. The train from Brussels to Tilsit always left at 1330h, but every time I presented myself at the administration building in Brussels to get the required signatures from the Lieutenant, I was informed that he was never in before 1430h. I had to come back around that time to get my paperwork signed. I didn't complain and said I'd be there on time.

My father who was wounded earlier in the war had his office in the same building, and I went to see him the day before my departure. Instead of saying goodbye to him I told him I'd be back in the afternoon. Neither he nor the Lieutenant or any of the other men of his service knew about the train schedule. The first thing I had to do was to go home and put on civilian clothes. I told my mother not to come with me that afternoon since I had to be there by 1430h, however my train would leave one hour earlier. My mother was in a panic as she saw me already being court martialed, but I was pretty confident that after three years of faithful service I actually risked nothing at all. It simply sufficed to put the next day's date stamp on my paperwork, just as easy like that. I couldn't do anything about the Lieutenant's absence and the paperwork that he had to sign. He was surprised to see me in civilian clothing when I went to get the stamp and his signature. "Why the hell are you dressed like that?" he demanded with a severe tone. I explained to him why I was dressed like this and that all of this was part of my plan and that it was my responsibility. "You could've told me this morning that 1430h was too late for you!" But I was the strongest that day and I finally won the argument. I told my father about my plan and that I would see him at home that night. He laughed because he knew that I managed to get one day of extra leave. I said nothing to my mother because I didn't know if my plan would be successful, and I didn't want to give her false hope. I knew that all the soldiers that went back to Germany had to be in possession of a medical certificate attesting that they didn't suffer from any mental illnesses.

The day of my departure my mother accompanied me to the station, and around 1300h I boarded the train. Exactly at 1315h there was the document control, and I showed my marching orders when they asked me for my medical paperwork. *"Sanitätsschein, bitte."* ("Medical pass, please.") *"Sanitätsschein?* I don't know what that is" I replied. He apologetically explained to me, due to the circumstances that I was required by law to have them on me all the time and that I could easily get them at the *Soldatenheim* at the St-Jean hospital. I mentioned that the train would leave in 10 minutes and that I would never be back in time. He went to explain my case to the officer of the German Feldgendarmerie in the station, and at the same time my mother, not knowing what we were talking about, again thought that I was in big trouble. It certainly was a human reaction, but foremost a motherly reaction. I've served three years of war in Russia before, but now she was trembling because I was amicably talking to an NCO of the Feldgendarmerie during a document control. Then I took my baggage and told my mother that we had to go to see the officer of the Feldgendarmerie for some paperwork formalities, but I said nothing more. Of course she suspected something since I had a smile on my face and I had no issue telling the officer about my situation. The officer of the Feldgendarmerie dated my marching order for the next day, and stamped it with *Feldgendarmerie Hauptbahnhof.* In ten minutes I presented myself at the St-Jean hospital where I got medically cleared and I got an extra day off. Afterwards I explained o my mother the nature of my operation with the results that I was hoping for. You should've seen the look on my father's face when he got home. This kind of pleasantries were the best, but the next day I was on the train to Tilsit. Have a nice trip, as a certain song mentioned, and 24 hours later I arrived in Debica.

Since I was still unfit for regular duty I was placed in a convalescence unit under 1st Lieutenant Renier who also had been the officer at Starosillya who had me evacuated in his Sanka. About 50 men were waiting to be put back into a combat unit. They passed their time there doing light duties and light exercises under the supervision of three German Corporals. Why Germans, I don't know, and the only thing that interested them was the disinterest of the company commander whose sole mission was to go back to the war. After his discharge, there was no more fun and I wasn't too eager for another medical examination. My wounds were nicely healed, but this visit was just a formality that I had to go through whether I wanted to or not. These were the rules and they had to be followed. It took these three Corporals exactly three days to start getting on my nerves; they lacked so much interest and they were so lazy that it became intolerable for me that I had to correct them a couple of times, and two out of the three understood where I was coming from.

Roll call was exactly at 2200h, even for the instructors. I also showed these three how to clean their room, and I made them very clear we had to maintain a certain discipline. So with my helmet on at exactly 2200h I entered their room with my Corporal. Two of them were sitting in the room on their chairs, staring at me as if I was a strange animal. The first thing we teach new recruits is to stand at attention when a superior enters the room, but in this case there was no reaction at all. And these men were instructors! They knew the drill, but they thought that a Walloon Sergeant would be happy with their smile. Boy were they wrong! I told them clearly that I'd be back and that I expected them to be at the position of attention when I entered the room. I also told them to consult their military instructions manual in case they forgot something. Then I left the room and 10 minutes later I entered their room again. This time they seemed to have understood, and the two of them were standing at attention. However they didn't explain to me where the third man was. They only told me that he wasn't there, but at roll call or inspection every absence had to be mentioned with a brief explanation why that particular person was absent. I asked them where the third man was since this was a room occupied by three people, and who's permission he had to be absent. "No permission at all Sergeant!" "When he comes back make him come to my office at once!" I bid them good night and I left. It was around 2300h that the missing German Corporal presented himself in my office where I was laying on a field bed while I was chatting with my Corporal. My Corporal was also a survivor of Cherkasy.

The way this German acted made me think he was ignorant but also very mean. I always thought that ignorance was more dangerous than being mean, and you always had to defend yourself against a mean person by using the same tactics. Against an ignorant person there was not too much you could do because they would always find another person where they could go cry like a baby while blaming all the others for being wrong. Most likely he went to his room before coming over to my office, and I bet his comrades told him about the incident during the inspection. Now if this would've happened in a German camp with a German Adjutant, things would've been very hard for him. Knowing this he probably thought that an impeccable presentation and a good explanation would've excused him for being late. I had already shown the two others that I wasn't ignorant though. So he came into my office with a briefcase in his hand, and he sat down on a chair next to my companion. And this was a German instructor who told me three years ago that you couldn't even sit down in front of a Corporal? And now a German Corporal, completely in the wrong, totally ignored an NCO in charge. Joke or not, he overstepped the boundaries, and when I stood up I showed him that you didn't have to be Prussian to make the walls of the room tremble. It seemed that the German Corporal was still conditioned because as soon as I opened my mouth, he stood there at attention and it was in this position that he listened to me for several minutes. My Corporal who was sitting at the table had a hard time to not start laughing. I told the German corporal to leave his military pass with me, and that he was dismissed. I would keep his military pass until the next morning, and then I would give it back to him. I wouldn't write anything in it of course but in this case he would have a very bad night. He knew if I took this to 1st Lieutenant Renier that this wouldn't be in his favor at all because the commander was not a man to would like to have presented a case of insubordination and lack of discipline. When the German Corporal left he told me that he went to visit a local farm and that he had taken some eggs and bacon from there and that they were in his briefcase. I wondered what he was trying to do, especially with a witness present. Even if I were very hungry I would never have accepted his peace offering. Undoubtedly this guy was ignorant, and I told him that tomorrow at 1300h we would present ourselves to the commander after I chased him out of my office.

Now I had no choice but to do a report, even if I didn't like it. It was the second time in my career that I had to go this far. The first time was after my return from the Caucasus when I was still a *Caporal-Chef.* One day I was the acting day Sergeant, and I took my company to the mess hall for dinner when one of the men broke formation to go and clean his mess tin. He made two mistakes: his mess tin had to be clean already, and he had no permission to break formation. I told him that this was not acceptable, but in front of the entire company he told me to go fuck myself. I was completely blown away by this, as I wasn't expecting this type of reply. Since I was the acting Sergeant I presented myself with the soldier at the commander's office where the soldier was still having the same attitude as before. He got eight days in the cell, the maximum a company commander could give a soldier. I thought he would've behaved in front of an officer, but apparently I was wrong. Since I knew 1st Lieutenant Renier very well, the German Corporal would get eight days in the cell as well. He spent the next week in jail, but until today I'm still convinced that he didn't steal the eggs and bacon from the local farm. I never saw the German Corporal again because I left the unit a couple of days later against the will of the commander, but I had to go on a mission as an assault pioneer.

I was called to the Kommandantur of the camp where I met two other Walloon NCOs and three German NCOs. I had never seen these Germans before, but the Walloons were Adjutant Sommeville and a Sergeant from the province of Luxemburg, but I can't remember his name. We were lead into the office of a Captain who explained to us, while holding several maps in his hands, what was expected from us. The advance of the Russian armies was progressing to the west, and even if they thought they would never reach our region we had to start thinking ahead, and this the impossible.

Our mission was to place a line of defense for heavy weapons between a wooded area and the town of Ropczye, located 20 km east of Debica. The positions would be constructed under our supervision by 200 Polish workers from the neighboring villages. They would all be gathered by Polish translators every day at 0900h, and then taken to the village where we were staying with the locals. We were the only ones that didn't have to work. Captain Proschinsky gave us strict instructions on how we had to manage our quarters: two men per house, and our houses had to be located in such a position that they could be easily defended against attacks. Each and every one of us was armed with an MP of a large caliber and a submachine gun. A full case of grenades was placed in our rooms to which entrance was obviously restricted, even for the Polish owners of the house. The doors had to be able to be locked at all times, and the windows had to be equipped with blinds capable of being locked from the inside.

In the village we took all safety precautions, and we made sure that the mayor would help us with that. Maybe our measures were a bit excessive, but we obeyed the orders of the Captain. And when one left the house at night the other one would remain awake sometimes for the entire night. Even if the Russian Army was still far away, they were still making progress and they were coming closer and closer!

The Polish partisans were bold and courageous like all other resistance fighters, but the region where we were posted had never been under real German occupation except for a brief moment in 1939. The locals never suffered from the indirect presence of the enemy. We were Walloons, we were dressed in the uniforms of the Waffen SS, and we made Poles work who never volunteered for this kind of work. I spent six weeks in the village of Ropczye without encountering any problems with the locals nor with the workers whose lives and working conditions we didn't make difficult at all. But we were always on guard, and we were always equipped with our submachine gun; also when we went out for a drink we were never drunk. Never did I take off my duty belt to which my P38 pistol was attached, and in my pockets I always carried extra magazines. The next story will show that one always had to be cautious no matter what.

The resistance was there and was always close. The Russians however, were still too far, and the actions of the resistance were isolated and didn't compromise the safety of the villagers. The spring was beautiful and the work progressed as planned. The workers were already used to seeing six young boys dressed in shorts with a P38 pistol around their waists and a forage cap on their heads. There was absolutely no hostility from the locals until one day…on a nice evening in May.

It must have been around 2200h when I went back to Ropczye to see my friends, and I walked by a small chapel. The chapel had two linden trees in front of it, and behind it there was a wheat field, so blond and shiny like the lady that I just had left. Also in the back, about 50 m away from the chapel there were some pine trees. When I was walking under the linden trees I had the impression that a wind blew from one tree to another, but strangely there was no breeze at all! It is crazy what kind of tricks the mind of a young soldier can play. So there was no wind at all, a cat couldn't make that kind of noise, and the cows were not hiding in the trees; there were no monkeys in this part of the world so my conclusion was that it had to be a person. And a person was there, a man standing right in front of me! By the time I took put my pistol he was already running in the field, heading towards the pine trees. I fired a couple of rounds in his direction. The pistol shots broke the silence of a quiet evening. I didn't follow the man into the pine trees because I was convinced that there would be a welcoming committee waiting for me. My friend who had heard the gun shots joined me at the chapel. Besides him no one else in the village had heard the gun shots, and the mayor was surprised when we told him that from now one nobody could leave their houses between 2100h and 0600h, and that all lights needed to be out.

But nothing happened until Sunday. It was around noon and I went for a beer to the only pub in the village. When I returned to my quarters, at least that was my intention, I passed the mayor's house and it seemed that there was a party going on. I was invited in and there were about 20 men and women present, all unknown to the village. They were dancing and the vodka was flowing like water in a river. I didn't take my belt off and I kept my eyes open. Deep down I knew nothing would happen to me because they all knew if something would happen to me they would pay for it dearly. I pretended to drink and every now and then I emptied my glass in a vase. The only thing I didn't really resist was when a nice young lady approached me and started talking to me in a broken German. Then the dancing was over and all went to eat. At the party I met one of the most beautiful girls I've ever met, and I was going to meet with her later at 1600h, and guess where? In the little pine tree bush behind the chapel! Did they really think I was this stupid, that I was going to meet her there and walk into a trap? Instead I went to write my parents a letter saying that I was 200 km away from the front lines and that I wasn't in any danger. I never saw the girl again.

As I said before, we had ordered a curfew and lights out after the first incident at the chapel. This was respected by all the villagers except one evening when after 2100h I came back to the village with Richard

Sommeville. We passed the famous chapel and close to a house I noticed the silhouette of a man, totally immobilized. I alerted Sommeville and we hid in a dark corner. Sommeville took his pistol and fired two shots, causing the silhouette to collapse. Immediately we went to have a look at the man, and at the same time a lady came out of the house, crying and yelling because she saw her husband laying on the ground. We looked at the man and we noticed two things: one, he was dead; two, he had been taking a leak outside of the house. Even though this seemed very inhumane, we didn't care anymore and we went back to our quarters. It was the day after that I called Captain Proschinsky. I prepared myself to provide him with an explanation about the curfew, the justification for what happened, etc. The Captain simply replied: "Is the man dead? Yes? Then burry him and move on!" War is war and unfortunately mistakes were made. Believe me that a mistake like this one is incomparable to the murderous bombings of Dresden.

A few days later I was called in for a medical check at Heidelager and I was declared fit for duty. I was assigned as an instructor of an assault pioneer platoon which was about to leave for Dresden. I was going to see my fiancé, so I packed all my things and said goodbye to the guys in Ropczye. I was replaced by an NCO that I had known very well, Jean Daoust, who was also a veteran of August 8, 1941. However he was less careful and he couldn't resist the charms of a nice young girl. Two days later he disappeared without leaving a trace. So I was declared fit for duty again, and the day after I was on my way to Dresden where I would find my new assault pioneer platoon.

The cadre were all veterans and the commander was our excellent comrade Lieutenant Sapin. He was promoted to officer for bravery shown on the battlefield in February during the battle of Cherkasy. For training my new platoon, I was accompanied by NCO Max Minnen who was also a good friend of mine and a veteran from August 8, 1941. He was one of the men who blew up the Van Eyser bridge when the Russians were about to cross it. I was very happy to be reunited with old friends, but what interested me the most was spending a couple of weeks with Irmgard.

Thanks to my two friends, these two months that I spent in Dresden were a real vacation. Friday evening around 1800h I would leave the barracks and they wouldn't see me back until Tuesday morning 0800h. Irmgard had multiple vacation days which she took every Monday. On those days when she was working I would go and see her in the evening; I would leave the barracks at 1800h and I would return the next morning. Many times they wouldn't see me on the training grounds before noon. Usually I was in my room preparing the next day's classes, and I used to do this in the laying position because that works better when you have to think.

One incident in particular compromised one of my free weekends. Friday July 20, early in the morning we were confined to the barracks like all the other soldiers. During the day all troops were gathered, and when we returned to the barracks we received weapons and ammunition, and at night we were not allowed to leave. Not even me! We were allowed to sleep, but in full uniform and with our weapons close to our bed within hand reach. Saturday the situation returned to normal, and we learned about the failed assassination attempt on Hitler by von Stauffenberg. From that day on the party officials had decided that all military personnel had to use the same salute as the SS, that particular salute that later would be called the fascist or Nazi salute, Hitlerian as some like to call it, but which had already been used by the Roman emperors. Even today athletes still use it! I ignored all the commotion around the assassination attempt, and I spent Saturday afternoon with Irmgard in a little cabin in the mountains close to the Czech border. There we had no newspapers, no radios, nothing, just the two of us. When we returned to Dresden on Monday afternoon I was surprised when a *Kriegsmarine* member gave me "the salute." The second one to salute me like that was a Wehrmacht soldier. I had no idea why they were all saluting me like that, and I asked him why they were all doing this. It was through him that I learned about this new rule. In the meantime the Allied landings and their advance towards Germany worried Irmgard and her parents. After all they were Germans, and whatever ignorant people may think, at that time Germany was still far away from its defeat. Personally I wasn't too worried about that, and I was a volunteer after all so my fate was already sealed. Whatever the outcome of the war was, I'd have to live with it.

One day we learned that Léon Degrelle was on a recruiting tour in Saxony where there were lots of Belgians working in the local factories. Since there was a Walloon platoon in Dresden, it was in this city where he would start his tour. We had to cross the entire city to attend the event in the reunion hall, and with a marching band in front of us playing Walloon songs, we marched through the city. And I can assure you that it was a big city to march through!

The assault pioneers started to know their job very well, and they became specialist soldiers however, their infantry training was mediocre since they were only told the basics. We had only two days left, and Sergeant Minnen and I had to teach these boys the proper drills to handle a rifle during a parade. We suspended all the other exercises, and within two days we taught them how to present arms, order arms...on and off, on and off. Since the rifle had to rest on the left shoulder during the parade we didn't teach them how to switch the rifle to the right shoulder. So with the rifles on their left shoulders the platoon, led by Lieutenant Sapin and three NCOs, marched through the city to finally arrive at the reunion. Lieutenant Sapin led the platoon behind the building out of sight of the public that had gathered on the square and who were waiting for Degrelle's arrival. Behind the building Lieutenant Sapin would give me command of the platoon so he could go join the boss inside. It was out of the question to order a regular "order arms" since all arms were aching because of the rifles that had been resting on the same shoulder for more than an hour. Because the left arms were stuck in the same position for that long it made it very difficult to make certain movements. So it was in a military fashion that I ordered my men to rest easy while they were still carrying their rifle on their left shoulder. I told them to grab the rifle with their right hand and to bring it down to the ground. In the meantime they had to bring down their left arm which was very uncooperative at that moment. It took them several minutes of moving their arms to get some blood circulation back in their left arm. If a German officer would've seen our sacrilege, he surely would've dropped dead where he was standing. After a couple of minutes the platoon was ready, and we would enter the hall where we took place in front of the podium where Degrelle would address the people. When everything had ended the assault pioneers would return to the barracks.

But before that Léon Degrelle told me to assemble two NCOs and 20 men to accompany him during the tour. And so it was done, and for four days I travelled with 20 men and Léon Degrelle. At each event we would put ourselves in front of the podium, resembling a security detail which of course always made a good impression, especially after the event when we could talk to the workers that came to listen to Léon Degrelle. Several volunteers were recruited in July 1944 during these events in Saxony. After a couple of days of vacation with Degrelle, we returned to our barracks and we picked up where we had left off. The moment that I had to join the officer cadet school in Prague was coming closer and closer, and even if Irmgard was kind of prepared for this, she wasn't looking forward to it. She knew that the training would take seven months which I wouldn't be spending at the front. We also made arrangements to get married as soon as I had graduated. It had been since January that I had been evacuated from the front, but I highly doubted that it would've been the last time. On the day of my evacuation I saw Russian soldiers from very close and many of them paid the ultimate sacrifice until the that last one who had me properly eliminated. Yes, properly eliminated is the correct word for my wounds; it was embarrassing but not life threatening. I'm pretty sure it would've meant a certain death if I weren't evacuated, knowing the circumstances of the event and my inability to walk.

On July 16 a *Kampfgruppe* of 500 men was sent to Estonia and commanded by veteran officers and NCOs. I found myself in Dresden with the assault pioneers, and we weren't part of the *Kampfgruppe*. Apart from the evacuated wounded men from the Estonian campaign at the end of September, only 215 legionnaires would return. It was during this horrible campaign that one of my good friends of August 8, 1941, Lieutenant Gillis, commander of an anti-tank battery won the *Ritterkreuz*. Gillis, Jacques Leroy, and Léon Degrelle were the only Walloon legionnaires that have been awarded with this prestigious medal. From this point until April 1945, the Legion would distinguish itself again in combat on the Eastern Front. Again I would be spared from that. From April 3 until May 5, 1945 many of my classmates from the *Junkerschule* would die while commanding their infantry platoons during the last battles. My destiny would be different again.

The long-awaited day arrived and I would leave Dresden on August 15 for Breslau where the Legion Wallonie was stationed at that time. This seemed a bit early for me to be on my way to Prague where I had to present myself at the *Junkerschule* on September 1. But orders were orders, and the next day in the evening I presented myself in Breslau. The next morning I was working on my curriculum vitae for the *Junkerschule*, and in the afternoon I was called to the general staff where I was given a marching order to go to Brussels. There I would be at the disposal of the commander of the Legion for a period of 10 days. Since June 6 all vacations had been suspended in the

German Army, and my marching orders were more like a disguise for an unofficial vacation since I would be spending 10 days at my place with my parents. I arrived in the middle of the night, and from the North Station I walked to Uccle. This was at the end of August and the Allies had already captured Paris, and they were on their way to Belgium.

SS-Junkerschule Kienschlag

After my stay in Brussels I went back to Breslau to get all my belongings. I would arrive in Prague a couple of days later with about 10 other comrades who came from different training schools. They had most likely benefitted from a special mission to Brussels just like I did. About a hundred veterans of the Legion Wallonie had already arrived at the school, and there were another hundred comrades of the Charlemagne as well. The school was located 50 km from Prague, and it was part of a large training unit established in this region of Bohemia. This area had been cleared of all its inhabitants as a repercussion for the assassination of Reinhard Heydrich, the *Reichsprotektor* of Bohemia and Moravia.

The school was located in the town of Neweklau, and it had also an engineer school, a tank school, and three other specialty weapon schools. There were two rivers crossing the region, and one flowed through Prague and became famous through the music of Smetana. This river was the Moldau, or the Vltava River, which would finally flow into the Elbe. The Moldau is a magnificent river which flows through the most beautiful regions of Europe, Bohemia, where I had the privilege of staying for seven months of my life when I was an officer cadet *at SS-Panzer-Grenadier-Schule/Junkerschule Kienschlag.* On multiple occasions I saw the river flowing through the beautiful city of Prague, and I was always happy to see her again in my dreams or in the music of Smetana.

We arrived at Neweklau on a Sunday afternoon, and in the evening we were already outside for our last nightly exercise led by 40 graduates which would leave the next day. We had to take off our shoulder boards and decorations for the next two months, after that we were allowed to put them back on after the first exam, or better put, after the first eliminations. No matter what your rank was before you entered the program, your shoulder boards were replaced by two new silver ones, marking you as an officer cadet. We were more than 200 at the beginning, but only 40 of us would make it to the end. Life in Bohemia was nice in musical pieces at the opera or in literature, but as an officer cadet of the Waffen SS it was completely the opposite.

The first selection happened during the first two months which was called the *Vorbereitung* or the preparation. As far as the Walloons were concerned, we were all veteran NCOs decorated with the Iron Cross 1st Class. Most of us had at least one year of service. At Cherkasy I had been in command of a group and a platoon of assault pioneers during battle, but during these first two months at the Junkerschule without our ranks and decorations were treated worse than new recruits. The future SS officer had to be capable of physically and mentally supporting everything that was possible and impossible, especially the impossible. The goal of the operation was to eliminate in two months all those who were not able to go through all the hardships. Even before the end of these first two months, about 100 candidates, half of them Walloons and the other half French, had already voluntarily left the program since they were not officer material. It is with a couple of anecdotes that I will try to describe my life at Neweklau.

From the third month when we were officially wearing the insignia of officer cadets, failing an exam wasn't that horrible. The student would be sent back to his previous unit with a higher rank than he had before when he started the program. But when a student would be sent back for a sanction or for an error that he had made, it was evident that this person wouldn't get a higher rank but he would return to his old rank. Seven months to make an officer might not seem that long, and actually it wasn't, but you have to consider that it was a special training, and during the war a training period of two or three years was simply impossible. They wanted to have officers ready to fill the gaps at the front because the war consumed many officers which had to be replaced as soon as possible. To attain this goal they suspended all the non-military courses, and only veterans with commanding experience in battle were sent to the Junkerschule. Most of these veterans could consider their shoulder boards already acquired in the last two months of the program, except in the event that they would commit a serious error. The first five months were the hardest when the selection of future officers was made.

Apart from the two exams one had to pass to get into the final stage of the program, one also had to prove his abilities and qualities as an officer. The physical endurance was one. For example, in all military barracks the hours of service would be posted, but at the *Junkerschule* it was an unnecessary formality since the hours of service were from 12 a.m. until midnight. Frequently we would get up at 0100h for an exercise and come back at 0400h-0500h. That gave us just enough time to get ready for roll call at 0700h. In that short period of time we had to clean our uniform, boots, weapons…basically everything that we used during the exercise. Another exercise was that we were brought to a local lake and we all had to line up at the river bank. When the signal was given we all had to jump into the water, and it didn't matter if you were able to swim or not. Two of the non-swimmers didn't jump and they were removed from the program. Once you'd pass a certain degree of physical fatigue, there would be only morale and your nerves left to you hold up. Physical endurance was tested and completely destroyed within a couple of weeks, and many would just continue the program on their nerves, which resulted in a couple of breakdowns. The sanction for a breakdown would be removal from the program. Others wanted to continue at any cost, and if they had a nervous breakdown they made sure it was out of sight of the instructors.

The discipline was unbelievably rigorous, and was also exercised in the punctuality of the candidates. I remember that one day a communication had to be made at 2100h in one of the lecture rooms. That night the entire village was obscured due to a power failure and the duty officer, a Frenchman, thought to wait until the instructor would say something to him and postponed the communication due to the lack of light. Lieutenant Genoet who was our history professor, arrived at 2100h at the lecture room and found it to be empty. Now the storm was coming! The duty officer was called on the parade grounds, and he had to assemble all the students. The darkness didn't make things easier, and the officer waited a couple of minutes before he started firing off his stern speech. He was obviously furious and we were going to have a bad night for sure.

Around midnight the alarm sounded, and in our combat gear we spent two hours outside in the bush. Upon our return we were completely covered in mud from top to bottom. We were put back to sleep, however ten minutes later the alarm sounded again. This exercise would be repeated one more time to finally finish at 0600h. But at 0700h we had roll call, and our uniform had to be immaculate with weapons ready for an in-depth inspection. The only one who didn't participate in this exercise was our comrade who was the duty officer; as soon as he finished his shift he was sent back to his previous unit.

The only German officer at the school was a young Lieutenant named Kleindienst who was also the commander and head professor. He was a very capable soldier and his impartiality was impeccable. For whatever reason he was very close to one of the students, but when this one particular student was on guard duty he decided in his own stupidity to fire a shot at a rat that was crossing the street. This would mean the end for him, and even with all the praise and good words of Lieutenant Kleindienst, he was found unfit to become an officer of the Waffen SS.

After our last exam that would lead towards the final exam, we had a *Kameradenschaftabend* (camaraderie evening). Actually this was an evening in a military school where each and every one of us would end up drunk and under the table. However this exercise had the objective not to fall under the table which would've been very easy even if one wouldn't drink at all. But this was easier said than done because every time an officer would bring a toast to an individual, he had to drink and he had to be polite enough to drink for the next 10 minutes. An officer would stand up and called out: "Section X!" and 20 men would stand up and drink in cadence. A couple of minutes later, the section leader had to bring out a toast to the officer. I tell you, one really had to be capable of withstanding the alcohol, and then we had to present ourselves fresh and sober at roll call at 0700h. I've gone through a *Kameradenschaftabend* before in May 1943 when I was in training as an NCO, actually on the last evening of my training. The next day we all had to go to the range for some pistol shooting. I don't have to explain that the results of that shooting practice were really terrible. But I was trained well, and only one didn't make it that evening as he fell on the ground because he was so drunk. Later the poor guy lost his life in Cherkasy.

Then there was something called "guilty negligence". I believe that every army in the world would consider the loss of a weapon a serious error. During the war at the front the consequences for losing a weapon were not that serious. There were enough weapons laying around at the front that a weapon could be replaced without any problems. The important thing was to have a weapon at the front. In the barracks the most important thing was that the serial number of your weapon would correspond with the serial number written in your *Wehrpaß* and in the registry of the army. It would be difficult to replace a lost rifle with one of those from your comrades. And one of the weapons one had to have with him all the time in the German

Army, from soldier to Adjutant, was the bayonet. Normally starting with the rank of Sergeant the bayonet was left off the belt, however at the *Junkerschule* we had to carry our bayonet again. After a while of having not carried one on the left side, I had to get used to it again. When one of the instructors asked Freddy Jacques why he wasn't carrying a bayonet he replied that he had lost his. Freddy was an excellent student and we were certain that he would be in the group that would make it to the final exam. But the loss of his bayonet would mean three days in the cells which could mean the end of his military career as an Adjutant. The sanction was pronounced by the section leader without emotion because he was simply following the rules and he was just doing his job. Most likely he was feeling bad for giving Freddy this kind of punishment because he was a top-notch student. The execution of his sanction would be postponed for two days because Léon Degrelle was visiting the school. Léon Degrelle was welcomed by the commander of the section with all the respect for his rank since he was a Lieutenant-Colonel or *Obersturmbannführer*, and for the respect the German Army and civil entities were showing him. He would become the future leader of Belgium after all. Degrelle had some personal conversations with some section members since they knew each other very well. He also had a conversation with Freddy and he asked him: "So Freddy Jacques, how are you?" "Not good, Chef, because I'll be incarcerated tomorrow," replied Freddy. "Why?" asked Degrelle. "Because I lost my bayonet." Léon Degrelle, allergic to anything military and to the Prussian discipline turned towards Lieutenant Kleindienst and visibly agitated, he said, "If such sanctions are spoken out to this man, I suppose this would've been the last bayonet of the German Army then?" "Absolutely not, *Obersturmbannführer*!" replied Kleindienst. "I understand why this sanction was given to this man, however I propose to withdraw all sanctions due to my visit!" said Degrelle. "Absolutely, *Obersturmbannführer*!" Freddy was more than happy and so was the Lieutenant who had had to make this decision against his will. The incident was now closed and we moved on. That day was also the second day of the German offensive in the Ardennes. We were just a couple of days away from Christmas, and Léon Degrelle told us, in the presence of the German officer, that he had the intention to follow the offensive so he could arrive in Brussels as soon as the Belgian capital would be reconquered. That way he could assume his position as leader there and to prevent the Germans from committing any more stupidities like they did for the last four years.

The most minor default in the discipline could generate such a catastrophe for the entire effective, and a minor detail could also cause a major disagreement between its authors. One day when everybody was out on exercise the chief instructors found that the rooms' cleanliness didn't correspond with that of officer candidates. Result: cleaning of all the rooms after dinner so we could digest our food while doing this and inspection at 2200h by Lieutenant Kleindienst himself. We already knew the outcome before the inspection even started because they would always find a little piece of dust in your room or on your weapon. They always compared our rooms with dirty stables and the barrels of our guns with dirty pipes. We had already gone through so many of these inspections that we knew how to handle them properly. In the units, only the commander had the right to punish a soldier and not grant the permission to leave in the evening or on the weekend. However, the platoon commander or head instructor, I had been both of them, who inspected the rooms and weapons at the end of the day had the right to make a soldier clean his room or rifle until it was clean. So every now and then I was presented with a clean rifle that I didn't want to declare as being clean and that for the following reason. If one of the men had really worked on your nerves during the day without getting a report from the commander, I made him clean his rifle after revoking his evening pass. This little game lasted so long until the soldier didn't want to leave anymore. Now in the Junkerschule we spent most of the night presenting our cleaned rooms to the chief instructors until they were basically tired and wanted to go to sleep. But we knew from experience that sometimes they wanted to continue with the inspections, and that they simply wanted to give us a bad night. Because I was the highest in rank as NCO and the most experienced soldier, I was the room captain and I had to present the room to the inspecting officers. I was also responsible for the execution of the cleaning duties of our room. The presentation of the room was rather a formality, but it was of high importance in the German Army, especially during officer training. A couple of minutes after 2200h, after the chief instructors had already inspected a couple of rooms, they entered ours followed by a couple of Belgian officers. I reported to the commander together with my roommate Marcel Envote. Knowing that this inspection had nothing to do with the cleanliness of the room or our weapons, it was rather an attempt to undermine morale and the nervousness of the students. But both of us were veteran soldiers and we were used to these types of things. Were very disciplined and Marcel had gone through the same training as I did at the Assault Pioneer School. During an inspection all military regulations were yelled at us making the windows tremble. With a smile on his face the German officer turned towards the Belgian officers and said: "When a presentation like this is made the room has to be impeccable!" Then he addressed us and said: "The inspection is over, good night!" The victory was ours because we wanted to do better, never doubting the result or outcome. For the others this circus would go on until 0200h and the inspections were also graded on the reaction of the students.

After three months we spent a lot of time around the sand box for tactical exercises. Everybody had to imagine and develop a report about a day and night time exercise which at the end had to be executed on the terrain. Everything was in the hands of the one who put the exercise together and one small mistake could compromise everything. The preparation was to be done in the smallest details, and the school commander together with the tactics professor had to review and approve its valor. The student had to explain the exercise in the sand box, surrounded by officers who were asking numerous questions like, "Why would you place these men here? Why would you move that way?" And one always had to be prepared to justify his actions while the officers were observing his reactions to the questions, on the situation, etc. Sometimes the exercise would be infantry only and the commander would choose a specialist to execute the exercise. For this reason, he chose me because of my qualities as an assault pioneer. The exercise was called Stosstrupp.

There had been four other assault pioneers that were officer cadets, men of great capability and quality, but they left the school because they couldn't take it anymore. They thought that spending seven months in this environment was not what they wanted as NCOs, so they returned to their units. They didn't want to be treated as recruits or just like simple soldiers since they were veterans with an extensive service record. But when you looked a bit farther down the road the *Junkerschule* wasn't that bad. Most of the exercises were done while using live ammunition and only on rare occasions would we use blanks.

There were two stupid accidents that cost the lives of two students: one Frenchman and one Walloon. In both cases it was because of negligence, incomprehensible though since we were all seasoned veterans. The

Frenchman committed an inexplicable mistake after a day at the range with a submachine gun. He forgot to inspect the chamber, and when we all assembled on the parade grounds and we put our rifles down during drill the round in his rifle went off. The bullet went through his chin and exited through the top of his helmet. The unfortunate man didn't even have time to realize what happened. This was not the case with my comrade Dethy, also a veteran of August 8, 1941. He did his night exercise with blank ammunition which was already odd. We were at the end of the winter in a snow-covered landscape, and it was very quiet and calm outside. I found myself at the edge of a bush to figure out the movement of the enemy. In the last phase of the exercise we had to attack the enemy and take their weapons. The progression through the snow happened very quietly and our excellent camouflage permitted us to get really close to the enemy positions. Then we opened fire on the enemy and initiated the attack under MP fire. From the first "Hurrah!" my comrade and I realized that one of these idiots was using real ammunition because we could hear the distinct whistle of the bullets. Two or three minutes later we could hear the whistle of the instructor and he was yelling to cease fire. We knew something had happened, and we thought that it certainly had something to do with the projectiles that had flown over our heads. We joined the others when we learned that one of the bullets hit one of our comrades. It was Dethy! The bullet had penetrated just above the belt buckle and exited through the back. We were 2 km from the village, and we made a gurney with two rifles and jackets to transport our wounded comrade to the infirmary. He was a brave man, but he must have suffered quite a bit since we had to march through uneven terrain while he was laying on that make shift gurney. He was conscious and he was talking to us calmly without complaining. From the infirmary he was transported to Prague the same night, and at the school there was a lot of disbelief and rage while the officers were trying to find a justification about what happened. All the ones that were positioned behind Dethy during the exercise were interrogated. The next day my comrade and I, already cleared by the officers, were picking up the brass casings but no real bullets were found. It must have been an accident, however the one that fired the real bullets must have known that he was using live ammunition. Of course, to prevent himself from being severely punished he remained silent. The culprit knew what he was doing because the recoil of a real bullet was a lot more powerful than a blank round. HE must have felt the recoil and most likely he must have cleaned up the brass casings before the exercise got stopped. Three days later, accompanied by a couple of Walloon officers I attended the funeral of our comrade Dethy in Prague.

Landucci's fiancé was Belgian and mine was German, and we both required permission to get married after our training. For this we had to undergo a medical and racial examination just like our future wives. We found ourselves in Prague where we presented ourselves to an SS Captain who examined us from every angle. We were wearing the berets of an officer candidate, and when this formality had ended we were seated in front of the SS Captain in his office. Since Landucci didn't speak German I was the interpreter. The Captain looked at us and stated: *"Meine Herren, Sie sind Germanen!"* Landucci and I looked surprisingly at each other without moving our heads, but this didn't escape the eye of the Captain. He then addressed us in perfect French: "Are you gentlemen surprised to be Germanic? Because I am Germanic and my name is…" He gave us a name that I can't remember exactly but it sounded like Santili. Our loud laughing must have been heard throughout the entire building, and it was almost in a friendly manner that we received some vacation days from the Captain. But the entire story didn't end up so well since neither Landucci or I married our fiancés, while his fiancé was pregnant. When Landucci graduated from the Junkerschule he was killed in action on the Oder front somewhere around April 20 while he was leading his platoon.

Graduation and the Last Days of the Reich

We came towards the end of our training and we all obtained the rank of *Standarten Junkers*, and we would be promoted to Lieutenant a couple of weeks later. The primus of the class automatically got promoted to Lieutenant immediately after graduation. In this case it was Roland Devresse, a veteran of March 8. We left Neweklau on March 31, 1945 to rejoin our Division which was now located at the Oder. During the night of April 1 I was on a train to Dresden where I would wake up my fiancé and her parents. While I was drinking a cup of coffee with Irmgard, well if you could call it coffee, I was told that during the night somewhere in February more than 200,000 women, children and elderly people had been killed by the bombs of democracy. Irmgard accompanied me back to the station, and there we said our goodbyes. I held her in my arms for the first time, and after that we would never see each other again.

When I arrived back at the Division I was waiting for the assault pioneers to come back from Czechoslovakia where they were training under 1st Lieutenant Merguin. In the meantime I was given the command of a platoon of conscripts in a reserve company, and we occupied the positions in the second line with a limited number of weapons. One MG for the entire platoon with only 50 rounds! I trusted this device to one soldier whom I thought would use it well. My Adjutant, Marcel Beaudinne was a fellow graduate from Neweklau, but they made me platoon commander since I had more seniority in years of service and in rank.

One day one of the men had to relieve one of the guards in a fox hole, but he refused to do so. He took place in front of the fox hole but he didn't go in it. Half of the platoon was watching us and so was our company commander De Goy. But I didn't see him since him since he was hidden behind some bushes. I pivoted to the right, I took my pistol, and before I knew it I was on top of him inside the fox hole with my P38 to his head. I simply told him: "Leave, I dare you!" He remained in the fox hole and he was right to do so because I would've shot him without hesitation. One can say what he wants, but I was the platoon commander and I was responsible for the discipline and well-being of a unit of 40 men. If I hadn't reacted to this type of behavior the next day more of the men would have disobeyed my orders. So if one would ask me to put me in that soldier's place, then my answer would be that he had to put himself into my place and see how he would react. It was as simple as that.

A few days later we released all the men from my platoon with the proper paperwork because all the assault pioneers had come back, and I would see all my old comrades again. Since all the positions of platoon commander were taken, the company commander made me his Adjutant. On April 20 the last Bourguignons fell at the Oder, between them Hector Landucci and the third brother Detlers who were my companions at Neweklau. Madam Detlers had lost her third son on the Eastern Front. This was the last retreat of *Kampfgruppe* Derricks, a pathetic retreat which brought us to the gates of Schwerin on May 5, 1945. There we would surrender to those that had liberated Europe without knowing the first line of its history. After I threw my pistol on the pile of weapons in the middle of the road I was walked with my comrades by two American soldiers. They looked at us in a strange way and I could hear one of them saying while pointing at us: "Hitler's supermen!" Personally it felt like an ice cold shower. I tried to keep myself composed and yes, we were conquered and we had lost the war. We lost everything. Actually not everything because I was physically and morally intact. I was alive! This was the most important part of all, being alive. But I can assure you that after that American soldier's comment I wasn't happy at all to be alive.

What followed was a black hole, a nothingness of 63 months which I don't want to discuss since I don't want to relive these five years and three months that I didn't live. My dreams came to an end in Schwerin on May 5, 1945. It was during the last days of the Reich that Walloons and Flemish volunteers fought the last stand at the Oder front, dying for their ideals and for a better Europe. Twenty-five hundred legionnaires found their final resting place somewhere in between the Caucasus and the Baltic Sea; 2,500 dead which in 1945 would be posthumously condemned as traitors. And since that day I've been very proud of what I did and I was never so happy to be classified as a traitor amongst these great men! During the years of incarceration we remained silent, and when we were finally released we didn't look back and we went to work completely on our own without any help. We always fought against hate, the name calling and the expulsion out of society on our own terms with the same courage and the same sheer will that we had before.

We remember and honor our soldiers despite the hate some people would show towards us. No service in their honor was allowed because they had loyally worn the enemy's uniform. These were soldiers that gave their lives to protect women and children against the barbaric hordes from the east.

How many faces do we see again? How many voices do we still hear of comrades that are long gone? How nay apocalyptic visions do we still see of a time long gone while we still hear our old friends talking to us in their particular accents? How many places do we see again, and how many battles do we relive and fight over and over again? Those places where the soil was colored red with the blood of our comrades…our respect for the ones that lost their lives on the battlefield will always be there, bigger and stronger than ever. Oh, how I respect you all Walloons and Flemings that were on the battlefields during the war on the Eastern Front!

Endnote

The study of such a recent and controversial period of history creates unique difficulties and challenges. This book is not an apology nor is it intended to serve as a condemnation of Waffen SS soldiers/veterans. The time for judgments - be they judicial, political, or even moral - has passed and, more than 75 years after the end of the war, it is appropriate to adopt a more dispassionate and - so far as that is ever possible - objective approach. After the war, nearly all Belgian Waffen SS were prosecuted under a system of military justice established by the Belgian government upon its return from London. A few were executed while many others were sentenced to long periods of imprisonment. Upon their release, some chose to settle abroad while others lived in retirement in Belgium. All paid dearly for their "crimes" and only a small minority still choose to glorify their wartime activities. A few who evaded prosecution - including Léon Degrelle - lived on in exile as the irrelevant relics of a historical process which has long since passed them by. Some of these sought to justify their past adventures, but for the most part, they too accepted that a page of history had been turned and had wished only that their deeds and motives be recorded.

In the ranks of the Waffen SS there were many opportunists as well as a significant number of brutal, evil men. However there were also, especially amongst the foreign volunteers, those who had joined this new army and who did believe that this new order, which was created in Germany, would offer the best hope for their country. After the war most of them realized they were profoundly mistaken as they had been fighting for a regime responsible for some of the darkest actions in human history. But bewilderment, ignorance, nationalism, religion, and prior loyalties all played a part in their choice. It is all too tempting for historians and others to impose a false clarity on events which at the time seemed complex and confusing. As for myself, belonging to a generation too young to have experienced the war first hand, I have sought to treat the Waffen SS like any other historical subject. By doing so, I intend neither to rehabilitate or condemn those involved, but to provide an accurate record for those who may wish to understand the volunteers of the Waffen SS and their crusades during WWII.

Raymond Lemaire

Nationality: Belgian

Joined the Waffen SS on July 1, 1943

Promotions: Legionnaire corporal/Gefreiter: March 10, 1942

Unterscharführer: 1943

Untersturmführer: November 9, 1944

Raymond Lemaire was born on October 13, 1922 in Dampremy (province of Hainaut, Belgium). He joined the "Legion Wallonie" on August 8, 1941 at the same time as his father Marcel and his Rexist leader Léon Degrelle. He was attached to the 1st Platoon, 1st Company, as a MG gunner. On December 15, 1941 he became sick and he had to be hospitalized returning to his battalion after December 25.

He participated in the battles of Gromovayabalka, also known as the "Valley of Thunder." He was wounded during combat at the end of June 1942 and was transported to a hospital in Bayreuth where he stayed for one week. After his stay in the hospital he benefited from fourteen days of leave in Belgium. He rejoined the Legion Wallonie in Belgium at the end of July 1942. In November 1942 he was evacuated from the front where he had contracted jaundice and passed several weeks in a military hospital in Rostov. He returned to the front in December 1942 where he found the last Walloon unit, a company under the command of Léon Closset. The withdrawal of the German troops in the Caucasus started at the end of January 1943, and the Walloons were evacuated by air in February 1943. During the summer of 1943 he was trained as a pioneer NCO for three months near Dresden. After his NCO training he joined the Sturmbrigade Wallonie in Wildflecken in September 1943. There he was attached to the platoon of the pioneers of Sturmbrigade.

Hit by shrapnel in his legs, he was seriously wounded at the beginning of January 1944. Unable to walk, he was evacuated by air to a military hospital on the Polish-Russian border. He rejoined the Sturmbrigade at the beginning of April 1944. In the summer of that year he went back to the SS Pionier School in Dresden for two months. Then from September 1 1944 to March 31, 1945 he went to the SS-Panzer-Grenadier-Schule

Kienschlag. During that time he became an officer of the Waffen SS. Before rejoining the Division "Wallonien", he passed by Dresden to see his fiancée for the last time. There he learned of the Allied bombings of the city. Later he joined "Kampfgruppe Derriks."

On May 5, 1945 he was captured by the Americans and convicted for treason by the Belgian authorities. Raymond Lemaire died in Brussels on December 26, 2001, having left his memoires on audio. His father Marcel was born in Uccle (Brussels) in 1895. He was a WWI veteran, Rexiste, and an NCO of the Legion Wallonie. He was wounded in combat in Gromovayabalka and repatriated to Belgium. He was convicted after the war just like his son Raymond.

Raymond was the holder of following decorations: Winter 1941/42 Medal, Infantry Assault Badge, Wounded Badge, the Iron Cross 2nd Class, and the Iron Cross 1st Class (March 1942).

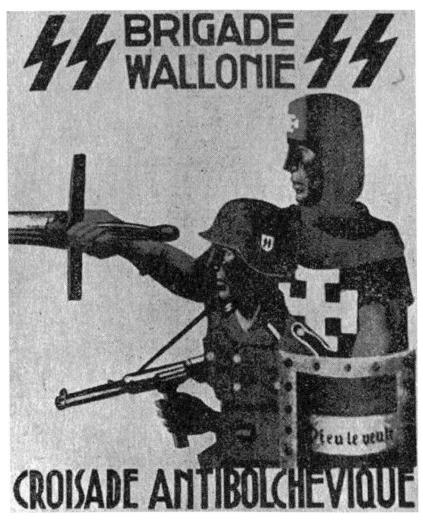

Anti-Bolshevism Recruiting Poster

Commanders and Knight's Cross Recipients

Commanders

Capt-Cdt. Georges Jacobs (August 1941 - January 1942)

Hauptmann B.E.M. Pierre Pauly (January 1942 - March 1942)

Hauptmann George Tchekoff (March 1942 - April 1942)

SS-Sturmbannführer Lucien Lippert (April 1942 - 13 February 1944)

SS-Sturmbannführer Léon Degrelle as political leader of the unit.

SS-Oberführer Karl Burk (21 June 1944 - 18 September 1944)

SS-Standartenführer Léon Degrelle (18 September 1944 - 8 May 1945)

Knight's Cross Recipients

Léon Gillis

Léon Degrelle

Jacques Leroy

Order of Battle

SS-Freiwilligen-Sturmbrigade Wallonien

- Brigade Stab
- I.Bataillon
    - Kompanie
    - Kompanie
    - Kompanie
    - Kompanie
- II.Bataillon
    - Kompanie
    - Kompanie
    - Kompanie
    - Kompanie
- I. StuG Batterie
- II. StuG Batterie
- Kriegsberichter Zug
- FlaK Batterie (8.8 cm)
- FlaK Batterie (2.2 cm)
- Panzerjäger Kompanie
- Nachrichten Kompanie
- 1.Feldersatz Kompanie
- 2.Feldersatz Kompanie
- I.Kollone

28. SS-Freiwilligen-Grenadier-Division Wallonien

- SS-Panzergrenadier Regiment 69
  - I./SS-Panzergrenadier Regiment 69
  - II./SS-Panzergrenadier Regiment 69
- SS-Panzergrenadier Regiment 70
  - I./SS-Panzergrenadier Regiment 70
- SS-Artillerie Regiment 28
- SS-Panzerjäger Abteilung 28
- SS-Panzeraufklärungs Abteilung 28
- SS-Nachrichten Abteilung 28
- SS-Pionier-Bataillon 28
- SS-Nachschub-Kompanie 28
- SS-Flak-Kompanie 28
- SS-Verwaltungskompanie 28
- SS-Sanitäts-Kompanie 28
- SS-Veterinär-Kompanie 28
- SS-Ersatz-Bataillon 28
- SS-Sturm-Bataillon
- Kampfgruppe Capelle

Bibliography

Conway, Martin (1993). Collaboration in Belgium: Léon Degrelle and the Rexist movement, 1940-1944. New Haven: Yale University Press. ISBN 978-0300055009.

Littlejohn, David (1972). The Patriotic Traitors: A History of Collaboration in German-occupied Europe, 1940-45. London: Heinemann. ISBN 0-434-42725-X.

Estes, Kenneth (2013). A European Anabasis: Western European Volunteers in the German Army and SS, 1940-45. Solihull: Helion. ISBN 978-1909384521.

Plisnier, Flore (2011). Ils ont pris les armes pour Hitler: la collaboration armée en Belgique francophone. Brussels: Renaissance du Livre. ISBN 9782507003616.

Cook, Bernard A. (2005). Belgium: A History (3rd ed.). Peter Lang. p. 118.

Griffin, Roger (1991). The Nature of Fascism. Pinter. p. 132.

Griffiths, Richard (2005). Fascism (2nd ed.). Continuum. p. 117.

Feldman, Matthew; Turda, Marius (2008). "Introduction". Clerical Fascism in Interwar Europe. Routledge. p. xvi.

Richard Bonney Confronting the Nazi War on Christianity: the Kulturkampf Newsletters, 1936-1939; International Academic Publishers; Bern; 2009 ISBN 978-3-03911-904-2; pp. 175-176.

Gerard, Emmanuel; Van Nieuwenhuyse, Karel, eds. (2010). Scripta Politica: Politieke Geschiedenis van België in Documenten (1918-2008) (2e herwerkte dr. ed.). Leuven: Acco. p. 112. ISBN 9789033480393.

Brustein (1988). "The Case of Rexism".

Étienne, Jean-Michel (1968). Le mouvement Rexiste jusqu'en 1940. Armand Colin.

Griffin, Roger (1991). The Nature of Fascism. Pinter. pp. 132–133.

"Geheim akkoord tussen Rex en VNV" quoted in Gerard, Emmanuel; Van Nieuwenhuyse, Karel, eds. (2010). Scripta Politica: Politieke Geschiedenis van België in Documenten (1918-2008) (2nd revised ed.). Leuven: Acco. pp. 119–20. ISBN 9789033480393.

Capoccia, Giovanni (2005). Defending Democracy: Reactions to Extremism in Interwar Europe. Johns Hopkins University Press. p. 114.

De Wever, Bruno (2006). "Belgium". World Fascism: A Historical Encyclopedia. 1. ABC-CLIO. p. 86.

Paxton, Robert O. (2004). The Anatomy of Fascism. Alfred A. Knopf. p. 74.

Richard Landwehr (2012, 5th edition). The Wallonien - Chapter 2 - The formation and first engagements of the 5th SS-Sturmbrigade "Wallonien", p.11 - Merriam Press - ISBN 978-1304906236.

Richard Bonney Confronting the Nazi War on Christianity: the Kulturkampf Newsletters, 1936-1939; International Academic Publishers; Bern; 2009 ISBN 978-3-03911-904-2; pp. 174-175.

di Muro, Giovanni F. (2005). Léon Degrelle et l'aventure rexiste. Bruxelles: Pire. pp. 151–3 and pp. 160–1 ISBN 2874155195.

Domenico, Roy P. (ed.); Hanley, Mark Y. (2007). Encyclopedia of modern Christian politics: L-Z (1. publ. ed.). Westport, Conn.: Greenwood Press. p. 163. ISBN 0313338906.

Brustein, William (February 1988). "The Political Geography of Belgian Fascism: The Case of Rexism". American Sociological Review. 53 (1): 69–80. 10.2307/2095733.

Conway, Martin. Collaboration in Belgium: Léon Degrelle and the Rexist Movement 1940-1944. ISBN 0-300-05500-5.

de Bruyne, Eddy; Rikmenspoel, Marc (2004). For Rex and For Belgium: Léon Degrelle and Walloon Political & Military Collaboration 1940-45. Helion. ISBN 1-874622-32-9.

Littlejohn, David. The Patriotic Traitors: A History of Collaboration in German-occupied Europe, 1940-45. ISBN 0-434-42725-X.

Streel, José. La révolution du XXème siècle (réédition du livre paru en 1942 à la NSE à Bruxelles), préface de Lionel Baland, Déterna, Paris, 2010.

Report on military units 1 July 1943; Propaganda Abteilung Belgien 1944.

C. Chevalier 'La presse francophone et l'eglise catholique en Belgique sous l'occupation allemande (1940-1944)' (University Catholique de Louvain-la-Heuve Memoire de licence 1986).

M. Claeys-Van Haegendoren 'L'eglise et l'Etat au XXe siecle', *Courrier hebdomadaire du CRISP* Ho. 542-543 (1971).

M. Conway 'Le rexisme de 1940 *a* 1944: Degrelle et les autres', *Cahiers d'histoire de la seconde guerre mondiale* X (1986).

J. Culot 'L'exploitation de la main d'oeuvre beige et le problem des refractaires', *Cahiers d'histoire de la seconde guerre mondiale* I (1970).

A. Dantoing 'La hierarchic catholique et la Belgique sous l'occupation allemande', *Revue du Nord* LX (1978).

The Great Soviet Encyclopedia, 3rd Edition (1970-1979).

The story of this Walloon volunteer was transcribed from more than 11 hours of voice recordings left by the volunteer himself. The recordings date from 2001 and were recorded in Brussels at the veteran's residence. He passed away in Brussels shortly after recording his WWII memories, leaving the recordings for future generations as a testament of his experience from the Eastern Front during WWII and the Legion Wallonie. No copyright was found for the recordings, and numerous attempts to find and or contact any surviving relatives were unsuccessful.

All pictures in this book are obtained through open source media or through personal contacts (private collections). The pictures found on open source media are not the property of a specific body or entity. Tracking the original owner of these pictures is as good as impossible. Pictures are used as a reference for this book and are not specific to the soldier's story. Picture of Lemaire provided by Grégory Bouysse and used with his permission.

The Crusade of a Walloon Volunteer: August 8, 1941 – May 5, 1945

ISBN 978-0-359-41204-4
BISAC: History / Military / World War II

All inquiries can be addressed at:
ghost-division@outlook.com

© Gerry Villani 2019 - All rights reserved
Ghost Division Historical Research

Published in the United States of America - 2019

Made in the
USA
Middletown, DE